WHAT I REALLY WANT TO DO IS DIRECT

WHAT I REALLY WANT TO DO IS DIRECT

SEVEN FILM SCHOOL
GRADUATES
GO TO HOLLYWOOD

BILLY FROLICK

A DUTTON BOOK

DUTTON
Published by the Penguin Group
Penguin Books USA Inc., 375 Hudson Street, New York, New York 10014, U.S.A.
Penguin Books Ltd, 27 Wrights Lane, London W8 5TZ, England
Penguin Books Australia Ltd, Ringwood, Victoria, Australia
Penguin Books Canada Ltd, 10 Alcorn Avenue, Toronto, Ontario, Canada M4V 3B2
Penguin Books (N.Z.) Ltd, 182-190 Wairau Road, Auckland 10, New Zealand

Penguin Books Ltd, Registered Offices:
Hardmondsworth, Middlesex, England

First Published by Dutton, an imprint of Dutton Signet,
a division of Penguin Books USA Inc.
Distributed in Canada by McClelland & Stewart Inc.

First Printing, November, 1996
10 9 8 7 6 5 4 3 2 1

C. P. Cavafy's "Ithaka" from *C. P. Cavafy: Collected Poems* (revised edition). Copyright © 1992 by
Keeley/Sherrard, transl. Reprinted by permission of Princeton University Press.

REGISTERED TRADEMARK—MARCA REGISTRADA

CIP data available.
ISBN 0-525-93770-6

Printed in the United States of America
Set in Bembo

This book is dedicated
to my father

S. J. Frolick

who 30 years ago
dedicated his first book to me

INTRODUCTION

Mother Teresa spends a lifetime serving others. After decades of feeding and sheltering the world's hungry and homeless, she is visited by God.

"Selflessness has long been your way of life, Mother Teresa," intones God. "Now it is your turn. What would you like? To feast on the bounties of the earth? To live in an opulent palace? To wear a crown of gold, diamonds, rubies, and emeralds? Name your desire, and it shall be granted."

"Well, since you're asking," Mother Teresa replies, "what I really want to do is direct."

The notion of a career in filmmaking conjures an aura of power, glamour, mystique, and immortality. The very word "director" connotes authority. A painter paints; a writer writes. A director . . . directs. And by effectively communicating his wants and needs to actors, editors, screenwriters, and dozens of others, a director brings his vision to life. At the studio level, this requires an average investment of over $30 million per film.

Those who have the chance to direct professionally often question those who can only dream of the opportunity. "To direct, you have to get up very early in the morning," said screenwriter Lowell Ganz in the BBC documentary *Funny Business*. "And you have to speak to people all day long with whom you have absolutely no rapport whatsoever. It's a very cool job because you're like the king. But it's not a very *good* job." *Twenty Bucks* director Keva Rosenfeld agrees: "What is the big deal about directing? Why is everyone dying to do this? It's incredibly stressful and incredibly hard. It isn't like I have a blast every day at work."

During the 1930s and 1940s, the infancy of talking films in America, crew members often graduated into journeyman directors-for-hire. Others developed loyal relationships with certain actors and/or gravitated toward specific subject matter: John Ford practically invented the Western, while Preston Sturges favored wry, screwball comedies performed by a regular ensemble.

As studio product was continuously churned out, filmmaking was considered more a craft than a vehicle for creative self-expression such as writing, painting, and other fine arts. If anyone claimed a motion picture as his own, it was usually the producer. In a newspaper advertisement, D. W. Griffith once called himself "Producer of all great Biograph successes, revolutionizing Motion Picture drama and founding the modern technique of the art."

That perception changed in 1954, when François Truffaut published a provocative essay in the French journal *Cahiers du Cinéma*. Truffaut, later a director of greatness himself, built on views of fellow critics Alexandre Astruc and André Bazin, who believed a director was a film's true "author." American critic Andrew Sarris dubbed this "the *auteur* theory." It held, in essence, that a film was part of a visionary body of work distinguished by a director's signature *mise en scène*, or "placing in the scene." This gestalt incorporated all of the motion picture's aesthetic concerns and authority over several creative disciplines. To this day, artistic possession of a motion picture has been universally recognized as that of the director.

In fact, some directorial styles have become so etched in our consciousness that adjectives have been specially created to evoke them: "Chaplinesque" for sweet, sentimental comedy; "Capraesque" for stories of small-town people with big-time dreams; "Felliniesque" for an imaginative, outrageous, and surreal world, often seen through the eyes of a child; "Hitchcockian" for the chilly layer of fear over a seemingly tranquil situation; "Spielbergian" for an uplifting sense of wonder.

The magic of film lies in its unlimited possibilities. Each season, several dozen would-be auteurs debut their unique visions. And perhaps, among them, is a director whose name will someday become an adjective.

Film school is commonly thought to be one of the better routes toward directing professionally. But if there is a more worthless college degree than in Philosophy, it might just be in Film.

Just don't tell that to the thousands of yearly entrants, students, and graduates of the American Film Institute and the nation's four other most prominent film schools: Columbia University, New York University, the University of California at Los Angeles, and the University of Southern California. There, students are unabashedly encouraged to pursue a singular goal—a successful career in the movie business—against ridiculously high odds.

Most film school students are driven by arrogant, at times delusional, beliefs about themselves. They believe they have stories to tell, but that writing is too limiting; that they are not simply actors or dancers but can manipulate performance; that they understand visual composition but cannot find in still photography the third dimension they need.

One afternoon in a darkened movie theatre, when they were eight or ten years old, at a matinee of *The Wizard of Oz* or *Close Encounters of the Third Kind*, the seeds of a dream sprouted deep within. They may not have understood the sensation at the time. And as they approach college age, their parents may have other plans for them—law school perhaps, or entrance into the family business. But all other possibilities pale in comparison to the notion of making movies for a living. So to film school they go.

There they meet dozens of contemporaries with similar interests and dreams. People from small towns and big cities, people who have crossed oceans, all with reverence for the art of the motion picture. They all know who Tim Burton and Quentin Tarantino are, but some also are familiar with the work of Ernst Lubitsch, or Howard Hawks. For many of them, their seminal prepubescent experience wasn't learning to ride a bike, or hitting a home run in Little League, but seeing *2001: A Space Odyssey* for the first time.

This homogenized rush splits off in many directions as a film school education unfolds. Students start to model their own reputations while categorizing others. As documentarians or comedians or animators or propagandists. As egomaniacal or selfless or highstrung or compassionate. And—ultimately—as talented, mediocre, brilliant, or simply kidding themselves. Because creative filmmaking requires collaboration, these judgments of others become crucial.

Film school, of course, is a microcosm of the professional world. Students write scripts and proposals, pitch projects, and try to earn the opportunity to realize their cinematic visions. Raising production and/or completion funds—if they are not supplied by the artist's family—often requires business savvy, a different type of creativity. If one approaches the dean or the department chair for extra resources, it must be with conviction and just cause.

After blood, guts, sweat, tears, and money are processed into a graduate or senior film, the student's work is graded. Far more important, though, is the subsequent use of this amateur production as a professional calling card.

The mid-1970s changed the perception of film school as a haven for the avant-garde or bohemian. Alumni like USC's George Lucas, UCLA's Francis Ford Coppola and NYU's Martin Scorsese offered dynamic evidence that a working knowledge of cinema history did not preclude—and might actually complement—rightbrain brilliance. Though wunderkind Steven Spielberg never attended film school, he was grouped with this collegiate new wave.

Perhaps it was Spielberg's youth, and the baseball cap, glasses, and beard, which seemed in those days to be the graduates' unofficial uniform. But it was also his attitude, a fierce drive to break new aesthetic ground coupled with an encyclopedic knowledge of film history. Incredibly, Spielberg admits to having "referenced" all of his movies before *Schindler's List* in 1993. That is, he used specific shots and styles of other directors to inspire his own work.

None of the so-called movie brats could claim instant success. Coppola directed a nudie film called *Tonite for Sure*, and made his "legitimate" debut with *Dementia 13*, produced by the notorious low-budgeteer Roger Corman. One would have been hard pressed to predict multiple Oscars for the auteur of this ax-murder bloodfest, complete with microphone shadows.

Martin Scorsese, after serving as an editor on the watershed concert film *Woodstock*, also toiled for Corman, as the director of *Boxcar Bertha*. However, with that film—a Depression-era spin on *Bonnie and Clyde*—Scorsese was able to distinguish himself. He followed it with *Mean Streets*, a raw, personal work for which he had prepared by writing autobiographical stories like *It's Not Just You, Murray*, a short subject produced at NYU, and *Who's That Knocking at My Door?* The latter, Scorsese's first feature, was actually produced by his mentor, NYU film school head Haig Manoogian.

Even before the 1970s, film schools turned out successful writers, directors, cinematographers, producers, and editors. And increasingly, as new work is released by film stylists like the Coen brothers, David Lynch, Oliver Stone, James Ivory, Spike Lee, and Jim Jarmusch—and mainstream hitmakers such as Chris Columbus and Robert Zemeckis—Hollywood takes film school that much more seriously.

Film schools take themselves pretty seriously, too. The number of annual applicants to NYU's Tisch School of the Arts Graduate Film Division has almost doubled, to close to nine hundred, in the past ten years. Once it was known as the Junkyard for its outdated equipment, but in the mid-1980s NYU spent $30 million on a twelve-story building. Its cameras and editing systems are now fully digital.

USC, whose number of applicants has also mushroomed since it first offered film classes in 1929, has a reputation for competition as well as craftmanship. The first university to offer 70mm projection facilities and the THX sound system, its hi-tech complex has been referred to by students as the Death Star. As of 1993, USC graduates had won thirty Academy Awards.

A year's tuition for FEMIS, France's top film school, is under a hundred dollars. At USC or NYU it's well over fifteen thousand. Professional studios, talent agencies, and film and TV production companies actively pursue relationships with these colleges through donations, grants, and sponsored events. Cable networks such as HBO and Showtime have often acquired student work for use as interstitular programming.

Formal screenings of college work, a relatively new phenomenon, are well attended by industry professionals. There are more than twenty-five annual student film festivals in the United States, and almost forty amateur festivals. Often sponsored by studios and/or major agencies, the events offer a head start to filmmakers lucky enough to have their work chosen. Young and established agents alike compete in currying favor with their naive but wary targets. Once they've signed, an important rite of passage has occurred in the life of young "players." They've got something to tell their parents. They're *represented*. They're legitimate.

But things don't get that much easier.

This project began as a short newspaper article. I originally planned to report on new faces emerging from the country's five top film schools. Since the orientation of the story was not criticism but reportage, it was unnecessary for me to see the graduates' films.

Brief telephone conversations with the filmmakers piqued my curiosity, however. As a film school alumnus myself (NYU '79), I recognized not only their collective hope and enthusiasm as they approached the professional workplace but their concerns and fears as well: Am I old enough to be taken seriously? Too old to change careers? The right color? The right gender? Is my work mainstream enough for Hollywood? Will the film industry force me to compromise the creative freedom I have enjoyed as a student?

For me it was, in Yogi Berra's words, déjà vu all over again. In 1979, I had driven from Long Island to Hollywood with many of the same questions.

So, outside the confines of my assignment, I wanted to see the filmmakers' work. I wanted to meet them and hear their strategies for getting from Career Point A to Point B—and beyond. The movie business has always been intensely competitive. But in the '90s, during a creative slump in an adverse economy, the odds of succeeding seemed to be off the chart.

Such curiosity prompted me to begin this work of narrative nonfiction about a cross section of these would-be "players." In it I track the career progressions of seven graduates over three years. Their reports to me, conveyed by telephone and at intermittent meetings (and my attendance at key events), have been held confidential until the book's publication.

I chose three years as the term because it often takes that long simply to assemble the elements for a feature film, let alone begin production, and obviously it would be especially interesting if at least one of the moviemakers was making a movie by then. A young director might succeed in getting the opportunity to do a picture, but the inability to accomplish this within three years would hardly qualify as failure.

The chairpersons of the major film schools recommended approximately two dozen candidates for my project. Most were winners of awards and fellowships; all had somehow distinguished themselves from a crowded field. I contacted each of the graduates and they sent me videocassettes of their films, along with brief biographies or letters.

The filmmakers had vastly disparate backgrounds, and had made ambitious, unique projects. My guess was that they also had unique expectations and strategies—and would experience unique results after knocking on Hollywood's door.

Three major requisites guided my search for the group of seven subjects. The first was their work. This in itself speaks volumes about an artist's interests, concerns, tastes, and sensibilities.

Second was cultural and gender diversity within the group. Fifteen years ago this book would have been about seven white males. The movie industry has since changed its attitudes and practices regarding minorities in high places. It is no longer a novelty (though far from commonplace) for a person of color or a woman to direct a studio picture. I wanted the demographics of the book's subjects to reflect the dawning of this relatively new era of Hollywood "correctness."

The third requisite was a perceived spirit of cooperation, a difficult element to sense in the early stages of the project. I knew that self-promotion and image modeling for Hollywood directors were far more important than ever before, but I wasn't sure whether that made my proposal attractive or repulsive to prospective subjects. The book would showcase their professional activities, but what if they didn't have any? It would quote them, but what if they didn't like what they had said? And it would involve their direct participation, but each candidate was informed that he or she would not have copy approval, nor receive even token financial compensation.

The next step was to spend some time with each of the graduates, introduce them to my nonfiction work, and address their concerns. These meetings took place in coffeehouses and diners, and in the case of two New York–based individuals, we communicated by phone and fax. I sent each filmmaker copies of industry-related articles I had written for *Premiere*, the *Los Angeles Times* and *Entertainment Weekly*.

Virtually everyone I approached to participate in the book seemed to be—in no particular order—flattered, curious, and suspicious. Over breakfast or lunch I was asked the same questions by each of the two dozen people I contacted. One of the toughest was: To what could I compare this book?

My answer was, in Hollywood story-pitch terminology, fairly "high concept"—*The Real World* (MTV's popular documentary series about six college graduates' lives) meets *The Player* (Robert Altman's postmodern movie-business movie). There were also elements of *The Big Picture*, Christopher Guest's slice of life after film school, and the *35 Up* series, Michael Apted's documentary spanning the lives of several Brits. (Today, I would say it's closer to 1994's *Hoop Dreams*.)

Three of the candidates quickly took themselves out of the running. One had directed a pair of award-winning gay-themed student films, but had not yet come out to his family, and felt that the book would be an inappropriate forum in which to do so. Another was an animator for whom the "deal breaker" was potential embarrassment over several unproductive years after college, during which he lived with his parents. I considered it impossible to ignore; each participant's past would be as important to look at as his or her present and future. The third decliner was genuinely shy, preferring to let his work speak for him rather than vice versa.

Although most of the candidates expressed interest in participating, almost every one raised some degree of resistance. And it didn't help my cause that, at the very time that I was asking people to open their lives to me, a prominent filmmaker was the unwilling focus of international media attention. The director was Woody Allen, named by many of the graduates as a major creative influence.

Whether or not they were willing to sign the legal release I (and my publisher) required, addressing their concerns and considerations became the first order of business.

No one in the group openly cited a desire for publicity as a motivation for their inclusion in the project. In fact, several made a point of denigrating media manipulators. But many of the graduates also claimed to observe a craving for such attention in their colleagues. I was amused by this conundrum—it was all "so very Hollywood."

A few candidates said they wished a book like this had existed when they were considering film school and moviemaking as a career. They may have seen the project as an opportunity to share their knowledge and feelings. One graduate, however, thought he would feel like a guinea pig. He resented being one of a group and wished that the book could express his *opinions* of the industry (despite his lack of professional experience in the field). He and I agreed that he would not be an appropriate subject.

It didn't matter to me what the graduates' specific reasons were for signing on. I was only concerned that they understood my expectations and that their commitment of time and energy would not flag after the process began.

At issue for many of the graduates was not necessarily how their own words might later haunt them, but how they might be portrayed personally, and how they would fare in comparison with their peers as artists and businesspeople. The graduates were faced with a career decision that, each one realized, contained an element of risk. I agreed and did not attempt to convince them otherwise. I knew that the more aggressively I tried to talk someone out of a reluctance to participate, the more likely those concerns would be to resurface in the ensuing three years.

I continued to open up discussions with new graduates as others dropped out, but consciously tried to limit the number in the pool. The more I had, the more I would have to reject. For many of them, there would undoubtedly be enough of that ahead.

A few of the students knew each other, and I encouraged them to discuss the project among themselves, while assuring complete confidentiality about their comments to me.

I also suggested that the graduates discuss their possible inclusion in the book with their families and representatives—despite my suspicion that most agents, personal managers, and lawyers would try to dissuade the young filmmakers from participating.

They did, and it's no wonder. In most books about the industry the agents, personal managers, lawyers, and studio executives are depicted as Ray-Ban-wearing, Perrier-guzzling buffoons. (When reports surfaced in early 1993 that cellular phones might cause brain cancer, the joke circulating in L.A. was that most of the people who used them had no reason to worry.)

In fact, the "suits" expressed a spectrum of reactions. Most recognized the promotional opportunities such exposure could bring, but warned their clients of the possible dangers. Mentioned more than once was *The Devil's Candy*, Julie Salomon's 1992 recounting of the troubled journey of *The Bonfire of the Vanities* from best-seller to big screen.

I reminded the graduates that this was a journalistic endeavor. The subjects could censor themselves; "off the record" would mean just that (although sometimes "off the record" means that there is a privacy the speaker would like, for some reason, to share with the writer).

Despite statements of my good intentions, the issue was trust, and one realization for some of the graduates was that no matter which agent, lawyer, or manager was "handling" them, the most important decisions are ultimately their own. Directors, in fact, are *expected* to be decisive—to know what they want and to be skilled in getting it.

After almost a year, I had found seven people who seemed like the right "cast" for this book. They signed their releases and our process began. Just as it did, I happened to see the movie *32 Short Films About Glenn Gould*. In it, Gould says, "Never interview your subject about what they do."

I didn't listen.

A NOTE ON STYLE

What *I* really want to do is *be* direct. My intent has always been to employ a simple, conversational style for this book, allowing the seven subjects to tell their own stories in the most straightforward manner. Thus, their narratives in sections II through IV—culled from hundreds of interviews conducted from 1992 through 1995—have been edited for clarity only.

The text is interspersed with my own italicized commentary and with excerpts from interviews with working film industry professionals, conducted especially for this book, which provide context for the new directors' thoughts and activities. (For a list of these agents, writers, directors, producers and executives, and their credits, see page 355.)

Lastly, because this book is not an exposé, a handful of names have been changed where noted. However, the interpersonal dynamics of the film business transcend such specifics. In Hollywood, a town both built on dreams and fueled by mythology, the role playing and power games among directors, agents, studio executives, and producers often border on cliché. And—as the cliché goes—the more things change, the more they stay the same.

I

SPRING 1955–SUMMER 1992

As you set sail for Ithaka
hope the voyage is a long one,
full of adventure, full of discovery.

—C. P. Cavafy, *Ithaka*

PHOTO: LALEH SOOMEKH

LIZ CANE

Big + Tall, near Liz Cane's West Hollywood apartment, is like most independent bookstores—coffee, tea, and designer espresso drinks are more profitable than the reading matter, which is perused by a twentysomething, bohemian clientele.

Cane, naturally shy and girlish, likens being profiled in a book to an 8mm movie she made as a teenager in Palo Alto, California. The high school opus featured her contemporaries reflecting on their lives; with some embarrassment she recalls titling it *Forever Young*, after the Bob Dylan song.

"There was no synch sound. I was, you know—young," Cane shrugs.

This leads us to the topic of Hollywood's obsession with youth. Cane, a product of UCLA's graduate film program, is twenty-eight. Many of her friends, though, are in their mid-thirties and wonder whether the industry will perceive them as "over the hill" or (they hope) "late bloomers."

Cane's just-completed short, *That's What Women Want*, is a

surreal black-and-white odyssey into the psyche of the '90s male, at least through her eyes.

"The film had many inspirations, from a magazine article on the men's movement to someone telling me about the practice of penis piercing," Cane laughs. "It's exactly how I experience life—as a random, disconnected series of events that make a story."

That's What Women Want has not yet been entered in festivals, but she's already won the Jack Nicholson Distinguished Student Director Award and was a finalist for the Paramount Directing Fellowship.

"I was selected by UCLA—only one person was selected for each fellowship category by each of the five schools. I met with Michelle Manning, who's a V.P. at Paramount, about the fellowship.

"Her male secretary seemed uptight. He got me a bottled water. Michelle had just been massaged and was self-conscious. She made a remark about how wonderful it was—that she had used some oil on her.

"I was wary of revealing original ideas. I was asked who my influences were, and favorite films. I told her Scorsese, Altman, Allen, Kubrick, Gilliam. She wanted to know how I felt about working in TV. I said, 'What I really want to do is write and direct feature films. I don't watch TV.'

"I saw her face drop. I said, 'But I think *any* directing's good experience—maybe there are some good things going on in TV.' Michelle said, 'You ought to know that ninety-eight to ninety-nine percent of what we do here is TV.' It was just an awkward moment.

"I said, 'I'm sure whatever you do here I'd find fascinating.' I probably sounded like a snob—it's an on-lot fellowship! But I was true to myself. I never regretted what I said. I felt like UCLA fucked up a little bit. They didn't even tell me I was chosen until way late. And the fellowship would have been as good for them as for me. They just sent the tape [of my film] out without asking if I wanted to send it out yet. The guy who won had a clean, polished film. But it probably wouldn't have made a bit of difference.

"I'm always awkward in my exits, and she said, 'Really nice meeting you,' and I didn't say anything. Michelle shook my hand, and I was just thinking, 'Oh shit, I don't think I quite did the right thing back there.' I get really spaced out. USC ended up getting the directing fellowship. Columbia got the screenwriting one."

Now Cane's looking for work to make ends meet while writing a feature script. In a couple of weeks *That's What Women Want* will be screened with a few other UCLA films at Universal Studios for agents, producers, and executives throughout the industry.

Cane wants to make wild, wacky movies; she freely admits that her graduate film was greatly influenced by Martin Scorsese's cultish nightmare-comedy *After Hours*. But she is concerned that independent, offbeat filmmakers get fewer opportunities and have to work harder for each deal.

"Who knows?" she shrugs. "My film is 'commercial,' from what I've been told."

When she was growing up in Palo Alto, Cane's parents frequently took her to movies—"heavyweight European" stuff by Fellini, Bertolucci, Bergman, and Godard. She saw *2001: A Space Odyssey* several times and, with a friend, memorized all of the dialogue in *The Sting*.

Cane claims to have been "neurotic and obsessive" about getting a 4.0 grade point average, graduated from high school a year early, and attended the University of California at Santa Cruz as a Sociology major. As she was finishing her undergraduate studies, Cane wrote a thesis on fascism in American cinema. After considering the topic as a doctoral thesis, she decided instead to learn how films were made.

"In 1985 I applied to graduate school at UCLA in Critical Studies, then opted for Film. I had heard that USC was a lot like a studio, and that scared me. I didn't really want to be competing. And it was expensive. NYU was attractive, but I heard they only invited forty percent back for the second year. And the out-of-state tuition there was very high. So the most economical seemed to be UCLA.

"When I entered UCLA, I was just happy to be part of the production program. I was high, thinking that maybe I could make films. It was the first year that the 401 project was switching from Super 8mm to 16mm, and it was the first year the so-called 'pilot' program became *the* program.

"Ten students were picked, to make five films in ten weeks, rotating crew positions. There was a lot of optimism and enthusiasm in the department for this new program, and we were the first people officially in it."

Cane's first film at UCLA was *2½ Weeks*, a comedy about a woman who falls in love with a man after she sneezes and he says, "God bless you." "It was really cheesy," she recalls, "but it was a rush to hear people laugh at my work for the first time."

That's What Women Want was developed with input from Cane's father.

"We're really close. He's fifty-three. He looks young and has a lot of young friends. I often rely on his feedback. We brainstorm and have collaborated a lot. Some of the new ideas for the rewrite came out of our discussions. We'd have conversations and go off on these tangents, I'd write things and go back to him. He came across an article on computer pornography. All these weird things were strung together into this wacky script based on all kinds of different influences."

In January 1990, Cane began assembling her crew and applied for use of a Panavision camera, which she was granted for twenty-one days. After several unsuccessful attempts to cast the male lead—a daring role which required partial nudity and full fearlessness—Cane found her man in her own backyard.

"My friend Greg Watkins, who was a film student, auditioned. I told him I wanted him to crew on the film. I was close to hiring a theatrical actor for the part but he was uneven, so I brought Greg in. He had codirected a feature called *A Little Stiff* that was made for ten thousand dollars. Greg liked acting and had taken a couple of classes. I just had him do the first scene, and he really did well. I was a little worried because he was a good friend, but now I think I was really lucky because he was perfect."

That's What Women Want was shot in L.A. in three weeks and for about $15,000, which Cane had saved working as an assistant editor. The half-hour film won the Nicholson Award (and $5,000 cash) and the Lyra Award for Sound.

"I felt good about the film—it was the first one that closely matched my original vision. I did an edit on video first. I broke up with my boyfriend, so I had to leave the house where we shot part of the film, and I had to give the Marxes a rough cut to see if I needed any pickups before I left. [Richard and Barbara Marx, Academy Award–winning sound editors whose credits include *Terms of Endearment* and *The Big Chill*, are instructors at UCLA film school.] Richard called and told me it was a wonderful film. That was really encouraging."

The film was shown at UCLA's year-end Visions Festival, and at the prestigious closing night of the Directors Guild of America's Spotlight Awards screenings.

"I got a mention in *Variety* and a few calls," Cane remembers. "There was somebody from Interscope, and from Paramount. Alberto Garcia, who was from Sundance, recommended it to a producer at Warner Brothers. Someone from New World called, but he wanted ideas for game shows. [Laughs] Michael Manheim Productions. Most of them wanted scripts, which I didn't have. No agents called.

"A couple of agents saw it at a screening, and some called for tapes because they hadn't come. I haven't sent the tapes out, though, because I don't have a feature script. I sent it to some of the producers, and they want a script. Monika Skerbelis [an executive] said she'd show it around at Universal, but I haven't heard from her.

"What's hard for me right now is I feel like I'm judged in an instant. I have to be 'on' all the time, and I don't always know how to present myself. My natural tendency is to be pretty laid back, talk slow, be kind of shy and introverted. I feel like I need an acting class for this stuff—improvisation and acting are good skills to have in this business.

"I'm terrified of pitching. I've never done it. Our group, the 401 [UCLA filmmaking class] group, is trying to come up with a name. Our slogan for the production company will be 'They Shoot Films, Don't They?' We're going to try to practice pitching to each other, and even *that* terrifies me.

"It's hard to figure out where to put your energy. I freelance for five different people. Tutoring on sound and editing, and actually doing some sound cutting. I'm a technical consultant to someone who's trying to make a documentary. A lot of it, like the sound cutting, is through school—I'm doing that for another student's film. I enjoy doing sound effects, and it doesn't tax my creative energy. I'd much rather do that than wait tables."

Cane is considering a production assistant job with director Donald Petrie *(Opportunity Knocks, The Favor)*, for which she was recommended by UCLA film chair Robert Rosen.

"I'm trying to avoid it and just scrape by with other things. It would be long hours, six days a week, and there's no time to write.

And because I know how hard it is to make a film, I would be doing my best to try to help the director.

"I have mixed feelings about it. I mentioned one of his father's films, and that wasn't too good. He just said, 'No, that's my father,' and I said, 'I guess I have you guys confused,' and then I didn't know what the hell Donald had done, so I couldn't talk about his work at all. He didn't act very taken aback, but he is getting references from three film schools.

"So then I rented a couple of his films and tried to call him but got his machine. *Grumpy Old Men* is the film, shooting in Minnesota with Jack Lemmon, George C. Scott, and Sophia Loren. [The picture was eventually cast with Lemmon, Walter Matthau and Ann-Margret.] It sounds like a great experience on the one hand, but I feel like I should really be writing and screening my film at festivals. But it's easy to put writing on the back burner—it's so hard to write.

"I've just started getting going on the feature version of *That's What Women Want*. The P.A. job would pay like four hundred dollars a week, which is okay, but . . . I don't know. I'm not really going for it like I would if it were for Scorsese.

"I'm also not really good at pitching myself over the phone, or in a cold interview with a stranger. Donald and I spoke for ten or fifteen minutes. He asked me what I wanted to do, and I told him, 'Direct.' He said, 'If you could direct any film, what would you be doing?' I said, 'The feature version of my short film.' And he said, 'No, no, no, if you could direct *any* film that's out there, like *Die Hard 2* or *Beethoven* . . .'

"I got really tripped up because I couldn't think of any contemporary films I would want to say I'm directing. So I talked about films from the past that impressed me. I guess I'm not that impressed with what's out there right now. I *was* impressed with Woody Allen's *Husbands and Wives*—he's able to get at the complexity of people's relationships in a deeper way than a lot of films—a combination of humor, pain, and honesty. The characters were totally believable, the direction was authentic, the dialogue was great. I rented *GoodFellas* again, too. Very entertaining.

"Life is like a roller coaster, aside from just being in the film business. It's what I wanted to capture in my film, how we're kind of taken on this ride in the process of finding out who we are, and trying to figure out how to relate to the opposite sex, and how to learn to integrate parts of ourselves that we're accepting and denying. I'm hoping the feature-length version will deal with those ideas in more depth. People are really unstable.

"This woman Laura, who just moved in with me, is really cool. She's a receptionist at a postproduction house, and she's trying to get on a Percy Adlon [director of *Bagdad Café*] set. She's really interested in film. She eventually wants to be a director."

Cane contemplates what her life may be like in two years.

"I think the feature version of *That's What Women Want* could be really commercial. There'll be some interest in it, definitely. And I think the people in this [UCLA alumni] production company are driven, and that among them someone's going to get a deal to do something, or we'll do it guerrilla style—some people have equipment.

"I'm optimistic about the future. The money thing is always an issue but I'm not as worried. About a month ago I was a little bit panicked. I don't know if I'll be directing in two years, but I will be participating creatively with someone else if I don't get it off the ground.

"I've heard that sixty percent of those normally employed in the business are out of work. So if the economy doesn't improve, we're in trouble. But Gregg Araki does all of these films for nothing. If you have a strong idea that doesn't require too much fancy stuff, with good people . . . I feel like I have a lot of talented friends, and we're lucky to have each other and have this kind of support."

JOHN KEITEL

October 23, 1992

The Sixth Gallery, in the heart of West Hollywood, is a coffee-house with a split personality: part '90s Beat poetry den, part yuppie hangout. John Keitel, the manager of the place, knows every inch of it.

As I walk in, Keitel is behind the counter making his own break-fast, unfiltered apple juice over a bowl of granola. He offers me the same—which I negotiate into something considerably less healthy—and we take a table in the front room.

John Fitzgerald Keitel was born into an obviously Democratic household in 1964 and raised in Highland Park, Illinois, a northern suburb of Chicago.

He remembers going to the city with one of his six siblings to see *Chitty Chitty Bang Bang* for his fifth birthday.

"Another film that was important was *One Flew over the Cuckoo's Nest* for its treatment of questioning authority and the establish-ment," Keitel says. "I saw that on a family outing—an important thing to keep in mind, since as a kid I saw that film's themes sanc-tioned within my family."

Between Keitel's junior and senior years of high school he attended the National High School Institute of Theatre Arts, a five-week intensive summer program. There he performed with Jami Gertz, now a successful film actress, in a theatrical adaptation of a Eudora Welty short story.

"I lived on campus with all of the other kids. That was where I had the awakening, not about being gay, but about sex. Nothing happened, but there was this lifestyle—I hate that word, but—*there were gay people*. It was a possible condition that existed within myself! The sexual tension between me and many of the guys who were there was intense."

After high school Keitel attended Stanford as a Human Biology major. Though his parents saw medical school in his future, Keitel was increasingly drawn toward Theatre, which became his second major.

"In the mid-eighties a lot of people were going off to work on Wall Street, and firms came to interview on campus. It was tempting, but I ultimately decided it was not for me. I thought about advertising. The CIA came to campus and I thought, 'Maybe I'll join the CIA.' But given the development of my sexual orientation, that was probably not a good idea."

Before moving on to graduate school, Keitel went back to Chicago—knowing he could live there cheaply—and sought commercial and industrial film work. After interning for several theatre and production companies, he was hired as the personal assistant to Julia Cameron, a writer-director, ex-wife of Martin Scorsese (and the author of a current popular creative self-help book entitled *The Artist's Way*).

"She was in postproduction on a low-budget feature she had directed. I wasn't even in Hollywood but I was indoctrinated into the ways of Hollywood. Being an assistant sucks, and I got it out of my system. I think Julia's a really good person, but I was doing everything from walking the dog to picking up the daughter at school, and it was all volunteer. She kept saying, 'The most important thing is the credit—the credit is all that matters.' [Sarcastically] Riiight!

"It was sort of the seamier side of the business. I was twenty-three at the time, and this job demystified the names for me. I realized that working in this industry and making films wasn't some unattainable goal, because I was dealing with the people who did it. You can be an assistant to someone and work your ass off to make them famous, but you're still just the assistant. I knew pretty quickly that was not what I wanted, and she figured that out, too. She said, 'I know you want my job.' I had my indoctrination, and then I decided, *adios* Chicago, I'm going to L.A. to go to film school.

"I wanted to go to USC, because of it being in L.A., and its reputation as *the* film school. That carries with it tremendous legitimacy for someone concerned about their future. There are also negatives, though. In many ways it's more of a business school than it is an art school. A lot of people with liberal arts degrees from good schools go there because they don't want to go to law school."

Shortly after his arrival in L.A., Keitel contacted a close friend of Cameron's, actor Nancy Allen (*Blow Out, Robocop*). He soon became conscious, though, of their difference in status.

"I really got the strong feeling that until I could come to the table as an equal, I wasn't going to mess around.

"At the end of my first year of film school I had a six-week relationship with a prominent studio executive, Brian Simms [name changed], who was only a few years older than me. But I realized quickly that I didn't need to 'get in' with people that way. I didn't need to become somebody else's person. I felt strongly—and still do—that it had to be on my terms.

"The first time I met Brian he saw me in [the nightclub] RAGE. Months later we were both at Studio One, and he just grabbed me. I found out later all his ex-boyfriends are Wilhelmina models and I thought, 'Where do I fit into all this?' He said, 'Oh, you're a different person.' Like I was in another class.

"Brian worked really long hours and at eight o'clock he'd call me to say he was picking me up to go to dinner. He was making a lot of money, driving a Mercedes convertible, and I was in my first year of film school! He really encouraged me to drop out and get a job at the studio as an executive. It was tempting because I saw how he lived, and it wouldn't have taken that long to make the same money, if I was good and put in the hours.

"I didn't pursue it, and the relationship ended, and shortly afterward I met Carter [Keitel's current boyfriend]. Brian did call me and we kept in contact. He called and said a job opened up working for the Executive Vice President of Development at Warner Brothers. I didn't really want it, but I didn't want to say no. He finally called me on the car phone one day and said, 'All right, John—you wanna work at the studio or don't you? There's a job, and this is what you need to do. Can you come by, pick up and read the screenplay? I'll give you samples of the notes we use. We wanna see what you do.'

"I read the script and wrote the coverage, and nothing came of it. I didn't want to work at the studio and I think he finally sensed that. I realized I would be forever frustrated on that side of the table. I wanted to be the writer or the director, not the 'suit.' I see Brian every so often. He may have seen my film, but, I don't know . . . there's a certain level of antagonism. I *defied* him. But I worried about it for about a half an hour and then said I'm not going to anymore."

Every semester, under the course number 480, USC's graduate film school finances eight productions—five narratives and three documentaries. Keitel's, *An All-American Story*, began as a documentary about the resurgence of U.S. patriotism during the Gulf War.

"The process of selection for the 480s is long and involved. You submit proposals, and you have to take certain prerequisites. For the documentaries, you submit a two- or three-page proposal. Then they choose a group and invite these people to pursue further development by writing a ten- or twelve-page treatment. From those they select another group, another cut is made, and the chosen ones are invited to pitch their idea.

"For the pitch you videotape a trailer—your vision of the film. You go out and shoot a bunch of stuff, come back to a pitch meeting that lasts about a half hour, and talk to a committee comprised of the documentary faculty and the student representatives. Usually there are about nine people who make it to that point, and from that group three are usually chosen for production.

"My pitch was for more of a concept film than a traditional documentary with one or two main characters. They don't normally go for that type of thing. They were willing to take that risk, and when the shift went personal, that was a really big risk. I wasn't always sure the film would come together."

Ultimately *An All-American Story* became Keitel's own story, as he filmed himself returning to Stanford for his five-year reunion. No longer "closeted," Keitel brought his boyfriend, Carter Bravmann, and much of the documentary's impact—and humor—comes from their conflicts at the event.

An All-American Story cost either $11,000 or $35,000. The first number represents the direct costs, what USC paid outside vendors for film stock, processing, and coding. The $35,000 incorporates indirect costs, "funny money" or "soft dollars" charged to the production by the school but never actually changing hands. This method of accounting is a way of educating future professional production managers, production accountants, and line producers.

Screened at the Gay and Lesbian Film Festivals in L.A. and San Francisco, *An All-American Story* has also been featured in festivals in London, Hong Kong, and Honolulu. At the Chicago International Film Festival it won the Golden Plaque for Best Student Production, Nonfiction. Keitel's film was also awarded the Independent Documentary Association David L. Wolper Student Documentary Achievement Certificate, as one of seven winners out of eighty international entries, chosen by a panel including Michael Apted and Saul Bass.

"It screens at the Academy November fourth. Twice a year USC films are shown there. And this Sunday it will be seen at an AIDS benefits in the Hollywood Hills. I also got a call that someone from Samuel Goldwyn is trying to track me down.

"A festival in Hong Kong will show it in January. I've yet to be offered to be flown anywhere. I do know people who have. I'm going to start charging the festivals. The first few, I was just grateful to get it in. But there's a lot of work that goes into this—keeping the contacts up, getting prints to them."

Keitel had recently attended a party at the home of Alan Hergott, a prominent entertainment lawyer. The gathering was organized to discuss ways to encourage films dealing with gay and lesbian issues both in the industry and at the university level. Keitel represented USC.

"At the dinner I met a lot of agents, producers, and executives—

one of whom was this person at Warner Brothers whom I had dated, Brian Simms. I thought he'd be there. It's a small world, as they say.

"You couldn't have asked for a better Hollywood experience. The party set my expectations in line about what happens after film school. Everyone thinks their film will show, someone's going to see it, they're going to sign with an agent, and they're going to get a deal. Doesn't happen. Very few people do. I met these people, I talked to some of them on the phone, those that hadn't seen the film did so and liked it, and that's that.

"Alan Hergott said that Peter Guber told him that the reason the studios have yet to make their gay-themed film is they've yet to find their gay John Singleton. Not to take anything away from Singleton, but the machinery was put in place for him. They decided to create a star, and he was at the right place at the right time and he had a script [*Boyz N the Hood*] that was good. But you have to place him in the context of black filmmaking, and he came along at a time when they were willing to take that chance. I think his agent and Stephanie Allain [then a Columbia Pictures executive] had a vision, and that enabled John to get *his* vision on the big screen.

"At the party, I said, 'This is going to take one of you who's in a position of power to have a vision as well. You have to be willing to take a risk, and not spend a lot of money on it. They didn't on *Boyz*. So don't give me this garbage that you have to have a twenty-million-dollar film or it's not worthy of taking to your boss, because it's not true.'

"My film is a documentary, so they don't know quite what to think about it or how to handle it, but as far as getting work from that film, I'm not. I'm going to have to create my own work.

"Whatever film you're pursuing, you have to be so passionate about it that you will do anything to get it made. You can't waffle at all. You've got to convince them it has to be made. You can't go in and say, 'I've got this really great idea, what do you think?' It has to be, 'This thing is leaving the station—get on the train now.' But that means you have to come up with or find that story or script that you want to get made.

"I see filmmakers' expectations for this First Look Festival that's coming up, and they're like, 'I've got to have a script. Got to graduate from film school with a film, and a full-length screenplay.' But what are these projects *about*? It's not about just satisfying some requirement.

"A screenplay isn't a job application that says you can sit down and type out a hundred and twenty consecutive pages and you know the format. I knew a guy at film school who would say, 'I just finished my horror script!' A month later he's saying, 'I'm almost done with my thriller!' So what is he going to do, have a representative from every genre?

"Maybe it works for some people, but I realized that whatever made me make *An All-American Story* in the first place is what's got to be there for the next film. Something burning, that I need to see get done. Luckily, I know what that is now.

"I want to do an ensemble film with seven primary characters. The working title is *Ground Zero*. Before you can go anywhere you've got to start at ground zero. And Ground Zero is the name of the central location of the film, a café in an urban environment, which is opened by two friends, one gay and one straight. The four other main characters are two Mexican busboys and the two love interests of the owners. Spending so much time in this café, I'm part of this extended family.

"A lot goes on—rawness, creativity. There are also a lot of different people that come in contact with one another. And I want to put these people from discordant backgrounds and upbringings together and force them to deal with each other—force them to get to know and appreciate one another.

"What happens when you take a middle-class white boy from the suburbs and have him work with a black militant lesbian from the inner city? How do they form a working relationship, and get beyond their preconceptions of one another and create new conceptions? The premise is, what happens when you take a group of people from diverse backgrounds and throw them into a seemingly adjunct community?

"What I mean by that is a community that doesn't form for any particular reason—it just sort of happens—and everyone's reason for coming is different, either to work for money, to get a shot of caffeine, or because they're lonely.

"Before they know it, this community has developed a momentum and a character all its own. Amidst the crises of L.A.—

social and political tensions and economic woes—how do they support one another? Two of the main inspirations have been the escalation of gay-bashing and my fascination with two Mexican cousins at Sixth Gallery. Both are saving money to bring their families up here, both come from this very Catholic country and work in this gay coffeehouse. They are the backbone of this place—they know it better than any of us.

"I want to include them in this community in a way that we usually don't, because most of the time these guys are invisible. They do their work and they kind of move like ghosts among us, yet they live with the very real threat of being deported. What happens when one of them is picked up by the INS? A friend of mine was, and it was a terrible experience. I had no idea what an awful organization that is.

"I'm under an extendable but strict schedule because this is being made as my thesis film at school. *An All-American Story* was made within the context of a graduate production workshop, so it is not my thesis film. The new script will be finished by January, and then the film will be made. It *must* be. And I do have means to raise a certain amount of money.

"Ideally, someone will say, 'Great, make this film.' Samuel Goldwyn, whatever. But I can't sit around waiting, so I did a nuts-and-bolts budget of fifty-seven thousand dollars. Primarily in one location—someone just said it would be like *Return of the Secaucus Seven*. This will be my first feature. So people have said, 'Let me see what you're going to do next,' and this is it. If they can help me, great. If not, I'm going to do it anyway.

"I'd much prefer Goldwyn or New Line to Warner Brothers. I knew after the festivals that there were people making careers out of one festival film. But I'm over *An All-American Story*. It's done. I still want it shown, like at the Berlin Film Festival. But *Ground Zero* is what I'm doing next, and however it happens, fine.

"I think Hollywood's at a critical juncture and it's going to change dramatically. We're going to see all new stars, all new actors. The Arnold Schwarzeneggers and Bruce Willises are going to be gone. The eighties are going to be *really* dead soon, and with it will go that style of filmmaking and the content of those films.

"The economy will have a lot to do with it, the election. If Clinton wins in a landslide, the social agenda in this country will shift. With that will come a change in the content of feature films.

It'll be much more like the seventies—*Easy Rider, Harry and Tonto, Nashville.*

"High-concept storytelling doesn't take long to master, and when you do, it's so predictable. If Bush loses, it'll be a sign we need to shift. I have that sense.

"Maybe it's just optimism."

MARCO WILLIAMS
October 23, 1992

Motor On Inn, on Motor Avenue in Culver City within spitting distance of the former MGM (now Sony/Columbia) studios, is a funky cappuccino and muffin joint decorated in thrift-shop chic—burgundy velvet couches, gold-plated lion statues. Its walls are covered with obscure images of retro pop culture.

Marco Williams, T-shirted and dreadlocked, is slightly late for our breakfast but extremely apologetic.

Born in Philadelphia one Halloween, Williams cites ageism as the reason he keeps the year of his birth a secret.

"Everybody is asking me my age these days," he says. "I tell people that in the fifties you didn't ask women their age, and in the nineties you don't ask men."

Williams's was the fourth generation of fatherless households in his family; his father fled before he was born. An only child, Williams moved with his mother to Manhattan's Lower East Side when he was very young. The arts were not part of his childhood, as he grew up without a television or exposure to classical music or museums. Instead Williams listened to the radio and read, and lived for street games: punchball, stickball, ring-a-levio, roundup, hot-peas-and-butter, hide-and-go-seek.

"I didn't know anything about movies, really. When I was a kid, at the St. Marks Theatre I can remember—thirty-five cents for kids, fifty for adults—seeing *Cat Ballou*, and sneaking in to see *Barbarella*. I was a big Bruce Lee fan, and would go to the Academy of Music and watch all his films. I remember my mother told me a story that fascinated me about movies, about a guy who makes a bet that he can eat fifty hard-boiled eggs in an hour. I was captivated by the concept—whether he did it or not, my mother didn't tell me. The film, obviously, was *Cool Hand Luke*."

When Williams turned eighteen, his mother moved to Paris to pursue her dream of working as a French chef. He was accepted by several colleges including Yale, Brown, and the University of Pennsylvania, and chose Harvard, which offered a better scholarship.

At Harvard, a humanities class on Alfred Hitchcock's work sparked Williams's interest in cinema.

"I was impressed with Hitchcock's precision and intent. I had never before appreciated that there was a whole art form of film. But the seed didn't germinate until a setback. I applied to a poetry class at Harvard. I submitted ten poems and was not accepted.

"I took a leave of absence from Harvard for two years. When I returned I was determined to make films. I had an interest in photography. I had taken a couple of classes while I was out, and I imagined that film was a synthesis of photography and poetry. So I went back to Harvard determined.

"You had to apply for the filmmaking class, and I wrote some sort of statement. I saw this piece of graffiti when I was in New York that said, 'Not art for art's sake but art for life's sake.' I culminated my statement by saying, 'That's why I have to take this class.' I got in.

"My teacher was Chris Gerolmo, who wrote *Mississippi Burning* and *Miles From Home*. I don't think Chris had yet been produced then, but for me his greatest credential was that he believed in movies.

"The first thing we did was a class exercise Chris called something like 'Ten Conversations in Ten Minutes.' We took a roll of film. There were ten people in the class and each person had a minute to introduce themselves and say something.

"I was trying to use film as a way to explore life, which is an emphasis at Harvard—documentaries—although through their archives and film studies classes you do have the opportunity to see all the classics. But in Filmmaking we watched a lot of documentaries and experimentals."

Williams earned a B.A. with Honors in Visual and Environmental Studies from Harvard, where he began working on an autobiographical documentary.

"The real genesis of *In Search of Our Fathers* was that in 1980 I decided I wanted to know my dad. My mom came back from Paris for part of the summer. There was a phone call for me, and I knew who it was—it was my dad. In speaking with him—which was a very strange, almost surreal encounter—I said that I was going to Ohio that summer. After hanging up and in the ensuing weeks, I started to feel that this was amazing—two adult men about to meet each other for the first time.

"I thought this should be documented, and what I would do was have someone come with a telephoto lens and a still camera and capture the snapshot. Then I realized it wasn't really just one moment but a series of moments, and that film captures a series of moments.

"I sat on it until the following spring, in 1981, when I had to do a final project in my Advanced Filmmaking class. I had ten minutes of film. I had filmed myself making another phone call to my dad, and had gone to Paris and shot some impressionistic stuff with my mother. When I started to put it together, it didn't gel. I was trying to make a movie in five weeks.

"After another year, I still thought that a future meeting with my dad was a good idea for a movie. I started to write some grant proposals, very sketchily. I worked and saved a little money. I had spent a year working as a T.A. in film at Harvard, which gave me the access to equipment. Then I sat on it again for some time."

In 1983, after several production assistant jobs on commercials, Williams was hired as a script supervisor (or continuity person) on John Sayles's *The Brother from Another Planet*.

"It was a great experience. Particularly given the fact that I was the script person, which meant that I worked fairly close with John. They bestowed a great deal of confidence on me, just based on my knowledge of filmmaking. After the fact, I realized that I didn't know half as much as I thought I did.

"John is a man without any discernible ego. That's not to say he doesn't have one, but he is always open to suggestions. He never said, 'I'm the director, leave me alone.' I respect that because that's how I am—open to things but in charge.

"It was Ernest Dickerson's first real feature as a cinematographer. [Dickerson is now a feature director whose credits include *Juice* and *Tales from the Crypt Presents Demon Knight*.] He had shot Spike Lee's first film, *Joe's Bed-Stuy Barbershop*, but *The Brother* gave him his chops. David Strathairn, who's now having a great year [with roles in *Sneakers*, *A League of Their Own* and Sayles's *Passion Fish*] was in it. It was just a real community of people, of which I have fond memories.

"John is very quiet. He could come on a set and not say a word to anybody until it was time to shoot. It was his third feature, I think. Low budget. John is an outstanding writer, and the dialogue is really believable for some Waspy white guy—it's primarily set in Harlem. I admire John because he is an American independent in the European tradition. He just does his stuff."

Hopes for additional production work were dashed as Williams was unable to land another job as a script supervisor or join that union. Determined to make a major life change, he pursued several grants for films, and applied to graduate school at UCLA for a master's degree in Afro-American Studies.

"I had this idea that I could specialize in film as a discipline. So I took some film classes and tried to edit my documentary, which I was still shooting.

"The first two grant proposals I wrote—one to the NEA and the other to AFI's Independent Filmmakers' Program—I was so worried that no one would be interested that I wrote it in the third person. I pretended it was about someone else."

Williams describes Springfield, Ohio, where he went to confront his father, James Berry, in 1987 as a one-horse town.

"It's got the proverbial railroad tracks, and blacks live on one side and whites on the other. When I first arrived there, I was looking for a store to find a map so I could figure out if I wanted to go there myself. I asked some approaching cops where I could buy a map, and they asked why, and I said I was looking to meet my father, and they said, 'Well, who is he? Maybe we know him.' They didn't, but it was that sort of environment—'We know all black men because we lock them up.' It had that feel.

"I hadn't seen my father in seven years. He said a lot of things I found unpleasant—fighting words—and my personality is such that when someone says something that bothers me I usually respond. But at that moment I was far more interested in getting the material than being thrown out. I was definitely working as a filmmaker.

"I think that my father was at a point in his life at which he thought he was invincible. He signed a release. He obviously had the power to say no, so it was a form of benevolence, because he had to grant me permission to film him. I think he was suspicious that [legal application of the footage] might have been what I was after all along. I just said, 'This is what I'm doing, making this movie about the black family.' I probably didn't say it was about meeting him, but at that point it was not a lie. The film *had* become about my family and the black family. The first time we spoke—on film—I told him I wanted to make a film about our meeting. So I just let him know that the scope of the film had broadened.

"Somewhere in our conversation one could infer that the subtext was whether or not I wanted something from him. I told him no. I didn't know enough about the legal situation to know if I *could* make any claim, financial or otherwise—but that wasn't what I was there for.

"I thought I had processed everything, but I was not really conscious. Once I met him, I had a huge amount of disappointment. I say in the film, less specifically, 'This is my father. He wasn't at all what I had expected.' You can hear in my tone that I was expressing disappointment. I was disappointed and dismayed—really flabbergasted by him. I hadn't gone with any conscious expectations, but I had expectations, and I think every child wants his daddy to be the best, the greatest. He had never really been a shit to me. He didn't know that I even existed until I was eighteen.

"There is something unresolved between him and my mom that has to do with me because I am the by-product of whatever was going on between them. I leave it for others to analyze the film. Psychology is complicated, and there's so much one needs to know to get at those cores. I'm in therapy now and talk about things and think about my childhood, but while I was making the film? No."

In 1990 Williams applied to direct a half-hour film, *Without a Pass*, for the now-defunct Discovery Program. Founded by Chanticleer Films producers Jonathan Sanger and Jana Sue Memel, the program chose four scripts for production each year. After completion, subsequent festival showings, and airing on Showtime, Chanticleer contracted for one year of "right of first refusal." This gave Sanger and Memel the opportunity to produce a feature project with the director.

From hundreds of applicants each year, Chanticleer would choose two dozen to direct two- or three-page, dialogue-heavy scenes on $3/4$-inch videotape. The director would be asked to cast the test, choose from a limited supply of props, finish the scene within four hours, and immediately edit over an additional four hours.

"You have to be interviewed by their whole conglomerate. Sanger, Memel, and someone from Showtime ask you about your script, and how you would shoot it. I suspect it imitates a studio system, and they pride themselves on being like a studio in terms of their product.

"We shot the test on a Paramount soundstage. You have a full crew, a D.P. and A.P., grips, et cetera. One of their producers is there. I had a very elaborate master shot and was able to get that and one or two covers, but I was only partway through my script. So I more or less had the goods but not really how I wanted to cut it. The producer said, 'Marco, you have twenty minutes—what are you going to do?' I said, 'Give me a second.'

"In the most critical role of my piece I had a great actor, Benicio Del Toro, who had played a villain in the James Bond movie *Licence to Kill* [and was later featured in Bryan Singer's *The Usual Suspects*]. My documentary experience helped in the sequence when his character was being executed—I had this whole thing about people watching an execution. He was the person being executed and I said, 'Benicio, I can't start and stop and re-set-up. I need you to just act.'

"We just rolled the camera for twenty minutes straight—it was the combination of his performance and the choice that I made. The set became very quiet. Everyone stopped and watched. When he finished, they all applauded. It was a real moment. It was exciting cinema.

"Chanticleer sits you in a room with twenty people and they all ask you questions. 'Tell us about your script. How would you shoot it? Who would be your D.P. if you could have anyone? Who would you love to act in it?' Then I was told I was accepted. I wanted Benicio to play a role. Unfortunately, I hadn't written a script for him. I have an idea for one now. There was a smaller role for him but he didn't want to do it. It was important for him not to be seen in a smaller role at that time. It was a career choice.

"The assistant director had to leave three weeks before the shoot, the production designer two or three weeks before. So suddenly it was in disarray. They brought on a production supervisor. If he had good intentions, which were to help me make a good film, he didn't know how to implement them. His intentions seemed much more to make a good impression so that *he* might be able to direct at some point. That created conflict. There was conflict all throughout.

"Intrusion and compromise and my naïveté are the crux of my dissatisfaction. I fought myself in a lot of ways for not sticking up for myself. But I didn't know enough about how things would work, and allowed myself to be compromised and sort of get trampled on.

"They also set me up to fail. My script for *Without a Pass* was big for a Chanticleer film. Most of their films are six-day shoots. Mine probably warranted eight—seven at least—and they refused to do seven. That, I think, meant I could *only* fail. Particularly as a first-time [narrative] director, I had to do so much work in such a short period of time, and I really needed at least one additional day. There are other films that have additional days.

"I will take some share of the blame, for not demanding to know more about what the budget was. I was having such a good rapport with the people that I believed that they believed in me. But I had an inexperienced line producer, and then my executive in charge of production, ten days before we started, got a 'real job' and left.

"But I learned, and because of that, it won't happen again. I'm very good at saying 'fuck you' when I understand the rules of the game, and sometimes I even say 'fuck you' when I don't.

"The disappointment was that the script was fabulous. It's a great story. It could have been nominated for an Academy Award if it had been made better.

"They all say that they're running the program fabulously because they've received two Academy Awards and three nominations. I think that the contradiction lies in that it's supposed to be a director's medium, but the producers intrude completely. So, unfortunately, all of the films look exactly alike, even though so many of the scripts are different. You'd think you'd have a chance to get some real independent expression in there.

"I get fairly good response to the film. It has a couple of really great moments. I made a mistake in editing by restructuring it. It starts off fairly slowly, a little too expositional. So you have to weather a good five minutes before you really get into the movie. After that it's a movie, with a fabulous climax that I know affects audiences every time. It was on Showtime, and it's been shown a lot in different places. But if it's shown with *In Search of Our Fathers*, people only want to talk about that. The documentary is a feature, and much more complex, like the difference between a novel and a short story. Even as good as a short story is, it is going to pale in comparison to a good novel."

Both *In Search of Our Fathers* and *Without a Pass* were selected for the 1992 Sundance Film Festival in Park City, Utah. Williams was accompanied by his mother—featured in *In Search*—who became a mini-celebrity. The only filmmaker screening two works, Williams met attorney Marcy Morris and Intertalent agent Chris Moore at Sundance, and subsequently signed with them for representation.

"If you have something in competition, Sundance pays for you to attend one of the two five-day sessions. I attended both as a treat to myself after ten years of working to get there. The first session there were all these people paying attention to me, excited about my film. The second five days the buzz changes—it became a meat market. It was clear that in the second week no one gives a shit about documentaries. All the industry people are there looking for the next *sex, lies and videotape*. So I just went skiing.

"I volunteered to be on the documentary jury this year, but I'm up against Oscar winners who have been invited: Barbara Kopple [*Harlan County, U.S.A.*], Rob Epstein [*The Celluloid Closet; Common Threads: Scenes from the Quilt*], and Steve Ozaki [*Days of Waiting*]. My film hasn't won shit—not one award, anywhere."

Also in early 1992, Williams was hired by HBO V.P. Sheila Nevins to develop a proposal for a documentary on the Rodney King riots.

"They don't pay you as a producer. What you're being paid is the opportunity to make a film. But it was enough money for me to secure an office and staff it with a part-time administrative assistant, a full-time researcher, and an intern. I budgeted for maybe two months, and I spent three months on the project. To my knowledge I was the only person solicited.

"They passed on my proposal, but I think it's very good. It might be a little too intellectual or creative for HBO and their audience. They said every step of the way that theirs is a 'six-pack-of-beer' crowd. I didn't strike while the iron was hot. By the time they got the proposal, two months after the riots, HBO's perception out of New York was that the riots were passé. I tried to make them see that all you had to do was be out here to know that the stuff was not over—and that my whole thesis for the project was, could it happen again?

"Then, this past spring, I was contacted by a headhunter for an executive position in HBO's documentary division. They flew me to New York to meet with Sheila. But I didn't get the job—I think because I was ambivalent about no longer being a creative person."

In 1991 PBS's documentary program *Frontline* had put up $50,000 in finishing money for *In Search of Our Fathers* and paid Williams a broadcast licensing fee of $25,000. The following year *Frontline* teamed him with a journalist to codirect a riot documentary for them, but the partnership ultimately fell apart. For the past year he has also been producing a documentary called *Nana*, set in South Africa, where he traveled for the filming. But Williams is still casting for the big fish—a Hollywood feature.

"I spent six or seven months doing the Hollywood two-step. I learned that I was willing to say 'yes' to anything because I wanted my foot in the door. I would do television, but it's not really where I want to reside."

Williams cites other African-American contemporaries who are making a reputation in films.

"Chris Gerolmo is a real good friend. I know Spike Lee from New York, I taught Reggie Hudlin at Harvard, and I worked for Warrington Hudlin. Charles Burnett is a friend, though I don't hang out with him. Charles Lane is a friend that way. John Singleton I've never met, actually. He wrote something about boxing for HBO and I tried to get a job directing it.

"I don't speak to John Sayles that often. I invited him to be in *Without a Pass*, with David Strathairn. I thought it would be kind of fun to have them play the cops in my film, because in *The Brother From Another Planet* they played cops. But their schedules didn't allow for it. When I had my screening in New York there were messages left for John, and Spike and Michael Moore. None of them came, but I know them well enough to call them.

"I think Spike is very good at playing the media. I liked *She's Gotta Have It* and *Do the Right Thing,* but I didn't really like his other films. I think he's filled with ideas. The films are short-changed in the writing. I admire Spike's abilities. He may be a spokesperson for a lot of blacks, but I don't feel he is for me. I get a little frustrated with that. But I feel he has something to say and he's making a difference, and I don't begrudge him in the least.

"Certainly Spike's success has suggested to people in Hollywood that you can make a buck on black-themed films. But I think what we're seeing this year versus last year is a regression—there are not as many films made by blacks this year. I have feared this all along. If the expectation is to do gangster films or light comedy fare, we are doomed.

"We're looking for a way to buck that. Here and there it's happening. It's typical of Hollywood that one or two benefit, though, instead of a bunch. It's a little club—you go with who you know.

"I've been to fifteen or twenty meetings, and all but one amounted to just meeting and greeting people. They want scripts. I have one, but it needs to be expanded. I wrote it with an idea for a TV movie. It could be a feature. I stopped because it dealt with black teenagers and after *Juice, New Jack City,* and *Boyz N the Hood,* I thought, 'Enough.'

"Chris Moore has set up a number of meetings for me, and I feel like a farmer in the spring, planting these seeds, setting up these relationships so people will know me, and when I have a script or something I'll have a number of places to go back to.

"I have to appreciate this as an investment venture, because it's a drag. You go to these meetings, and no one is offering you jack shit. They're there to say, 'If you have anything, my door is always open,' which I'm sure they'd say to anybody. That's not to disparage any of them. They've all been very nice.

"The highlight so far was Denzel Washington, who wanted to meet with me based on seeing my documentary. I had a couple of ideas I presented to him, but in the end it was just about connecting. We met at his office at Columbia. Denzel spent a lot of time watching and listening. Only after that did he offer his thoughts and feelings. He asked questions—he's someone who had a sincere interest versus somebody who just talks. That really touched me.

"Hollywood films are not that interesting—very formulaic, without much depth. I thought *Husbands and Wives* was really excellent. *Unforgiven* was flawed, but at least it tried to be about something. In the summertime you usually don't even get that. I didn't care for *Juice* or *New Jack City*. I knew they were successful and wanted to be impressed—which I was, in bits and pieces—but overall I was not that happy with them. I liked *Boyz N the Hood* as the best in the bunch.

"Things are sold with violence or sex. A gang movie allows a bunch of middle-aged white men to live out a fantasy for two hours. That was part of the popularity of blaxploitation. Even though white people were often the butt of the jokes, it allowed them to go in and be Shaft for two hours, and have the foxy girl. The detriment is the overwhelming perception that black culture *is* gang culture—that that's the extent of black reality. That's what I'm struggling against.

"I may not agree with what black filmmakers do, but I am inspired by the successes of my peers. You do what you gotta do. I have no judgments.

"You start to wonder who the hell you are, and how you face yourself each day. I do work hard, but it's my life, and I'm the boss. If I don't want to do something today, I don't. I'm my harshest critic, but the only person I have to face is myself.

"I'm definitely on the outside looking in. That's how I've been all along, and how it continues to be. It's partly out of choice and partly out of not being completely sure how to get in. And knowing that at some point I will be in."

PHOTO: LALEH SOOMEKH

JOHN MCINTYRE
November 11, 1992

The first thing I notice in John McIntyre's Santa Monica apartment is not the tenant but the duck. An enormous papiermâché duck suit lies in the center of the living room, so expertly rendered that it looks less like a suit than . . . an enormous, dead, duck.

Like McIntyre, his girlfriend Theresa works in the world of animation; her voice, appropriately, is reminiscent of Betty Boop's high squeal. Theresa serves up some homemade brownies and tea before excusing herself to watch a Bruce Springsteen concert on MTV.

McIntyre was born on April 1—again appropriate, he claims—in 1963. He lived in Jersey City, New Jersey, until he was nine, when his family moved to the suburbs. McIntyre's father was a writing teacher and basketball coach at Saint Peter's College; his mother raised her children, then attended university later in life.

McIntyre began drawing as a small child—first cartoon characters like the Flintstones, then a year of sketching only horses to master anatomical drawing.

"It wasn't until my father showed me how a flip-book works that I started to get to the next thing," he says. "I remember the first time I saw something 'change' on a piece of paper."

McIntyre also recalls his enchantment at seeing *Pinocchio* at a Jersey Shore drive-in. At thirteen, he and a friend monopolized the family's 8mm camera and started filming fifty-page flip-books.

"We convinced ourselves that we had reinvented animation, because we didn't know how it was really done. Instead of flipping these books for everybody, we thought, 'Why don't we place them each in front of the camera and take some single frames and save it on film and project it that way?' Sure enough, that's the essence of animation.

"The first one was a standard rocket launch that crashes into the moon. Later, in college, you see other people's flip-book films and it's always the same thing. I don't know if it's a phallic beginning or everyone's roots."

McIntyre considered and applied to several colleges, rejecting Rhode Island School of Design after visiting, and California Institute of the Arts due to its distance from the East Coast and an unattractive brochure. Despite being offered a scholarship from New York's School of Visual Arts based on a skills test, McIntyre chose NYU.

"I chose NYU because I liked Richard Protovin, the teacher I interviewed with. He convinced me that they had a more complete animation program. He was a painter who happened into animation and established NYU's animation department, an adjunct to their film department, in the mid-seventies. From the start he was an inspiration because I had never met an animator before, much less a successful one. He had made a few films and they had been shown and distributed. It was really attractive. That's when I started to think that I could make a career as an animator."

In 1983 the sophomore McIntyre made an animated short called *Scar* using a 16mm Bolex. He continued to adhere to the index-card style for a while.

"Flipping was easy to see immediately. I had a lot of trouble getting into the standard way of doing it, with paper that was twelve inches square. I felt like I had a novelty, a distinctive way that I worked, and I liked to be able to show somebody on the spot. With paper you have to flip 10 drawings at a time. It's kind of tricky, learning a new tool, and I was not fast to get into something different. I didn't know the advantages, then I realized when you draw larger you can get a lot more detail into it, a lot of variance."

After graduating as a Film and TV major from Tisch School of the Arts in 1986, McIntyre continued in NYU's graduate program. His agenda was twofold: teaching credentials and access to production equipment.

"Ultimately, I feel that graduate school was a disappointment, or a wrong choice. The real incentive was that I was offered a job staffing the new animation department, so with tuition remission, I could have gone to school for free. But the classes became redundant, and I had to work there full-time—a nine-to-five staff job. I was training people and troubleshooting on equipment, budgeting, and bookkeeping for the department from late 1986 through 1990. I was essentially running the place, and going to school at night."

NYU's two-year graduate program requires a seventy-two-credit minimum, and in Animation a finished final film is mandatory. McIntyre's, codirected with John Moynihan in 1990, was *Melbridge*, a live-action, period mock-documentary.

"The name 'Melbridge' is a hybrid of Méliès and Eadweard Muybridge, involving the transition from photography and magic into motion pictures. These two eccentrics inspired a twisted look at those sorts of guys.

"I was just juggling a lot of things at once. Making the film was the singular, courageous thing I was ready to do to really kick myself into gear. We were working day and night, one frame at a time, almost like animating—scratching and aging the frames.

"The cast was whoever we could find on each weekend we were shooting. We had girlfriends in it, friends, people who just liked the idea and volunteered to be in it. We shot on a big, cavernous old soundstage at 721 Broadway, with a loud hum from the air conditioning system and terrible light. It was perfect for making silent movies, because we could light it ourselves, and the noise didn't matter.

"I always felt that *Melbridge* was the perfect low-budget film, because it wiggled in all the cracks. We could use friends, we could use the soundstage, we didn't need synch camera because students would get those, and the synching we did do was single-shot interviews. And we had access to William Everson [an NYU Cinema Studies professor and noted film collector and scholar], who gave us stuff from his archive, which was also free."

Exteriors for *Melbridge* were filmed in Central Park's Strawberry Fields and in New Jersey; an ambitious East Orange train sequence was shot close to where the silent-film pioneer Edwin S. Porter made *The Great Train Robbery*.

"We also used the Erie Lackawanna. Edison used to film along the same railway, and as a kid I used to walk along its tracks. We built the train and the props and I said, 'We're going to get in a car and my parents will drive us, and it'll be real nostalgic.'

"We drove down to the tracks. We were mustachioed villains, all in whiteface and costumes. We pulled the train out. We got into the woods where the opening was going to be shot, but found that the tracks had been taken apart and peeled away years before. People in the neighborhood could see us through the trees from their houses. They were probably thinking, 'Here's a silent film crew that's come to film a train robbery, and there are no train tracks.' We ended up shooting at an active train track in Montclair, New Jersey.

"It became important to make a straight documentary with footage that really looked authentic. Later I felt this was a flaw in the film, because I thought it should have been more out-and-out funny. We could trust that the stuff looked period, so we may as well have done any joke we wanted, or gone even further.

"I was afraid of making a film that would just become slaphappy, and lose the integrity of the history, but I think we swung too far to the right and just made this historic thing. Distributors who have watched it say, 'It's really informative and very interesting, but we're not getting the humor of it.' It was *quietly* funny."

Melbridge had a well-attended, successful screening at Magno Sound in New York two days before McIntyre moved to Los Angeles in December 1990.

"I stayed with friends—I knew a lot of people. Folks had been moving out here for years. There are three generations of NYU students that I had watched leave, and lots of them were here. I lived in North Hollywood."

While in New York, McIntyre had sent his film reel to Duck Soup, a commercial animation company in Santa Monica. They responded with an offer over the phone: a full-time position as an animator with a salary of almost $50,000.

"It was great. I had been making a third of that at NYU. But I got the impression that business must be really good out here, so I didn't take the job right off. I made a demo reel, dubbed a dozen of them, and mailed them to studios all over New York and L.A.

"I called every place, but I think I got one other offer out of the nine other studios I went to. I went to Klasky-Csupo, the owners of which I had spoken to at an animation festival in Ottawa. They liked my reel, and they were starting this *Rugrats* program and gave me every indication that I could work there. In fact, they said I could do storyboard layouts—which is the closest to directing—and eventually direct. I had to go see them. But when I got to L.A. it was a different story. It was 'take this test.' They really put me off.

"A producer at Disney, Dan Rand, had the best sense of production and animation of anyone I had met out here. He talked to me for a while about the caliber of talent needed at Disney, and that I could probably fine tune what I did to reach certain levels, but that Disney is a major factory and I might get lost, and that perhaps it would be better if I started at Duck Soup.

"What makes holding Duck Soup off even more odd is that they had done a few ads with a really distinct look—loose, with this sketchy, animated yet artful look. It inspired me to use the same look in a short film I did, and I wrote to Duck Soup in eighty-five or eighty-six asking them if they had any work. They said they didn't hire anyone. There were six of them and that was it. I was rejected."

Accepting Duck Soup's offer, McIntyre went to work on commercials for Speas apple juice and for 7UP (Duck Soup created the "Dot" campaign) as an assistant animator.

"I was constantly fighting to get animation. Now I'm getting a lot more than I used to. But I don't even know if we're going to have any jobs next month. I was laid off at the beginning of last year for three months because no work came in.

"I didn't do too badly. There was the depression of being out of work, but I took that time to design stuff for Duck Soup. I hunted and got freelance work at Playhouse Pictures in Hollywood, and that sustained me for the three months.

"There are things Duck Soup encourages people to do. They have people doing ongoing logos to demonstrate different techniques and styles, put them on the reel and hope clients will say, 'Oh—let's do it *this* way.'

"I really like Duck Soup and the concept of the place, and I could go a long way there. I could animate there. They were talking about opening a live-action division, and I could segue into live action.

"Even if I was doing as well as I could, I didn't know if animation would be completely satisfying for me. I wanted to work the live angle as well. So I just started writing, and doing five different storyboards for various types of logos. I came up with these promotional flip-book ideas. I always wanted to publish flip-books. I have one week now to get them to a printer because we want to get them done by Christmas. I made five, and two of them have been accepted by Duck Soup.

"Right now I'm trying to jump-start various components, and create my novelty, the 'look' of what I do. Doing things that I've always wanted to do—build costumes, flip-books. I did some acting with an improv class called Up-Front Comedy. What I'm doing this year is shooting in different directions, and giving a lot of things a try, and it's been good therapy for me because I felt like I had become atrophied in what I wanted to risk.

"I'm exploring, expanding, becoming less specific but a lot happier. I think it's going to be the best choice I've made in a long time.

"[A while] ago, I was starting to feel old at twenty-eight. 'What am I doing?' and 'So-and-so had made it at that age'—that whole thing. Eddie Murphy was twenty-eight, or Chaplin was twenty-five when he started working at Keystone. The guy who did most of *The Seven Dwarfs* and created the look at Disney that pulled it out of the ancient era was twenty-five when he did that. Bill Titlow, who created *Night on Bald Mountain* and *Monster of the Whale* and all the incredible imagery of those early features, was in his early thirties.

"What is of interest to me is to do something that's pure and to the point, and not convoluted by the necessities of advertising and marketing. Just to make something that's genuinely funny, and not funny like I've ever seen before. I have a sense of humor that I feel like I've yet to exploit in a film. I'm starting to write feature scripts.

"I liked *Who Framed Roger Rabbit* when I first saw it, but it didn't have any staying power. It was a really violent experience, and I don't think back to how great that was the way I think back to, say, *Pinocchio*. Sweet, sentimental things stick closer to me, perhaps.

"*Roger Rabbit* was an incredible achievement, matching live with animated, like nothing before. It worked really well. The curse of

Roger Rabbit, I realized when I came out, is that ad agencies and clients insist on that look whenever they have characters. They want this full-textured, tonal, shadows-and-highlights feeling.

"On the high-paying jobs, half of the clients still want that, it hasn't stopped. And it's a nightmare to do tones and shadows—that's what I did for a year and a half. It was super-tedious. Some of the 7UP Dots I did for a year, putting the shadows on the sneakers, and highlights. I really overdosed on those."

McIntyre thinks about what his future might hold.

"In two years I want to have gotten enough experience in the commercial world, and to have directed some commercials, like the live-with-animated parts. I hope to have written a screenplay and gotten experienced in writing, pitching screenplays, and working my way into that end of the business."

PHOTO: LALEH SOOMEK

BERNARD JOFFA
November 16, 1992

When they first hit the Coast, aspiring filmmakers often move to the Hollywood section of Los Angeles, despite the fact that it is neither the safest nor the most desirable part of the city in which to live. My film school buddies and I did it, and I loved sending my friends and family letters with a Hollywood Boulevard return address. Now I wouldn't be caught dead in the area, although people are often caught there just that way. Sixteen years ago, perhaps I, as so many others, was seeking physical proximity to my dreams.

Downtown Hollywood does boast the few remnants of the town's history to be found. The corner of Hollywood and Vine and the footprints in the forecourt of Mann's Chinese Theatre can still inspire a newcomer, but other landmarks, like Schwab's, the Sunset Boulevard pharmacy where Lana Turner was (apocryphally) discovered, are long gone. Further east on Sunset, in the heart of an area in which Westerns were filmed seventy-five years ago, there now stands a minimall called Gower Gulch.

Hollywoodland, a small community in the hills just below the famous "Hollywood" sign, is where Bernard Joffa lives. His modest house features a picture window that offers him a spectacular panoramic view of the hills.

Joffa was born in 1955 in Johannesburg, South Africa. Until 1961, his family lived in Welkom, a little town in the Gold Field, a region of gold and diamond mines.

"I was born with a condition that's called 'a hole in the heart,' " he says, sipping tea. "When kids are born, there's a hole between their aorta and their heart which closes up, except for the blood and oxygen supply from the mother. In my case, it didn't close, which required major surgery. They cut me up at the age of eighteen months and left me with a scar of seventy-five stitches around my chest and back. More of me was stitched than was not. I had this horribly ugly scar all over me.

"The most uncomfortable thing was going to phys ed at school, where you had to swim. Anything that involved taking off my shirt was the worst. It was a nightmare.

"I pretty much became a director at the age of two. A control freak, that's what a director is. I was controlling my environment at the age of three, four. But it was a deception. Underneath a coat of armor was this Elephant Man, and only I knew it. Creativity is an expression of pain. You show me any good artist and I'll show you a person with a lot of pain.

"My parents were sensitive in some ways, but totally insensitive in others. My mother should have confronted the issue and let me know that it was okay to have a scar. When I wouldn't take off my shirt, she'd allow it."

Joffa's parents, first-generation Jewish liberal South Africans, sold jewelry and women's clothing in Bloemfontein, once the home of *Lord of the Rings* author J. R. R. Tolkien.

"It is the capital of Afrikaner conservatism, bizarre as any racist place can be. There was an eight o'clock curfew and sirens— WHOOOO!—all through the town, which meant that all black people had to be off the streets.

"Anti-Semitism was so pervasive. There was a group, a very close-knit community of Jews, which did pretty much what most persecuted people do all around the world—try to survive. However, we were white, and we were privileged. So if there wasn't a black problem there certainly was a Jewish problem. My parents still live in Cape Town, and I see them once every two years."

Joffa listened to the first moonwalk on the radio; television was banned for fear that it would spread liberal, Western ideas.

"My parents were part of a film club in the seventies. Most films were deemed inappropriate for us to see by the South African government. Any film with a black hero would be banned. Any film that had a black *name* in the title would be banned. It was ridiculous! They banned the children's book *Black Beauty*—about a horse—because of the title.

"People would smuggle in the films that were banned. I was supposed to be studying. I used to jump out of my bedroom and sit outside in the garden with a blanket and peek through the windows and see the films—*To Sir with Love; In the Heat of the Night; Goodbye, Columbus*—these films were all banned. *Bob & Carol & Ted & Alice*. Anything that was slightly sexual, as well. I used to go with my dad to fetch the reel. It was living on the edge—as brave as we got in our little town.

"It was the first time I saw film, a projector, a screen, light going across a room. I got into the mechanics of film, the scratches. It became something else."

Joffa spent several years after high school evading compulsory military service by maintaining his status as a full-time student. At various universities he studied business and drama. Then, in his early twenties, he enrolled in South Africa's only film school.

"The school, in Pretoria, was very practically oriented. They wanted to groom technicians to make films for the government. And politicians had recognized that television could be used as propaganda, but they had no one to train to become television producers and directors.

"It was a terrible school. We had an assignment to do a commercial, which I did. But they saw it and said I couldn't continue until I made another one because mine was an 'anti-commercial.' I just wanted to be creative."

In the late seventies Joffa finally agreed to serve in the army, out of fear that if he left South Africa he would never be allowed to return to see his family.

"Most of the kids went up into the border between South-West Africa—Namibia—and Angola. People were dying every day, like going to Vietnam, it was serious war. My time came, and I said, 'The only way I'll go is if I don't have to carry a gun.' That made my family so nervous.

"After weapons were issued, I went up and told the medico about my heart operation, and borrowed the urine of someone who I knew was diabetic, and tried to pretend my left ear was hard of hearing. So they tested me and found out my right ear *was* hard of hearing. Eventually, I got to the guy up front and he said, 'I've run out of rifles.' So I never got a rifle. It was never an issue."

Years earlier, as a news photographer in high school, Joffa had happened to photograph a fatal accident involving several paratroopers. On his second day in the service, he was called back to Bloemfontein to testify about the tragedy in court. After seven weeks of waiting, he confirmed that he had taken the photos and was dismissed.

"I was at home while everyone else had their basic training. When I got back, everyone had gone to the war. I never learned how to salute, or any of the military things. I told the colonel I'd been to film school, and he said, 'That's interesting. I'd like to start a film unit.' I spent the rest of my training buying equipment for a documentary film unit budgeted at two hundred thousand dollars. It was as fun . . . as it could be. My year was the last one-year compulsory period. Thirty days before I was to leave they called and announced that it was now going to be two years. That was horrible."

Joffa served the second year and left the service at twenty-three. Unable to afford film school tuition in England or America, he started his own television production company in South Africa. From 1982 to 1985 he and a staff of fifteen wrote, produced, and directed forty programs, each comprising between twelve and twenty-six episodes.

"I told everyone who worked for me that we would be closing in 1985. It was perfectly clear from the word 'go.' I was offered millions of dollars for the company, but part of the deal was that I would have to stay with the company for five years. It was very easy to close the doors. By coming to America, I gave up a very big business and a lot of money. But I think I gained much more."

In 1985 Joffa also met a woman and married her within three weeks; the couple moved to England, where he again contemplated attending film school. Joffa wound up making a Channel 4 documentary, "David Goldblatt in Black and White," about a photojournalist's coverage of apartheid. But the marriage was troubled.

"I went to San Diego, where my sister was living, and stayed there for two years. This was in 1987–88. I got divorced and went through a lot of nonproductive time. I cried for two years. I was a big deal in South Africa in the TV world. But I came to America and no one gave a damn about me."

Joffa applied to the American Film Institute. Though originally rejected, he was granted alternate status, and a few days before the Fall 1988 term started he was admitted.

"AFI is like a graduate school, a conservatory. They emphasize telling a story. You get an opportunity to make three stories in your first year, and if you get accepted into the second year, you then make one film.

"My first year cost six thousand dollars, my second year it went up to seven, and now it's close to ten.

"I never had any expectations of going the second year, so when I was selected it was a surprise to me. I didn't have the same competitive drive that everybody else had who was hoping to get into the second year. This turned out to be very good for me because I was able to be free and make projects for no specific reason. That's *how* I got selected for the second year. But a lot of people who go to these film schools bullshit on their résumés, and no one bothers to check. I was initially rejected from AFI because I didn't bullshit. A lot of people get in through bullshit and connections.

"You work in video the first year. AFI has no interest in technique. They don't teach you how to load a camera or anything. You get accepted into one of six departments: Directing, Producing, Editing, Cinematography, Production Design, and Writing. Editing is new—they didn't have it when I went. They take thirty-three of each position. They place you on a team— writer, producer, cinematographer, editor, et cetera.

"They tell you to go off and make a half-hour story, pairing you at random. Using video, you make a short film. You have a week to shoot it, a week to edit, and the third week you screen. Every week, four new pictures are made, with the emphasis on story. The cinematographers learn about cinematography privately. They have their own specialized courses.

"The first project, the director brings the story in. The writer works on the second. After you present the film you have one-to-ones with the teachers. I had Antonio Vellani, who was the head of the school, a teacher for nineteen years. He passed away in my second year. When you're shooting your project you can't go to a lot of the other classes during that period. We complained at one point that it wasn't fair. Tony said, 'That's okay. I talk about the same things every day.' He was a fine teacher.

"Those were the classes where you learn the most, when you screen the videos and pull them to pieces. Every week you see four new projects. There's great improvement between the first, second, and third projects. It's all based on going out and making mistakes. That's where you learn.

"The other nice thing about AFI is that they tend to accept people age thirty and up—which means people with some life experience are going to the school. Most college films deal with people in college, and it makes sense. But at AFI there's a wonderful blend—you have ten percent of the people coming from overseas. People came up to me: 'Wow! South Africa!' I met one guy who swam across a river in Czechoslovakia to get to Poland.

"You've got thirty-five-year-old people giving up careers in order to go to film school. One guy was a gynecologist. You can't work at the same time you go, though. AFI is full time. Classes sometimes start at nine in the evening. It's a big commitment.

"At the end of the year, after you've made three half-hour videos, they select up to eight people to come back to make one film each in the second year. You have the whole year to make one film. That becomes your calling card, and that's how you get your M.F.A. The first stage in Hollywood is to get *into* Hollywood—by train, plane, or automobile. The second is to get an agent. And the only way a director can get an agent in this town is by having a film. The only way to get a film made is by going to film school."

Joffa adapted the script for his second-year AFI film from a short story in a South African collection. Set in Soweto in 1980, *Senzeni na? (What Have We Done?)* follows a gardener, mistakenly incarcerated, whose life changes when he becomes intimate with the passionate struggles of political prisoners.

"The interesting question for me was one of identity—this theory that all black people look the same. I also liked that the gardener was a nonmilitaristic individual, an ordinary person. I'm nonviolent.

"It was all shot here, down the road. The crew came out of AFI. Wally Pfister was the cinematographer. He came out of documentaries and did a wonderful job. He's now shooting *Amityville Horror 5, 6,* or *7.* He also did a film for Showtime and a Corman film. Very talented.

"I don't make films so that I can control—I make films because I *can* control. Recreating South Africa was a huge job. It just turned out to be impossible for my production designer to go out and find what was in my mind. This, as it turns out, is what storyboarding is all about. I'd find pictures and show them to her so we all knew what we were talking about. The light in California and South Africa is the same. But whenever I'd see a palm tree in the edge of the frame, I'd say, 'No good, let's move.' When I went back to Soweto to shoot the opening, I was struck for the first time by the fact that there *are* palm trees there, the same type as in L.A.

"I love the process. I'm obsessive, and when you make a film you have to obsess for however long it takes to make it."

Joffa submitted *Senzeni na?* to several Hollywood agents; all returned it unseen, with letters explaining that their policy was not to consider unsolicited material. The film was then screened twice nightly for three nights at the AFI. Joffa sent two thousand tickets to agents and production companies and estimates that—appropriately enough, in the agents' case—ten percent came. A few weeks later, in February of 1991, *Senzeni na?* was announced as an Academy Award nominee for Best Short Film. Not the Student Academy Award—the Oscar.

"As soon as *Senzeni na?* got nominated, I got offers from ICM,

William Morris Agency, and Triad. CAA were the only ones that said to me they didn't think it would be to my advantage to sign with them, because I'd get lost. Which is a good thing, because I know someone from AFI who did go with CAA, and he was very upset. His name is Randall Miller, and his uncle is Danny DeVito. Randy's got talent, but it doesn't hurt to have connections. I had no connections, nothing, nobody whatsoever. The Academy suddenly made me a connection.

"I did a lot of heavy-duty dining at fancy restaurants—Kate Mantilini for breakfast, Orso for lunch, and Le Dome for supper. I had a Yugo, and it was always great fun to arrive at the valet parking, because *no one* would run up to my car.

"I hadn't lost the Academy Award yet, and I hadn't won, so that's the period when you strike—when you're nominated. Then if you win, the agent can take a big ad in the trade papers: 'We congratulate our client on winning the Academy Award. . . .'

"I had a choice of two beautiful agents, both wonderful people. In the end I went with Ronda Gomez at Broder-Kurland because she was the one who said, 'Bernard, I don't think you're going to work in the next year or so,' whereas the other one said, 'We're going to put you to work immediately.' It was much easier to believe what Ronda said! And it's true—I've been with the agency for two years and I haven't worked. She kept her word.

"It's a funny relationship because I'm so indebted to her, and everybody says, 'No, you're wrong—she's working for *you!*' And I say, 'You don't understand. She's my only contact with Hollywood.' I don't schmooze. I've never been to a 'schmooze party' in my life. The last ones were my bar mitzvah and my wedding.

"After we got together, in the spring of ninety-one, Ronda sent me to meet the town. I met with Zoe Fairfax at Carolco, Robert Lawrence at Fox, Helena Itchidowi at Danny Glover Productions. The next week, Peter Heller, Spring Creek Productions; Paula Weinstein, a producer [*The Fabulous Baker Boys*]; then Mindy Farrell at Paramount; Adam Klein at Caroloco; Dan Redler, RKO Pictures; David Vogel at Disney and Debra Neumeyer at Amblin. Lorenzo De Bonaventura, Warner Brothers, Michelle Satter at Sundance. These are all big deals, the people you really want to get to know.

"*Lunch Date* won the Oscar my year. Wonderful picture, beautifully done by Adam Davidson in New York. The big controversy was that everyone knew he didn't write it—it was based on an old urban legend. Adam's father is a very influential man, the director of the Mark Taper Forum [Gordon Davidson]. But it was a damn good film, very well made, smart."

Joffa was proposed for the Paramount Directing Fellowship by the AFI, and selected. He was given an office and full access to the studio lot for a year, as well as a salary of $25,000. Never having had the experience of seeing a feature get made, Joffa asked for the chance. He was set to observe Francis Coppola directing *Bram Stoker's Dracula* until the project jumped studios to Columbia. Eventually he landed on the set of Paramount's *Patriot Games*, directed by Phillip Noyce and starring Harrison Ford.

"Big picture, big people. I gained firsthand knowledge of the filmmaking process at a studio. It's quite different than anywhere else.

"Being on the set you learn so much. The hardest thing was to keep quiet. I did quite a good job of that except for one point, where I opened up my big fat mouth. It was on, like, day three of my 'fly-on-the-wall-ship'—that's what I call this period. Harrison Ford's character was being introduced. He was in a London hotel, and he was preparing a speech for the next day. The wardrobe department had given him a pair of shiny silk pajamas. He said, 'I can't wear these,' so they gave him another pair, of flannel. He didn't like them either.

"On take twenty-six, after a lot of deliberation, they decided maybe he should wear his shirt and pants from that day, and the shirt should hang over the pants. That didn't work, either.

"So I go up and whisper into the ear of Phillip Noyce, the director, 'Why don't you suggest he wear his underpants, with the shirt over?' Because that's natural, to be in your hotel room like that.

"So Phillip waited a few seconds and then said, 'Our intern here, Bernardo, has a wacko suggestion.' Everyone was quiet, and all the attention was toward us. He said that in case it was a bad suggestion—I would take the rap. 'He's got this really wacko suggestion that Harrison should be in his underpants.' Harrison closes his eyes for a few seconds, puts his hands to his head, looks up, and says, 'I

like that. I really like that. Now why didn't I think of that?' That's
how they shot the scene, and how it was in the movie. Quite a
strange, funny way of being noticed. After that I was known as the
Underpants Boy.

"There were two producers on the picture, Bob Rehme and
Mace Neufeld. Rehme was more of a gentleman, Neufeld more of
the aggressive 'producer type.' One day I was sent on an errand and
couldn't watch that afternoon's shoot, and I came back and Phillip
was sitting at a video monitor and he said, 'Come and look at this
shot.'

"The shot called for two doors to be in the frame. If the person
chose the wrong door, it would take him to his death in a base-
ment. If he chose the right door, he would have gone into the
bathroom. Phillip showed me the shot and you could only see one
door, which meant that the audience wouldn't know he had a
choice. I said, 'Phillip, it's not going to work—there's no tension
there.' He thought about it, then called an assistant to look at it,
who agreed with *him* that it was great. I said, 'I may have made a
mistake, but that's what I think.'

"The next morning—the first shot of the day—he was
reshooting that shot of the doors. He had obviously thought
about it and agreed with me that it wouldn't work. A few hours
later, Mace came running onto the set and called Phillip and
took him away, and Phillip came back looking very troubled and
worried.

"Then the V.P. in charge of the production from Paramount
came up to me and said, 'Bernard, you're in trouble.' I said, 'I
know I'm in trouble, I've seen it written all over the place.' He
said, 'This is the situation. Mace wants you off the set, and
Phillip wants you to stay on the set. We've struck a deal with
Mace. If you stand fifteen feet away from Phillip, you can stay.'
So I said, 'I certainly don't want to stay if Mace doesn't want me
to be here.' And he said it was actually Paramount's picture, so I
should stay.

"That afternoon they projected the dailies from the day before,
and Bob Rehme saw them. He said, 'Phillip, that's not going to
work. You can only see one door there.' And Phillip said, 'Don't
worry, Bob, we reshot this morning.'

"So I stayed on for the rest of the picture, and had to stay fifteen feet behind Phillip. It was ridiculous. I understood exactly

what Mace Neufeld's worry was. I cost the production twenty thousand dollars, by rescheduling the next day. You sneeze and it's fifty thousand dollars. I was costing them a lot of money by doing that. So I learned to stay absolutely quiet, even if I disagreed with what Phillip was doing. I realized there are thousands of ways to call a shot. One person's vision will push it through.

"That was the hardest time for me. Everybody warned me that I would be so frustrated watching somebody else make a movie. Very often Phillip was asking me to validate what he had done. He certainly wasn't asking me to tell him that it *wasn't* right. So I learned a little diplomacy in that year. It taught me a lot. It's difficult because you're an unpaid nuisance, running around in everybody's way.

"Observing the filming of *Patriot Games* is not necessarily going to make me a better filmmaker, but I won't have to go through some of the emotional problems that I might have gone through had I not known about it. Like the whole concept of 'don't take it personally.' That's purely a studio thing, and I would not have been able to deal with it had I not experienced it firsthand.

"The best example of that was that Phillip Noyce, the director, got his next feature at Paramount, *Sliver*. He asked me if I would like to be the second-unit director because we had built up a rapport. Of course, I was thrilled.

"It was a done deal. I met Howard Koch, Jr., who was producing the picture for Robert Evans. I was happy, we were all happy, and I was just waiting to finish the Paramount fellowship, which made a lot of sense. I would finish on a Friday and join them the following Monday. So I knew six weeks before the termination of the Paramount deal that I was going to be working on *Sliver*. The money was going to be fantastic. I'm in the Directors Guild, so the pay was at least nine thousand dollars a week, which is DGA minimum. And I was asked to be available for fifteen weeks, which translates into a lot of money.

"But more than the money was the opportunity to work as a director, even though it was second unit, on a big fifty-million-dollar picture. I was excited as hell, and it was wonderful that Phillip was giving me the opportunity and trusted me to do it.

"I finished the Paramount fellowship on Friday and was due to start work on *Sliver* on Tuesday. Monday I got a call from Phillip's assistant. 'Bernard, I've got really bad news for you. Somebody totally out of our control doesn't want you to do it, and has given us the name of somebody else that he would like to do the film. Don't take it personally. Phillip really doesn't want you to take it personally, but it's out of our control. Bye-bye.' And that was that—the beginning and the end of the job.

"I thought, Fuck Phillip. 'Don't take it personally'? Firstly, he should have called me to tell me. And secondly—of *course* I must take it personally! Here's this guy, his name is Richard Baskin, turns out to be a friend of Robert Evans. So I know that it was with good intentions that Phillip wanted me to do it, but when it came to the crunch, Richard Baskin had it. Now, I certainly don't take it personally!

"Ronda, my agent, was really upset, but from the word 'go' she had seen it as a long shot. She knew that nothing happens in Hollywood until it happens."

A fellow AFI graduate, Robert Mangenelli, recently hooked Joffa up with River Communications, a company trying to move from industrials and advertisements into motion pictures. Their first proposed film is the story of Sydney Maree, a runner who grew up in the era of the Soweto uprising and eventually won the New York Marathon.

"It's not political. It's all about a man who decides to find some kind of dignified life for his family. He wins marathons in Barcelona and New York, and still can't build a house for his mother—even though he has the money—because he's black. His challenges are the fabric of that society, which changes.

"I'm meeting Sydney in New York on Wednesday. The fact that River Communications sent me a plane ticket, and are putting me up, is good. I would want to write with Greg Latter, a friend from South Africa. I think he's right for the project. I can't write. I hate writing. It's a hard process and there's nothing natural about it. I want to work with a writer who finds it natural, but who will share ideas.

"Wesley Snipes and Denzel Washington have been mentioned [to play Maree]. Knowing how Hollywood works, they would be much happier with a name. But you have to learn how to walk. Black South Africans walk differently, they talk differently, they eat differently, they sing differently, they shout differently—everything's different. In my little film, when one guy bends over to write against the other's back, that's a very normal thing, and yet everybody was charmed by it."

Joffa considers what the next two years might bring.

"I'm thinking of going into therapy. I think it's time. I have a take on my childhood, but I just don't know how to deal with it."

LISA KLEIN
November 19, 1992

L ulu's Alibi, a West Los Angeles coffeehouse, is a "program place," a hangout where actors and writers often go after taking the meetings that *really* impact their lives—Alcoholics Anonymous meetings.

For Lisa Klein, who pulls up in a Cherokee Wrangler, it's just a place to get an afternoon caffeine jump start and think about her writing. At four-thirty she'll head down to Marina del Rey to work the dinner shift at an upscale dim-sum restaurant.

Like Marco Williams, Klein is coy about her age, which she'll only say is in the "late-twenties-early-thirties" range.

Klein was born and raised in Detroit, where she vividly remembers seeing *Funny Girl* and a double feature of *Klute* and *Wait Until Dark*. Her tastes these days run to Nora Ephron and David Mamet. More than once her mother, a newspaper reporter, waxed rhapsodic over her precocious daughter in print. Klein's memories put her ambivalent feelings about participating in this book in perspective for me.

"My mother did a column every week in the *Southfield Observer and Eccentric*. I'd sneeze a certain way and it would be in the paper. My friends would read it, and it got embarrassing. She did something about how I was trying to avoid seeing her and my father when they came to visiting day at my camp, by hiding in a dryer. She made up a lot of it.

"I loved going to movies, also tennis and swimming. My father had an 8mm camera. Mine was a typical Spielbergian story of making movies. But I was more into acting as a kid. I took lessons, and used to put on shows for my grandparents and parents. I was very much a ham, and then one day woke up shy."

Klein attended the University of Michigan as a Radio, TV, and Film major with an English minor. Within a four-month period during her sophomore year, both her father and her older brother died.

"At certain ages you're much more resilient and able to bounce back. But I was a mess, I couldn't do anything. I could barely talk for two weeks. I got mono. I couldn't sleep or eat. I was in pretty bad shape. I'm still trying to deal with a lot of that."

Upon graduation, Klein wrote letters to industry pros from Jim Henson to Jack Valenti, to no avail. Resistant about moving to Los Angeles, she visited friends on the East Coast and wound up staying there for several years.

"I got a job in cable TV, in Arlington, Virginia. I didn't know what the hell I was doing. I worked in sports and did all the on-air promotions. By the time I left I was making thirty thousand dollars. I was about twenty-six. During the last year I was there I would come home burned out—I wanted to do other stuff. I started writing poetry."

Leaving a boyfriend behind, Klein was wait-listed at her first-choice graduate school, NYU. USC admitted her, though, so despite reservations about L.A., she moved to Hollywood.

"The program at USC was very hands-on for the students and hands-off for the professors. There wasn't a lot of teaching there. We were sort of thrown into battle. I cried the first week I was in L.A., because I had broken off this relationship. I had left all of my friends again. I had already done that once when I left Detroit.

"The first thing they said—we were sitting in this auditorium—was, 'If you have a social life planned for the next three years, cancel it. You are going to eat, sleep, drink film school. That's it.' All these strange people. It was a horrible nightmare. I thought, 'I just made the worst mistake of my life. I left people I know for this vast wasteland.'

"But after a week or so it was great. It's probably something like war. You're in the trenches with these people, nobody knows what the hell they're doing, and you're in it together, so you make these fast, close friends.

"The first year I took an 8mm class and they said make five movies. Many people had never held a camera, which surprised me. I thought everybody there was going to be a creative genius. But they were much more scholastic, academic—Harvard, Yale—people were comparing their GREs and stuff. I thought it was going to be a real artsy environment, which it was not at all. One guy was an engineer. I didn't know there were so many career changers until I got there.

"Some people were kidding themselves. This one girl—to say she had a feminist bent would be an understatement. She did an animated montage of magazine cutouts in which she castrated men. I remember looking at some of these things and gasping. One was like some bad Andy Warhol movie. Another was about someone growing pot in his backyard. The lead actor, who was a dark Italian, with dark eyes, quit in the middle, so the director replaced him with somebody who was blond. It was a little confusing—we had to get that it was the same character.

"At first I thought, 'Wow. This stuff is really esoteric. It's over my head. I'm stupid.' Then, by the end, I realized it was just bad."

Klein next targeted USC's competitive 480 program.

"The 480 films are tough to get, politically, and the restrictions are getting pretty wacky. Someone was found with an HMI—a lighting kit—that they didn't get through the school, and there was some sort of penalty. You can only use a certain amount of film. They're all over you. You show your dailies after the weekend, and they're like, 'No, no, you can't use this, you have to reshoot this scene . . .'

"USC is a sort of microcosm of certain Hollywood studios in

that they're holding your hand—not in a helpful way, necessarily—and taking you through and being incredibly critical. It's a good school in a lot of ways, but much more Hollywood-oriented than what I've heard NYU is.

"It's a little more of a technical school. For a few years they went through a period of beautiful films with bad stories. When Frank Daniel [an Academy Award winning filmmaker who died in 1996] came in from Columbia [University], and brought a band of his writing people, that changed dramatically. I don't think you can learn to write, but certain screenwriting techniques that he taught in his classes were amazing. The writing program there became really, really good.

"Phil Joanou [director of *State of Grace* and *U2: Rattle and Hum*] had already left by the time I got there. John Singleton [*Boyz N the Hood*] was the star of my year, but I didn't really know him. The guy who wrote the first Van Damme movie was there. I didn't know any of the celebrities—I just knew the hacks. [Laughs] That was a joke; they're all really talented."

In 1988 Klein wrote a short script, *King for a Day*, which was chosen for production as a 480 film. Klein was disappointed when a friend, Peter Orenstein, was not selected to direct, and she virtually disowns the resulting product.

"The dailies would come in and I'd go 'Oh, my God—I didn't write that.' Even though the words were there, my sentiment was gone, my mood, my tone. It was an incredible learning experience, so I don't regret it."

Klein later had another script selected, but this time exercised her option to pull it from production after disagreeing on USC's choice of director. Then Orenstein presented her with an idea, which became another Klein script entitled *Radio Wars*. The film—an ambitious comedy set in the 1930s—was directed by Orenstein.

"We shot *Radio Wars* in twenty-two, twenty-five days, somewhere under a month but pretty much straight through. I think we stopped for three hours during that month. It was an unbelievable nightmare, just incredible. I didn't want to be a producer—I abhor producing—but I ended up being very involved anyway, just in terms of crew selection, casting, et cetera.

"Peter was clearly the director. I would take him aside and

whisper to him from time to time, and there were a couple of things he did that I wish he would have done differently, but for the most part I was happy with it.

"The actual shooting was very ambitious. It was a period piece. But we had a great crew and cast. After the first week and a half Peter fired the cinematographer. He was one of the most talented people I met in film school and I would work with him tomorrow. But he's very much a perfectionist, very slow. Every setup was a forever situation. He's apparently faster now because he's done some professional work.

"It took so incredibly long to do everything that we were operating on two or three hours of sleep. At the end it got sort of rough because we had the stage for only a certain amount of time. We were about to lose it and had to keep hanging on.

"Mostly at the beginning it was Peter's money. Postproduction is when I borrowed a lot. We actually spent close to sixty or seventy thousand dollars."

Radio Wars's first major screening, at the Academy of Motion Picture Arts and Sciences in Beverly Hills, was scheduled for April 29, 1992.

"We thought we'd save time by editing on the Ediflex, the video system. So we had to train an editor on that, and when it was finally cut, the tapes themselves were not coordinated with the sound, and everything had to be redone. Peter thought we could use this digital sound thing. We'd have to stop for a week and get some more money, and the screening date was looming. We had to do the mix in a minute and a half.

"On the morning of the twenty-ninth, we were running between PhotoChem [a film lab] and Cinesound [a postproduction facility]. We were transferring the sound and had to have the film to the Academy by three. The Academy screening is the one the agents and producers come to. We saw the film at noon on a flatbed, and totally slashed the mag track down the middle. Peter got beeped and found out that the Rodney King riots had broken out. We hadn't slept in three days, and we had a split mag.

"We hadn't made the USC screening only three days before,

because we needed every second. Every time something happened—and four times in the final twenty-four hours—Peter said, 'We're dead, we can't make the date.'

"We all had separate jobs to make sure we would be ready. The screening was going to start at seven o'clock. I ran to the Academy at five with the film—past the setup time. I begged the people to load the film on, and just as they were, at around six, there was a blackout at the Academy. I thought, 'Well, this is it. . . .' My sister was in Long Beach and we had to figure how to get her here. My mother was in town and I had to pick her up in Beverly Hills, go back to Venice, and then get back to the Academy by seven.

"The lights came on five minutes later, although it seemed like an hour. We checked the film, and I ended up being about an hour late. I was in a daze. It was like being in some sort of weird dream. I didn't know the impact of the riots. I knew that I was going to get up the next day and go to City Hall. I was incensed about the verdict. I didn't know anything about Reginald Denny yet. When I was driving to the Academy I started hearing stuff, and I was getting a little nervous, particularly since I have an open vehicle."

Klein and Orenstein had another industry screening in June, and were contacted by many studios and agencies. They met, individually and together, with Universal, Columbia, and Imagine, among others.

"They wanted to know what I was working on, and I pitched some things. I met with someone who had read this script I was revamping, and liked it, and called me in and said *she* had an idea. She told me about it, and asked me to think about it. I called her the next day with a whole outline—I was totally stoked—and I never heard from her again. She didn't have to throw me a bone. I had said, 'You can wait until you read my next script.'

"I had another meeting in which someone said, 'We're pretty sure we want to option Guardian Angels [Klein's feature script], I just have to talk to one other person.' It took a long time, and she finally called back and said, 'I'm going to be in New York. I think we're going to do this, I'll call you back.' Weeks later, her secretary called and said, 'Well, she's going to be gone this week, but she'll call you next week.' That went on and on and on. Finally, she told me, 'So-and-so isn't ready to do that now.'

"People have said the script is *Ruthless People*-ish. I would love Danny DeVito and Rhea Perlman for it. Supposedly Larry [Weinberg, Klein's attorney] has a meeting set up with Jersey Films [DeVito's production company] for next week.

"The script needs some work. I hate pitching, I'm terrible at it. I don't finish my sentences. My tendency is to either go into the story in great detail, or to gloss it over because I know it so well. Peter does a better job with my stuff than I do.

"We went in to Universal to pitch *Lovestruck* and another script I'd already written. I pitched *Lovestruck* and he pitched the other, and they loved it, even though Peter and I both thought *Lovestruck* was much more viable.

"I actually have a champion there who has believed in my stuff from the beginning—Monika Skerbelis. Monika had given me her name after that first film at USC was made.

"I've seen good coverage [studio readers' reports] on my stuff. The bad ones hurt, and you have to be kind of thick-skinned. I haven't had anything that's been blasted overall, like, 'This person should choose another profession.' Generally the dialogue's been well received, but I've had some story and character comments. A couple seemed like they were from an angry film student who hasn't been able to get anything produced, and wanted to lambaste somebody that day.

"Some of it was really mean spirited, not completely constructive. It's interesting, though, how everything is compared to something else. 'This is a cross between *Ruthless People* and *Last of the Mohicans*.' What's original, I wonder?

"My friend Kyle [name changed] and I are rewriting something called *Fat City*, and Peter and I have written a first act on something, and have some other ideas.

"I have a manager, James [name changed]. He represented David Mickey Evans [writer of *Radio Flyer* and writer-director of *The Sandlot*] and—I don't know if he still does—Bobcat Goldthwait. He's pretty well connected.

"I had an agent a couple of years ago who I liked, but she was the first person I ever talked to. We had a meeting to sign the contract and I chickened out. I didn't feel we were on the same wavelength. I didn't think her comments were harsh enough—I needed somebody to be tougher on me. Signing with the first agent you meet is like marrying the first guy you sleep with. Not that I wouldn't, of course. [Laughs]

"I don't know why I met with James. It could have been that he didn't say, 'Send a script first.' He loved *Radio Wars*. He took me to lunch. It was an instinct thing—it felt right."

Klein finishes her cappuccino and thinks about how her career might play out.

"In two years I'd like to have sold a couple of screenplays, and have some sort of control—not power—maybe *influence*. I want to keep writing things I want to write, not things that will compromise my values. I'd like to be making a living. I don't really have the mansion-and-Jaguar aspirations.

"I'm expecting the first thing I sell to be raped and pillaged. I'd like to have enough influence that I can stay close to the story. Eventually, I'd like to direct—smaller stories, my own stuff. I want to feel comfortable, though. Part of me feels like I should direct someone else's stuff—or something I've written with someone else—because I don't know if I can be objective enough. I've seen some movies by first-time directors who've been writers. The lack of objectivity can be disastrous.

"I may be naive, but I don't think I'm going to be discriminated against as a woman. Apparently there aren't a whole helluva lot of female screenwriters, for whatever reason. In terms of comedy, you look at Paula Poundstone and Ellen DeGeneres, and they're just as funny as someone like Steven Wright."

I tell Lisa about a quote of Nora Ephron's: "The hardest thing about being a woman director is becoming one."

"Directing is a man's world," she concurs. "It hasn't gotten that much better since I've been out here. The ratio is still high for the men. But if you're talented, and really good, you're going to do what you want to do. I don't care who you are. Randa Haines and Penelope Spheeris are pretty talented.

"The truth is, I'm only writing to further my waitressing career. [Laughs] It's more the respectability than the money, believe it or not. If somebody asks me to work their shift, and I say I'm writing, they say, 'Oh, so you're not doing anything today?' It bothered me at first. To me, *that's* the job I take seriously.

"I'm not good with authority. There's a powerlessness. Someone's controlling my career, all these people are reading my stuff, and they're telling me if it's good or bad. People are telling me what to do.

"I'm at a point where I have to get control over my life somehow."

P. J. PESCE

November 24, 1992

Pinehurst Road in Hollywood, where P. J. Pesce lives, is a narrow, winding street flanked by lush foliage. Its palm trees are unkempt, unlike those in Beverly Hills, which are manicured and checked regularly for the rats that often nest at the top of their trunks.

Pesce was born in 1961 in Miami, Florida, where he lived until he was eighteen. Both Pesce's parents were children of Italian immigrants; his father, a doctor, grew up in an orphanage.

In the kitchen of an apartment with dorm-room decor, Pesce lights a surprisingly good brand of cigar.

"In the back of my house was a lake," he remembers, "and at the bottom of the lake was this fine white clay, like what all the natives are covered with in *Apocalypse Now*. We would go down there and dig it up, and cover ourselves with it.

"I must have made this 8mm movie *The Attack of the Clay Monster* three times, minimum. I made it every year or two. The first time it was really primitive, just filming the clay monster going around, and picking my sister up and stuff. The second time I conceived a story. I didn't know about editing. I didn't even have the concept of a moving camera."

Pesce's awareness of the director's role grew in the mid-1970s, when he saw *Taxi Driver* and *A Clockwork Orange*.

"I started reading about directors, and decided at sixteen that I wanted to be a movie director. My senior year at Catholic high school my whole id was wrapped up in being funny, and I made this movie for some weird religion class. It was a really big hit. I thought, Maybe I can do this, maybe I can be a filmmaker."

Pesce applied to Harvard and Columbia and was accepted by the latter, where he was inspired by the core curriculum. By day he devoured St. Augustine's *City of God*, Darwin, Freud, Adam Smith, Hobbes's *Leviathan*, and *Mein Kampf.*

He considered a degree in Physics, then Architecture, but ended up graduating in 1983 as an English major. Pesce applied to Columbia's film school and was awarded a small scholarship.

"I had just broken up with a girlfriend. I cut all my hair off and I looked like Travis Bickle. I saw *Taxi Driver* again that summer and thought I was flipping out just like Travis. New York was getting to me and I thought, I can't go right back to school. I took a year off, even though I would have to reapply for the scholarship."

By night for most of that year, Pesce played guitar with a band whose members were once arrested for breaking back into a bar they had played the night before.

"Sitting in the jail cell at age twenty-six, I realized I was not a college student anymore, and this could no longer be considered childish pranks or youthful exuberance. I could actually go up the river for this kind of thing. And I realized it's a young man's game, rock 'n' roll. As a filmmaker, you can age gracefully."

Pesce flew to England and worked at a chocolate factory, where he claims he was miserable and—thanks to the perks of the job— acne-ridden. A stint as a bartender and some aimless hitchhiking followed. In 1984 he returned to New York and started film school.

"I came back looking like this real artiste, my hair shaved on the sides, and braids. All the kids at Columbia looked like they should be in business school. And they're like, 'Who the fuck is this character?'

"My first directing class I had a great teacher, Nick Proferes, who had been a cameraman for Elia Kazan. He gave us this book,

Harold Clurman on Directing, which was torn to shreds because I always was going through it.

"There was also a woman named Milena Jelinek, who was part of this whole Czechoslovakian connection, with Milos Forman and Frank Daniel, and Wojtech Jasny, who did *All My Good Country-men*. These guys were artists. They went to the Czech film school in Prague. They used Stanislavsky's theories, that you're not just an actor, you're an artist—which means you've got to sharpen all your senses, your sense memory, and your emotional memory.

"They approached making films and being a filmmaker as this total education. All these things I had been embarrassed about and saw as dilettantish about drawing and writing poetry and music and everything else—they were like, 'No! That's good! You should do that and you gotta keep doing that!' It was really amazing.

"I felt validated. By Milena, and Brad Dourif [an actor best known as Billy Bibbitt, the stutterer, in Forman's *One Flew Over the Cuckoo's Nest*] too. All of them were aware of what the others were doing because Frank and Milos had come up with this comprehensive syllabus—the way to make people think about movies to become a film artist. You had to act, write your own scenes, and begin by taking scenes from other movies and breaking them down, beat by beat, like Clurman and Strasberg.

"The first semester Milos was totally absent—he had become famous, et cetera, and he wasn't involved day to day. A friend of mine, Les Firestein, who's now head writer on *In Living Color*, would contribute articles to the *New York Post*. He leaked that Milos Forman was never at the school. It was this big scandal— 'Who did this?' They called me in. I said, 'I have no idea.' Nobody knew for years who had done it, and then Firestein told me that he had. Anyway, that embarrassed Forman into coming back and actually teaching.

"I sat in on the class and acted in a couple of people's scenes, just so I could be around and hear him do his crits. They were good. He would come in and make a couple of adjustments, he would direct the actors, and that was amazing to watch.

"I took a year off to work in a sound studio, and returned to Columbia in 1985. Scorsese came to teach and I was chosen to be in his class. They chose about eight people. Everyone else was sneaking, getting their friend the T.A. to let them show up and fake their name on the list. The first day no one wanted to talk.

"He was finishing *The Color of Money*. Our first class met at Sound One, where they were still doing postproduction. It was amazing—here's this guy who made this movie that was the most important movie in my life when I was sixteen, and still was—and I was going to meet him.

"All through college I was trying to erase my Italian-American heritage. I was embarrassed by it and didn't want to have anything to do with it. I thought Scorsese was going to be an austere Eastern intellectual. Not at all. I met him and thought, 'Wait a minute, he's like me! He's this GUY!'

"Marty is producing a film, *Naked in New York*, now, which is being directed by Dan Algrant. I sort of became one of Marty's favorites in the class, and Dan was the other favorite.

"Dan is a tremendous writer. He really has this ability to get the truth. I think that's when Dan became interested in me—'Oh, I better find out who the other of Marty's favorites is'—so we became kind of friendly. I haven't actually talked to him in a while, we just kind of went our separate ways.

"The first year he was in my writing class with another guy, Tom Abrams, who's now my writing partner. Tom's film *Shoeshine* won the short film award at Cannes and was nominated for an Academy Award.

"The first day we were all totally afraid we're going to say something stupid and Scorsese's going to throw us out or something. I had written this script the first year that I thought was kind of dopey. I thought I would read it. I didn't really want to do it, I wanted to write a new script with him, but I would read it because it never failed to get a laugh, something I'm comfortable with. 'Ha ha ha' . . . he'll know who I am."

Pesce's project, *The Afterlife of Grandpa*, was a comedy about an Italian man who returns from his grave in sexual pursuit of his grandson's girlfriend.

"I started reading this thing, and I was doing all the accents, and I was terrified. It was a total gamble. If it goes bad, I'm an idiot, and I'll never speak again in the class, and I've made a bad impression.

"But it went well, and Scorsese actually started laughing. He encouraged me to rewrite it, and then he pushed, and I did and said, 'Okay, let's shoot it,' and he said, 'No, no, no. You gotta rewrite it again.'

"In the original ending the girlfriend doesn't actually do it, and they go off all happy. And Scorsese would say, 'What do *you* think about the ending?' And I'd go, 'Well, I guess it's kinda sappy.' And he'd go, 'What would be the *truthful* ending?' And I'd go, 'The old man would fuck her, and the kid would be upset.' And he'd go, 'Yes! It's a comedy, but yes, that's the truthful thing, and in fact that's the funniest thing.' The simplest things Scorsese taught me were, when in doubt, you go for the truth to the best of your ability.

"So that's what Marty did, he would ask questions like that. About dialogue—is this truthful, would they say that? I had kids talking real, like, you know, muthafucka, and fuck this and fuck that. And he's like, 'Wait a minute, is that really appropriate for this?' And I thought, this is Mr. *Mean Streets*, this is Mr. *Raging Bull*, and he's telling me there's too many *fuck*s in this? But in fact, that kitchen-sink realism was inappropriate for the tone of this movie because it kind of pulled you out.

"Scorsese gave me an actor, Frank Vincent from *Raging Bull*. He was Joe Pesci's friend, and Pesci got him the job on *Raging Bull*. They used to have an act together. One day I was leaving class, which was always held down in the Brill Building in Scorsese's offices. His assistant came up to me and said, 'Here, Marty wants you to call this number.'

"I'd seen *Raging Bull* three zillion times. So I called Frank Vincent and set up a meeting, and I was this punk student, this dopey little would-be Orson Welles, a pretentious geek. He said, 'Well, Marty says I should do this, and I'm doing it as a favor for him.' Eventually we became friends, and he did the movie, and he was great. But that's how Marty would do things, like the maestro in *The Red Shoes*. He would have someone else do it for him.

"Making *The Afterlife of Grandpa* was stressful. It was shot in twelve days. I had never really done it before, yet in some ways it felt like I had been doing it all my life. I had never shot a 16mm movie. I didn't know anything about properly formatting a script. I became this crazy maniac, driving everyone into the ground. One day I shot twenty-two hours—if *I* was working for me, I would have stormed off or strangled me. I was this little Napoleon.

"I rehearsed with this actor [playing the grandson] for six weeks, and then we shot with him one day, and it was a disaster. He knew it wasn't working, I knew it wasn't working. The producer said,

'What should we do?' We'd wasted like a thousand dollars, which is a lot for a student film.

"I wrote it, I was directing, and I'd gotten all these great people. I found this great cinematographer Paul Gibson, who wound up shooting features like *The Refrigerator* and *Paris Is Burning*. As if I hadn't gambled enough, I fired the actor, came in, and did the role myself. I hadn't slept, I was stressed out of my mind, my girlfriend was coming back and forth from Spain and I was dealing with her. But I said, 'I'm not going to fail. I'm not going to allow anything to get in the way.'

"So I shot the movie and it came out okay. I am probably the worst thing about it. Rehearsing with these people for six weeks saved me because I knew what I wanted. Marty saw it and said, 'No, you're bad. Cut you out of it. As much as you can cut you out of it, cut out.' Of course, I was hoping he would look at it and go, 'You're brilliant! I want to put you in *GoodFellas*!' But he said, 'What are you doing? You're doing nothing! You're directing the film while you're onscreen! You don't do *anything*!'

"I had to get that film done. I literally had everything on the line. I had won a bunch of awards for the script which got me some money. I had all these student loans. Instead of putting them into tuition I went out and bought film stock, and food for the crew. The film cost twenty-eight thousand dollars.

"It ended up at twenty-four minutes but the first cut was forty-five minutes. I learned more about the economy of writing from the cutting of that film. I was in hock up to my ears and I borrowed money from everybody I knew to finish the film. I had to work as a plasterer. Scorsese's assistant hired me. Marty was moving out of his house, so I put all of his stuff in boxes. All of his books, all of his records, and an amazing collecting of videocassettes. I think all directors are pack rats."

Pesce also studied with George Roy Hill, and a close friend of Scorsese's, Brian De Palma.

"At the end of the fucking year Brian gave me an F, and he bragged to Marty about it. I was like, 'You wanna give me an F? I'm not going to complain. I'm going to take it like a man.'

"So one day I was at Sound One showing Marty my film, and he said, 'I hear you got an F from Brian.' I said, 'Yeah—how did you know?' He said, 'We were out at dinner the other night and he bragged, "I gave your pet an F." ' I said, 'What?' I couldn't believe that. I was amused, pissed off, like, what is *that* about? And I decided to never say a word about it.

"Brian *was* very generous in class. I did learn a lot from both him and Scorsese. From Brian, just about film grammar. He was a good guy, but a hard teacher. I always tell people, 'I got Honors from Scorsese and an F from De Palma—make of that what you will.' If that says what I think it says, I'm very happy."

The Afterlife of Grandpa won at the first competitive festival Pesce entered—the Student Emmy for Best Comedy, and $1,000, from the Academy of Television Arts and Sciences. Pesce took second prize and £1000 (approximately $1,800) at the Edinburgh Film Festival, and Grey Advertising awarded him $2,500 for the screenplay.

"I was invited by the Indian government to the Bombay Film Festival. They flew me over and put me up for eight days. It's amazing—here are all these filmmakers who are poor, busting their asses to make these movies and get some kind of appreciation. All of a sudden someone calls and says, 'Hey, come to this film festival and we'll put you up.' They go crazy. They get drunk twenty-four hours a day, and stay up all night arguing about films.

"And you're seeing all these films you'd never get to see, especially short films. In the U.S. there's no venue for them, and some of them are tremendous, beautiful and incredibly inventive."

Pesce got an agent, David Kanter of Bauer-Benedek, after the festivals. He then spent a year teaching film history at Columbia.

"In choosing my agent I thought, 'Who'll make the best friend?'—which is a dumb thing, but you're a film student, and you need to feel safe. So I figured, 'This guy likes the same music as I do.' Really smart way to choose your agent.

"There was also somebody from Gersh, and somebody from CAA called me. 'Hey, we heard a lot about your film, send it.' They returned it. A week later an assistant called and said, 'We're not taking on any new clients.' Thanks, I didn't ask to be taken on anyway! Send me a dead fish in the mail! Fuck you!

"Right after I signed with Kanter, Universal flew me out to California to talk about directing a movie. It was from a great script they gave me called *Danny and Randy*, about two kids, one a Catholic boy. I was thinking, 'This is going to be easy. I haven't even graduated and they're already flying me out and putting me up.'

"My friend Malia Scotch Marmo [a Columbia graduate,

screenwriter of *Once Around* and cowriter of *Hook*] said, 'You gotta go to the Sunset Marquis. I'll be staying there and you won't feel so bad. We can hang out.'

"At the hotel, before I went to sleep, I could check off what kind of coffee I would like—cafe au lait, espresso, cappuccino? Which newspapers would I like to read—the *New York Times*, the *Los Angeles Times*? Yes, this newspaper, and that . . . I'll need several kinds of coffee. I'd like a juice. I open the door and there's a basket of all this shit. I thought, I could live here forever. I will write anything you say, I will prostitute myself in any way, just so that every day I can wake up and you will bring me all this shit. *The Locust Eaters*? Fine—where do I sign? 'My soul.' 'Lou C. Fer.'

"I saw Bruce Springsteen out at the pool and thought, 'All you people back in film school, fuck you. I am to the manner born, I am a star.' Malia and I had breakfast and I was going, 'The Boss, man, the fucking Boss. I think I've got a tape upstairs of some of my songs. Think I should give it to him?' It was ridiculous—out of control.

"So I had a meeting with a Universal production V.P., Josh Donen, and I noticed he had a tattoo. It was, 'I'll show you mine if you show me yours.' The producers, Carol Baum and Jon Shestack, looked at me like, 'Who *is* this guy?' Afterwards, Shestack said, 'I thought you were going to strip to the waist and wrestle with bowie knives.'

"Unfortunately, the writer of *Danny and Randy* didn't want to let the script go. He was my age, and he felt like, 'Why should this guy direct? *I* can direct it.' It's too bad, because it's a good script. But in retrospect if I had made it, God knows what would have happened to me. I would have made a movie right away, it all would have gone right to my head, I would have been more fucked up than I am now. I would have been a bad person. Thank you, Jesus, for not letting that happen.

"I met Scott Rudin [producer, *The Addams Family, Sister Act*]. I met this one and that one. Howard Rosenman from Sandollar [a feature production company] told me, 'You're a genius!' I was like, 'Please don't say that. I don't want to hear that.' Then I saw Rosenman at a party. He's like, 'Who are you? Have I met you before?' I'm thinking, 'Yeah, yeah. A couple of years ago you thought I was a genius. Thanks.'

"I found out a month after I got back that the movie wasn't

happening. I starved for eight months. I was philosophical, because
it wasn't a script I had written. It just fell out of the sky, and I was
no worse off than if it hadn't. I figured if it were that easy, another
one would be right around the corner, right? I could handle it.

"Well, nothing was forthcoming. My agent sent people my short
movie, and they loved it but I didn't have a script. So I wrote one."

Pesce's and Tom Abrams's feature screenplay *The Trials of Leo* is
a character study of two Manhattan slackers. Actor Frank Whaley
[*Field of Dreams, Born on the Fourth of July*], a friend of Pesce's, has
expressed interest.

"My agent describes it as a 'festival comedy.' He says if I ever get
this made, it'll be great, it'll garner a lot of awards, and I'll go on
and make lots of movies. It's kind of a comedy, kind of dark—
'quirky' is a word I've heard many times.

"Fuck quirky! Quirky and a dollar twenty-five gets you on the
subway. Quirky and small—'It's a small, quirky movie . . .' Yeah,
well, what's [1991 Sundance Film Festival winner] *In the Soup*? A
'big, not-quirky movie'? It got made, and now everyone wants to
know these people and hire them. But until you actually make it,
fuck you.

"I need an Oliver Stone, a rabbi. Scorsese would be great. He
hasn't read it. He may have read it and hated it. His development
person read it and it was, 'Thank you very much, go away.' Who
knows? Maybe it's a terrible script and only me and Frank Whaley
like it.

"The script is totally not a Hollywood movie. I tried, but I
didn't know how. God knows I tried. I thought if I wrote this
really great script I could go back to the Sunset Marquis. Coffee,
newspapers, granola.

"I don't really know what sells. If I did, I'd probably be
pounding away right this moment. I just know that in terms of getting a movie made, it really has to be painting by the numbers. 'On
page twenty-one, you have to know this, dah, dah, dah.' You have
to be very clear in telling your story.

"David sent the script around. Nothing. 'Great, call me when
you write another one.' So I was in New York, just rewriting the
script on my own, not teaching. I was broke and I didn't know
what the hell to do.

"I was just about ready to work as a waiter or something when I
met these guys who made this film called *The Refrigerator* and had

like a three-and-a-half-hour cut. I offered advice on how to cut it, because we would all do that at Columbia, and I thought I would kill myself if I stayed home another day and didn't do anything.

"Chris Oldcorn, the producer, asked, 'Would you like to do it? We've been cutting for a year and don't know what to do anymore.' So I said, 'What the hell?'

"We had our own version of the Tribeca Film Center, our own crummy little space. No heat, freezing. They had a Steenbeck editing system in there that they hadn't paid the bill on in six months. Every day there was a call. We had to let the answering machine pick up because we knew it was the Steenbeck guy. 'Don't answer it!'

"They paid me thirty-five dollars a day, and it was the most ridiculous thing because Chris and Tony were just like me. They had no money, they had spent three hundred grand on this movie and shot it in Super sixteen. So Chris and Tony had to get jobs. Tony's girlfriend worked for a publisher and she was stealing books and giving them to Chris and Tony, and they went out on the street selling them to make money to pay me thirty-five dollars a day so I could edit the film and they could finally make their money.

"They also had these fundraising events and tried to convince their friends from Brown who worked on Wall Street to give them money—three thousand dollars, five thousand dollars, ten thousand dollars. It was hysterical. My first cut was, like, eighty-seven minutes long. They called me the Butcher. It was good, though. It saved my sanity to have something to work on."

In 1989 *The Afterlife of Grandpa* won another award, from Laurel Entertainment, a TV and film company which also hired him to direct an episode of their anthology series *Monsters*.

"I did the episode back in New York. They put an unbelievable amount of pressure on me. They gave me four days to shoot it—sixty shots—and they were breathing down my throat every minute. The pay was a thousand dollars. Alex Zamm [a colleague from Columbia film school] and Tom Abrams each did one, too.

"Basically, what they wanted to do was make a student film, go off and sell it, and make as much money as possible. They would not hire a fight coordinator, and we had all this blocking. They're like, 'Oh, you don't need a fight coordinator.' Okay, what do I know? I made all these movies when I was a kid that had fights in them. I coordinated them. So, I'll be the fight coordinator. Great.

"I rehearsed everything with the actors. They all donated their time, so I would make them dinner.

"We worked with the D.P., put paint down on the floor, knew where every camera position was. And we flew through the first day. We banged it out. We even finished early. Second day, we were like fifteen minutes over schedule. Third day—when all the prosthetics came out—we were dead in the water.

"The producers came out there for the first time, and they gave me so much shit. 'We're going to pull the plug, we're going to pull the plug. You're going to have to lose shots. Cut this out of the script. Too many shots. One master and one close-up, that's it.'

"I was flipping out. They did the *wrong* thing. So the third day things were getting really crazy, they were freaking out, and this lady said, 'You're going to be fired, do this, do that,' and I said, 'Okay, fine.' I was blocking a fight scene, and I showed this actor, Christine Dunford, how to do a stunt, and I said, 'No, I want you to *shove* her!' I shoved her, she went flying backwards. This woman was six feet tall.

"I said, 'Oh my God, I'm so sorry.' I ran over and she was looking a little weird. I looked down at her arm, and it was broken. It looked like a W. I was a wreck. I said, 'Don't look at it.' She looked at it; she said, 'Ohmigod—can't anyone just pull it and fix it?' I said, 'I don't think so.' Then she went into shock. We called an ambulance, and they took her away. It's perhaps the worst experience I've ever had.

"I'm very proud to say—remember when Orson Welles couldn't get the money for the costumes for *Othello*?—I redesigned all the shots and threw a jacket under the arm so you can't see the cast, and staged it so she was behind people, and we made it work. It was hell, really hell. That was the most difficult moment so far."

In 1990 Pesce won the first Paramount Directing Fellowship and moved to Hollywood. Despite being furnished with an office and a salary, he says he was ignored by the studio, which was undergoing a management change.

"June was coming up, when I would turn thirty. It's a thing for American filmmakers—got to make a film before you're twenty-six, which is when Orson Welles made his [*Citizen Kane*], so I missed that deadline. Now thirty was coming up and I hadn't made my first feature? I was going to have to hang myself!

"Lo and behold, around the time I turned thirty, I said, Fuck it. I was having trouble in the relationship I was in, I didn't know what I was going to do. Right before a trip down to Baja to see the eclipse I got a call from a friend, Chad Oman. He had seen my short movie and recommended me to Roger Corman."

A living legend to movie brats, Roger Corman is known for having given early breaks to Scorsese, Jack Nicholson, Francis Coppola, and Jonathan Demme, among others.

"I met with a guy named Mike Elliott, who was abrasive but I *liked* it, because I was tired of all this bullshit that everybody feeds you. I had had it with Hollywood. No one else was giving me anything, so my attitude was, Fine, fuck you too. I just gave it right back to him.

"They gave me this script called *Body Waves*, and it was just not very good. Not funny. No one who read could get through more than ten pages. I told them that I was going to Baja, and when I came back I had twelve days to write a new script.

"Corman requires nudity every fifteen minutes. Just a flash, a breast. My girlfriend read it—we were already not getting along—and said, 'Oh, my God! The woman takes her clothes off and then they play volleyball? You're going to direct this?' So I rewrote it and tried to make fun of the original script. I tried to write a satire of this comic movie, where the main female character had this whole long speech about this kind of movie.

"Corman didn't get it. He hated the script. Everyone else in the office thought it was the funniest script they had ever gotten. Elliott loved it. But we would get notes from Roger saying 'Who *is* this guy?' about me. This from the man who carved people up and chopped their heads off and strangled them and had sex with them! He was offended that someone called someone Mr. Vomit Stink Mouth. Taking the high road with me, after making movies like *T.N.T. Jackson*! Yes, he's the guru of young filmmakers. But he didn't like my script, so fuck him.

"Originally the shooting schedule was supposed to be eighteen days on a budget of six hundred thousand dollars. Then Elliott said, 'If you can shoot it in fifteen days for two-fifty, you can make the movie.' He also said, 'You're going to have a cut in salary.' Already he was giving me twelve thousand dollars, for basically six months of work. I figured out that I made less money than the P.A.s per hour. I'm not complaining, because I got to direct a movie. But I ended up making ten thousand dollars for writing and directing.

"There are parts of *Body Waves* I'm really proud of, and there are parts of it I'm really ashamed of. It was terribly uncomfortable to be confronted with a scene where you have to say to a woman, 'Look, you have to take your shirt off, really for no reason.' So we tried to make fun of ourselves, sometimes succeeding and sometimes not. But I stand by it now. The hardest part about it was that Corman didn't like it."

Body Waves was released theatrically for one week in San Diego and Atlanta and shown on the Cinemax cable channel in November 1992.

After the film was completed, Pesce was again contacted by Chad Oman, who had become a production executive at the independent Motion Picture Corporation of America. MPCA paid eighteen thousand dollars to Pesce and Tom Abrams to write a Western, *The Desperate Trail.*

"We turned out a tight, brutal, gritty script. The first draft had a lot of humor in it. We threw all that out for the rewrite and added a little more sex, with the understanding that I would remove the sex when I made it, unless it made sense to the story. We bent over backward to hit our due date and make this the script [MPCA cochairman] Brad Krevoy wanted. He went to MIFED [a large festival held each fall in Milan]. He didn't read it there, or on the plane back, or for three weeks after he got back to L.A. Finally he read it. 'I love it, it's great! Let's make it immediately!'

"The next day Krevoy went to a meeting at Columbia-TriStar to pitch some video deal. They said, 'Wait, stop. We don't want to hear about it. All we want to hear about is science fiction and Westerns.' He said, 'Westerns? I got a great one!' He proceeded to tell the story completely incorrectly, even misidentifying the gender of one of the main characters. 'There's these two guys, see, in the West . . .' What happened to the *Bonnie and Clyde* influence, and the strong woman character we had written?

"Now they have given me a tentative start date of April twenty-eighth. I'd like to not shoot it here in order to not be under Brad's thumb. They're talking about a budget of one-point-five million. No casting ideas yet.

"God knows if it'll really happen. At this point, after three years of being crushed under the ooze of despair and then coming back a couple of times, you feel like a boxer. Uh! Uh! You go back in and Uh! Uh! If you really believe that if you do not do this you will die, then you know that this is what you have to do. And I realize now, this is what I have to do, what I am best at.

"Scorsese said when it comes down to it, you have to believe in your talent. If you lose your faith in that, forget it. And there have been moments out here when I was just ready to toss it in. It's so brutal to live in this town and not work. If you are not working in this town, you're dog shit. You're worse than dog shit."

Pesce tamps out his cigar as he mulls his future.

"In two years? I'll be teaching high school English in Miami. I don't know. Where would I *like* to be? Not in this apartment, that's for sure. I would like to have made *The Trials of Leo*. I would like to be working on something I care about, something I can be proud of if I ever get married and have kids. I just want to work and have a family. I don't know if I see myself out here. Maybe back east, at least away from L.A.

"This place is a stinkpot of evil and excess."

II

AUTUMN 1992–SPRING 1993

I have spent my life just trying to have a career.

—Francis Ford Coppola, in
The Movie Brats by
Michael Pye and Lynda Myles

DAVID LETTERMAN: A lot of people may have thought,
"Oh, maybe I'll be an actor, or maybe I'll direct." How
do you actually do it?
MICHAEL MOORE: Get a camera and start shooting.

—*Late Night with David Letterman*, 1989

LIZ CANE

September 30

On September 17, 1992, at the Alfred Hitchcock Theatre at Universal Studios, Cane had premiered That's What Women Want *for the industry—or, at least, part of it. Three of her film school colleagues, Sharon Powers, Lawrence Trilling, and J. C. Bennett, screened their films as well.*

I asked Patrick [Drummond, a UCLA visiting professor] to introduce the films. I was his teaching assistant for a couple of years, and he's beloved at UCLA. Sharon did the food. I got the invitation lists. J.C. designed and printed the invitation. All four of us did the mailing. We got 280 RSVPs, and the theatre holds 300. About 150 people came. The theatre cost $1,000 to rent, so the whole thing cost us $370–$400 each.

I got there earlier, after running around looking for dress pants that I could afford. And I had to get the tables in the car. The projectionist was bad. He wouldn't do a sound check. I said, "Let's just do one." He put my film up. I tend to be hyperneurotic about EQ level and timing. I'm a perfectionist. The film looked purple and dark—*really* dark. I was worried. Even the projectionist ran to get another lens. I went to the car and got another print. It was a worse-timed but brighter print, and it worked great.

I got a message from Monika Skerbelis: "I saw your film, it made me laugh. Give me a call." I was nervous. We met at her office at Universal. I'm not sure how I should be in these meetings. I have friends who are vivacious and enthusiastic. I go the other way, as far as my presentation of myself. Should I be working on this?

The meeting was on Wednesday, September twenty-third. I didn't have to wait. It lasted about a half an hour. Monika is Universal's "eyes and ears person." She's been there five years and knows everybody. She said she had recently taken an interest in two USC students' script. Executives passed, though. They thought it was too derivative of *Thelma and Louise*. She told me all the details, I think because she wanted me to know that no matter how hard she pushes, studios are more conservative these days.

Monika encouraged me to keep writing. She also said she'd show my film around, and read whatever I write. I let her know that I was working on a psychological thriller and a road movie. She asked how I got the ideas for *That's What Women Want*. I told her I don't come up with the "high concept" and have the whole story. I don't know if that's a turnoff or not.

ADAM DUBOV, Director

My UCLA film, *The Grand Poseur*, took about four and a half years to make. It cost about thirty grand, made in bits and pieces, and took place in a completely fabricated universe—models and masks and sets. It was twenty-nine minutes long. Much to my great surprise, the movie ignited one of those berserk Hollywood feeding frenzies. The whole hype patrol pounced on it. Suddenly there was this attention—people from Hollywood were attending the end-of-the-quarter screenings.

After that, film school became sort of like going to West Point or something, which I think, ultimately, sucks. It's become much more that you go in a plebe and come out a second lieutenant in the film industry. I think that's lousy. That's not why people should be doing that. They should have careers, but in my opinion it's become too calculated. At the time I was there, UCLA was run like an art school insofar as it was run at all. It wasn't even being run—it was just sort of anarchy.

November 11

I have eczema on my hands. I get it when I don't have anything creative happening.

On two successive nights in mid-November, the Directors Guild of America presented its First Annual Student Film Screenings at its Sunset Boulevard headquarters. One hour of screen time was given to each of the six participating West Coast schools: USC, UCLA, Cal Arts, Loyola Marymount University, Cal State Long Beach and Cal State Northridge.

Chuck Workman, chairman of DGA's academic liaison subcommittee, moderated from a podium before a capacity crowd in the guild's three-hundred-seat theatre. Workman is best known as the compiler and editor of film clips for the annual Academy Awards broadcast.

"I've made it a point never to watch anyone's student film," Workman told the audience. "I usually tell people, 'I'll hire you—as long as I don't have to watch your student film!' Most student films feature two things—a not particularly attractive girl running towards the camera, and a suicide. If it's a comedy, it features a not particularly attractive girl and a dog. I should know. I made one, and so did my son. But these kids are stealing jobs from me, so they must be doing something right."

Workman, though clearly amusing himself, wasn't exactly slaying the audience, many of whom were the "not particularly attractive" cast members.

At stage right, a well-dressed Asian-American man signed for the deaf in a pool of light as the first of three films from California State University at Northridge began. A fifteen-minute black-and-white story of a woman who turns into her cat, it was neither hysterically funny nor effectively eerie, but competently made.

The second piece, however, was a cacophony of student-film clichés which seemed to validate Workman's barbs. A grade-D attempt at Scorsese, the half-hour film dragged considerably (though I did get a kick out of watching the signer as he mouthed along and signed lines like, "I'll bet these guys wouldn't care if their mothers was getting fucked up the ass as long as there was money to be made").

The last CSUN offering was a flawed but reasonably effective study of a deaf photographer's frustrations on the job. After a five-minute break, five Loyola Marymount University films screened, ending with a melodrama starring former teen idol Leif Garrett.

Between the final two hours—Cane's film would end the program—she told me, "I'm a little disappointed at the smallness of it all. There don't seem to be many industry people here. And a couple of the films really weren't very good."

Before introducing the last three filmmakers, from UCLA, Workman continued to push the hosting envelope. "I hope your films do well because then maybe you'll finally leave UCLA," he said. "[Chair] Gil Cates says you never leave." Upon introducing Cane, Workman smirked, "Liz Cane's film is last, but she wanted me to let everyone know it's really worth waiting for." In the audience, Cane smiled and, blushing, bowed her head.

Not surprisingly, the UCLA films were best. First off was Amie Williams's What the Water Gave Her, about a physically abused woman's flashbacks to childhood swimming lessons from a tormenting father. Literal and obvious in its depiction of "inner child" consciousness, the film was well crafted and affecting. Marco Williams was acknowledged in the film's closing credits.

The second effort, Ann A. Kaneko's A Shortness of Breath, about death and dying, combined documentary and narrative forms and was redeemed by a light, sweet sense of humor. Then came Cane's That's What Women Want, described in the program as "a roller coaster ride through the psyche of the 90s male." The audience response was enthusiastic.

NEAL JIMENEZ, Writer-Director

I waited a year to do the Project One, which is kind of a big testing ground at UCLA—your first Super 8 non-synch sound short film. It's throwing you into the deep end to see if you can survive. They don't teach you much about filmmaking—you kind of have to struggle to do what you can do.

Luckily, having already made a lot of films, I had done all of the clichéd stuff that first-time filmmakers do—the film that starts out in black-and-white and turns to color for the dream sequence; the stupid comedy; the wacky, trying-to-be-Woody-Allen comedy with the nerdy guy; the alienated youth film which inevitably ends with a dead woman's body. I had done all that shit.

November 23

The film played really well. I thought people really got into it. A lot of young people were there.

I haven't gotten calls from agents. A couple of people heard about it. One person called—Yoram Ben-Ami, an Israeli producer of low-budget films. He didn't actually attend, but asked me if the film could be made into a feature. I told him that's what I was doing.

There wasn't much of an industry turnout, which was pretty depressing. When you screen at the DGA, you have expectations. Over thirty films were entered from each school. There's this drawn-out selection process. They said they would advertise in the trades, then they never did.

I thought Chuck Workman's comments were cheesy and horrible. I didn't know why he was introducing student films if that's how he felt about them. He was totally out of line. I did go up to him after the first break and asked if we have to take a second break. He said, "Yes, we do." I said I was just being paranoid. Then he made two references to it that totally embarrassed me.

I met with Donald Petrie [director, *Mystic Pizza*, *Opportunity*

Knocks, The Favor]. I would like to get the job, assistant to the director on the film *Grumpy Old Men*. Jack Lemmon will star, maybe George C. Scott, maybe Sophia Loren. They're not sure of the casting of the Scott role. Petrie just went to Minnesota to scout locations. He seems like a nice guy. He's got a good sense of humor and someone I know said he's really great.

I don't know about this thing. I mean, I'd be going to Minnesota for four months. How could you do your interviews? We'd have to do them over the phone. I guess I'm just looking for a reason not to go.

He made it sound like I would be on the set a lot, and read material towards the end of the shoot. A previous assistant found this project. I talked to a bunch of people about this, and one of my professors thought it would be a good experience. It's unusual to get an assistant to a director job this quick and he thinks I would learn a lot, as opposed to a P.A. job, which a lot of us are considering because things are so tight. I should know within a couple of weeks.

KAREY KIRKPATRICK, Screenwriter

While I was in school, I met people working in the industry and they would always ask, "What do you want to do?" and I would think, "This is my chance!" and blurt out, "I'd like to write, direct, and produce, and one day have my own company, you know, like Amblin."

I later realized that it showed a lack of focus. Studio executives, producers, and agents don't care what you've been dreaming about since you were seven. They want to hear you say, "I want to write—that's all I want to do." So what if it isn't true? They want to know that if they hire you to write something, you aren't going to lose interest when David Cassidy calls you to direct his comeback video.

BERNARD JOFFA
November 27

I spent two days with Sydney Maree, the marathon runner, in New York. At 47th Street Photo, they all recognized him. He pulled out a photo and autographed it, and they gave him a discount. The production company put me up at the Gramercy Park Hotel and kept taking me out to meals. They were so generous. We saw Blue Man Group, and Woody Allen at Michael's Pub.

Now we have to make a deal. I've never been as passionate about a piece before. It's a little *Chariots of Fire*. The main thing now is not to be greedy about writing fees, but to be attached to direct. There is the fear of being squeezed out.

MARCO WILLIAMS
December 8–10

On November 24, PBS's Frontline *had aired the one-hour version of Marco Willliams's* In Search of Our Fathers. *The* New York Times *wrote, "[It is] the story of one special young man, and therein lies its special strength . . . The hourlong work, although very much in the tradition of a gifted young man's effort to understand himself by digging into his past, avoids self-indulgence."*

From the slightly less positive Los Angeles Times: *"[Williams] has made a film purely out of his control and dictated by events. . . . [He] is at least groping for some meaning. . . ." Both papers prominently featured a portrait of the filmmaker with their full-length reviews.*

Suddenly the film has taken on a new life. I got seventy-five calls and ten letters. The response has been of a different quality than I planned. An old girlfriend called while it was on and I spent the entire time talking to her.

The most impacting calls were from two nieces on my father's side of the family, and from my father's adopted son. I now have the possibility of having a whole other family. There's a reunion next August. It's a long way away but I really want to see all these people. I've joked in the past about a sequel, but I don't know— maybe this time I want to just *experience* something.

I plan to make video dubs of the film and sell them. The common route is theatrical, broadcast, educational, and then home video. Educational institutions could pay as much as $450 for a tape. A few other organizations, like Big Brothers, have also contacted me about using the film. I've been studying the video market. Volume over high price is definitely the way to go.

Simon & Schuster contacted me and asked if I wanted to write a book about being in a black fatherless household. *Iron John* and men's studies are in vogue, so I guess they want to capitalize.

Frontline may rerun the film for Black History Week. They are allowed to show it for a seven-day window—as many showings as they want—four times. Maybe for Father's Day or Mother's Day, or if some crisis develops around black families. I'd rather sell the tape.

I'm really intrigued by this. I've had something of a resurrection or revival. Maybe the cut-down film is a little better, but *Frontline's* imprimatur has led to me being taken much more seriously.

Having my face in the *New York Times* and *Los Angeles Times* was unbelievable. As a kid it never would have occurred to me that I would be in the *New York Times*, unless I fantasized that I would make it as a football player or something. Sheila Nevins from HBO called me to congratulate me. She said, "Most filmmakers aren't in the *New York Times* until their obituary appears."

Also, *Without a Pass* has been nominated for three Cable Ace Awards: Best Director, Actor, and Theatrical Special. Showtime is thrilled, because they're up against features. The ceremonies will be on January fifteenth and seventeenth, the second one being televised. I'll be at the award ceremonies. I have to rent a monkey suit.

I've got five new ideas. One is a touchdown. A Harvard graduate student asked me if I knew about Michael Apted's *7 Up* series, and would I be interested in making a series with black kids? The question is, who has the vision to get in bed with us for the long haul?

Now I really want to develop *In Search of Our Fathers* as a feature. I don't want to write it, though. I'm too close to the material. I would write a book, because that would be from a different perspective. I'm interested in Judy Ann Mason to write the feature version of *In Search.* She wrote a Disney project that they're going to turn into *Sister Act 2.*

JOHN KEITEL
December 12

During our first interview, Keitel was emotionally rattled; the day before, he had found a dead body in an alley near his apartment. Today, he had just returned from the courthouse in downtown L.A., where he was summonsed after Hollywood detectives found the killer.

I didn't actually have to do anything, but I have to go back down in January. The detective drove me home and I showed him the site where I found the body. And he starts looking for the slug! Do you believe that? He says, "They never did find that slug." Then he asks me if I've ever done this before. Yeah, right. I find dead bodies all the time. He kept telling me this was "good material."

The detective who was driving me home from the precinct said they call Venice Boulevard—my bike route to and from school— the Five-Yard Line. He said, "You're a lucky boy that they haven't killed you just for the fun of it." He's right. Particularly since the riots, I think they see me more. I don't blend in. Now I'm not taking my bike there anymore. I mean, this was a street-smart black cop, who's out there all the time.

They dropped off the witnesses en route. Two crackheads, a fortyish man and woman. The cop said to them, "I could put you away for six years and you'd probably live longer." He said to me, "Don't tell anyone here [at the precinct] your name and address."

Keitel had recently been contacted by Dan Gelfand, a vice-president at the Samuel Goldwyn Company. They discussed a possible compilation of four short films—including Keitel's An All-American Story—*which Gelfand had seen at gay-and-lesbian film festivals in different regions of the country.*

A business affairs executive at Goldwyn outlined to Keitel an arrangement in which Goldwyn would take a 35-percent distribution fee and the remaining 65 percent would be split among the filmmakers, with 10 percent of all earnings donated to AIDS organizations. Goldwyn would need legally cleared material, and own the rights for twenty-five years.

They feel there's a market for this and an appealing way to present the films. The hope is to premiere them at Sundance. The other films are *The Dead Boys Club* by Mark Christopher, *RSVP* by a Toronto woman, and one more.

I was so thrilled when they approached me that it doesn't even matter if it happens or not. I just said, "Tonight, I'm celebrating!" The film sold out at the Chicago Film Festival and there have been many calls for video copies. So if it's not this, it'll be something else.

Keitel ran the Goldwyn project by USC film school chairman Mark Harris, who gave it his blessing, and then called attorney Alan Hergott, who considered the deal too small and speculative to work on. But Brooke Warden, a lawyer who teaches at USC, offered to negotiate on Keitel's behalf.

Brooke laid her cards on the table. She said she wants me as a client, and that an agent is unnecessary. Hergott agrees, for the time being. Brooke is on her own and has been doing this for about three years. She told me that if I wanted to pursue a feature-length version of *An All-American Story*, she could get me a deal right now.

She keeps mentioning Stephanie Allain at Columbia as someone who should see this film. My gut feeling about Brooke is that my experience with her on this Goldwyn project will be a prime opportunity to see how it goes. Larry Auerbach, a veteran William Morris agent, is also working with us. He was hired by USC to provide a bridge from film school to the outside world.

Hergott said that trying to finance my feature film could be the risk of my life. But I think that's an odd notion. Artists are *supposed* to create and take risks. Brooke said, "Start it at a fraternity." I wrote fifteen pages and then thought, I don't want to do this. We've already seen too many of these "coming out" stories. So I will contradict my thesis objective. The two owners—best friends, one gay and one straight—are now both gay, with a very important supporting cast. I'll be gone to Chicago and Amsterdam December twenty-first through January eleventh, and want to have a showable first draft soon afterward.

At First Look, a film program at the Academy of Motion Picture Arts and Sciences featuring An All-American Story, *the thousand-plus-seat theatre was half full.*

Gail Begelman from Jerry Weintraub, Jeff Bynum from Scott Rudin's company, and someone from Todd-AO, who are developing features now, were all there. It was a mistake to show the first night of the four because it took time for word of mouth to build. But to be honest, after showing at international and national festivals, the Academy was anticlimactic anyway.

I won the gold plaque at the Chicago Film Festival, making my film eligible for an actual Academy Award. Now they're considering eradicating the awards, though. Why? Does it take too much time to screen and judge the films? I think it's a short-sighted decision, and somewhat arrogant.

In late 1992 the Academy announced that it was considering the elimination of short subject Oscar categories. The threat was rescinded after it met with extreme opposition from the film community and the media.

P. J. PESCE
December 15

Pesce and his partner, Tom Abrams, had recently been hired to write a sequel to Whore, *a 1991 Ken Russell film.*

For a low-budget deal, the fucking gyrations Trimark are putting us through are amazing. I can't tell you the number of ways they have tried to screw us. They got a free option for a year, plus they own everything. And there's no guarantee that I will get to direct it.

MPCA, meanwhile, won't guarantee me the money I made on my last deal for *The Desperate Trail*. But the production bonus will make it equal.

JOHN MCINTYRE
December 17

McIntyre was continuing at Duck Soup, one of the many commercial production companies found not only in L.A. but in all cities where major advertising agencies are located.

I've been working on 7UP "Dot" commercials during the holidays. And Pop-Tarts, in '30s-style animation. I'm animating exclusively, working with Jean Perramon, a great designer who worked with Richard Williams [a top animation filmmaker] in London.

A lot of work has come in. We could be busy through the spring. I may also be doing more of these flip-books as a separate enterprise with a friend, Joe Forte, an advertising copywriter.

P. J. PESCE
December 17

Brad Krevoy from MPCA called me to direct a movie. I figured I should call you and tell you all this because—who knows?—in another week it'll all be gone and I'll be so miserable. At least I'll be able to listen to the tape and know that it was once real.

He called and said, "Listen, why don't we put you to work right away, have you direct a different movie, and we'll push the Western back another month? Then we can finish that one and go right into the Western."

I said, "Okay, what is it?" He said, "The Barbarian Brothers [muscle-bound twins and occasional low-budget film stars]."

I saw a one-sheet in Krevoy's office with these fucking lunkheads on it. I think MPCA did *Think Big*, the Barbarians movie that Jon Turteltaub [later the director of *Cool Runnings* and *While You Were Sleeping*] did.

So all of a sudden there's that, and also the possibility of *Whore II* at Trimark. I can just see the headline—"Young Whore Directs 'More Whore.'" I keep telling myself, "Well, look, Howard Hawks, John Ford . . . all these guys worked with the Barbarian Brothers. It didn't hurt their careers." [Laughs] Those guys did knock out a lot of crummy movies in the '20s and '30s.

I said, "When would we start?" He said "Tomorrow." I probably could have said yes on the phone last night. Instead I said, "Send me the script, send me the other two Barbarian Brothers epics, and I'll watch them and think about it." I talked to a friend of mine who had seen these films. I asked him what goes on in them, and he said, "I don't know, they seem to drive around a lot in a truck." So who knows what I'm in for?

My friend Les says that what you have to do is give yourself eighteen days, then—without telling anyone—you use the rest of the time and budget and film to shoot your own movie. Corman did that all the time. *Body Waves* was shot on the sets of some thriller from the week before. He just said, "Write a dumb beach comedy, but it has to have a radio station set somehow."

By the end of the week I should be able to decide between directing *Whore II* or *The Barbarian Brothers*. How could anyone decide? Barbarians, Whores, Barbarians, Whores . . .

LIZ CANE
December 18

A week after the DGA screening, Liz Cane attended an open house at the Guild. A Q&A session was held with a panel including directors John Singleton and Arthur Hiller and an award-winning recent NYU film school graduate, Christian Taylor.

Christian is developing his short into a feature. Some of the students were not too bright and kept repeating the same basic questions—"How do you break in?" etc.

The subject of women directors came up, and Arthur Hiller had this lame response, mentioning Streisand, Jodie Foster, and Martha Coolidge. He's an older guy, so he didn't seem very concerned.

Singleton said that less than a year before *Boyz N the Hood* was filmed, he was an extra in *Darkman*. He admitted he didn't know a lot about filmmaking and is just now studying *8½* and other classics. He seemed really honest and comfortable with himself. Chuck Workman moderated again. I *really* don't like that guy.

I kept talking to Donald Petrie. He thought maybe Walter Matthau would do *Grumpy Old Men*. He never watched my film, and said he hadn't yet made his decision. I tried calling him today. The movie's been green-lit and he's on location.

We had started to talk in a more relaxed way, getting to know each other. But maybe I didn't come across enthused enough. I got the feeling Petrie was testing that, and I didn't pass. The person who got the job was, maybe, more determined.

I got a three-day educational video job. And the BBC is looking for someone to organize and edit a documentary. They gave ten or twelve people High 8 cameras and up to sixty hours of tape, and used them as sort of video diarists. None had any experience with cameras. They will stop filming in February, and they need someone to help five of the diarists. It will take two weeks for each person to edit their fifteen-minute section.

I would also be involved in the January shooting. They want someone with a filmmaking/directing background and to overdub audio, etc. I felt okay in the interview except for the fact that I'm this little blonde girl. I worry that they might think that I couldn't go into rough neighborhoods. The interview was Tuesday morning. The producer took my tapes to New York.

RANDA HAINES, Director

Women and minority filmmakers are still viewed as "special" somehow. But as long as you're viewed as "special," you're in a precarious position. You're not part of the mainstream, and always in danger of not being "special" enough anymore, disappearing and being extinct.

There are so many more women directing now, particularly in television. When I started directing, it was still so unusual. I remember seeing my first dailies and hearing a woman's voice say "action"—*my* voice—and that was a shock even to me. I was so used to a man being in that role. But there still aren't the numbers of women there should be. We're still moving too slowly.

When I was starting out, I think I must have put blinders on, so I wouldn't even be aware of prejudicial attitudes around me. If someone said, "Oh, she's too slow," I could work on that. But I couldn't change the fact that I was a woman, and would never want to. You just can't work in a state of anger, so I didn't see it or hear it. You need all of your energy for the work itself.

JOHN MCINTYRE
January 7

I've been doing shadows and tones on the Dots for weeks. There are like twenty of them, and each of them has sneakers with different treads.

MARCO WILLIAMS
January 8

We "hurried up to wait" on this treatment for *In Search of Our Fathers* as a feature. I met with Denzel Washington for the second time, and I wrote a seven-page treatment with Judy Ann Mason.

It's a little unrealistic for me to think that Denzel is going to star—as me—in the first film I direct. So he may be involved in another capacity, as producer perhaps. Frankly, putting the character in his mid-thirties changes the story. We evolve at every age, but I think an audience sympathizes more with a character going through this in his twenties.

I may go to Sundance and I'm thinking about some other festivals, like Paris again. And Hong Kong, if I can get them to fly me there.

FRANK DARABONT, Writer-Director

The lovely thing about writing and directing is that the more you go along, the more you start dealing with people you really respect and admire. And I've met more lovely people in this business than not. Tom Cruise is just a prince as far as I'm concerned. Rob Reiner is an enormous talent with an enormous heart, and I think the world of him. George Lucas is one of the best guys in the world. Dick Donner I wish was my uncle—he's the greatest guy. There are so many people who don't disappoint you when you meet them.

I recently met Spielberg, and that was really quite a thrill for me. I haven't lost the capacity to be thrilled by these people I admire and respect.

LISA KLEIN
January 20

We're having a lot of trouble getting *Radio Wars* booked into festivals. It's 35mm and forty-eight minutes long, which means it's too short to be a feature and too long to be a short. We're hitting a lot of brick walls.

At Ann Arbor, they insist the films be 16mm. So Peter and I have considered dubbing it down to 16mm. But that and cutting would take time and money we just don't have.

P. J. PESCE
January 20

I met Steve Soderbergh last night through this mutual friend, Davis Guggenheim, who was one of the producers of *sex, lies and videotape*. Davis had asked me to do a movie when I was still in film school. He really wanted me to direct it, but the script was bad—very bad. Of course, I really wanted to direct a feature while I was still in film school, and I was very tempted, but in the end I had to say no.

Davis to this day says, "Wow, I'm still impressed that you had that kind of ethical and moral . . ." and I'm like, "No, it's not like that." I was just afraid to make a real big mess of things, and thought it was cursed from the get-go. Anyway, Davis and I have become really good friends. He did a short film which I wound up helping him with when he was writing it. When he was cutting it, I spent a week in Washington, D.C., with him and his editor, as a sort of consulting editor.

Three days earlier, in conjunction with the upcoming Sundance Film Festival, a feature story appeared in the Sunday New York Times *entitled, "So, You Wanna Be a Director?"*

Bill Grimes from the *Times* called and said someone told him this anecdote about me, and he wanted to check its veracity. He didn't tell me who told him, but the anecdote was that I had been offered a three-picture deal at Paramount right out of school, and I stayed there for a year and turned it down in order to do a picture for Roger Corman. And I thought, "Wow! That's great! What a great story! I would like that guy a lot, whoever he is!" Unfortunately, though Davis may believe I am concerned with this higher good—which I am, to an extent—I figured if you let stories like that go around, they just come back to you in the end.

So I had to correct Grimes. No, I didn't have a three-picture deal. I had a deal that would allow them to make three pictures with me if they wanted to make one movie, but Paramount chose not to do anything with me because they were going through so much internal turmoil, and everybody was worried about their own jobs. They didn't really care about what I was doing.

It was really a fellowship for a year—I was paid—and at the end, yes, I asked to be let out of my contract three weeks early so I could direct a film for Roger Corman.

Well, apparently *that* was not interesting enough, so I was not featured in the article. It seemed like the standard "Film students get out of school and are wined and dined." I don't think things are like *The Big Picture* anymore. Seven or eight years ago, the studios were doing a lot of stuff like that. But very few people get out of school and then their student film gets all this attention and someone gives them a three-picture deal as the result of it. Or *any* picture deal. If they don't have a script—a solid feature script—they don't get anything.

Even Dan Algrant was lucky, because in our class with Scorsese he had already written a feature for hire. Marty was interested in producing features for other people at that point. I don't know if that's the case anymore, but Dan had a short that Marty rather liked and encouraged him to turn into a feature [which became *Naked in New York*]. Well, he developed it into a feature, four years ago at this point. It was on again, off again, on again. He got it all together and Scorsese agreed to be the executive producer.

So it wasn't just "Hey, you're out of film school and everyone's wining and dining you." That wasn't even the case with him. I don't know her, but Stacy Cochran [director of the well-received indie film *My New Gun*] sounds like she is someone who managed to get a feature done very quickly right out of film school. I think the person it happened to most like in *The Big Picture* was Adam Davidson [*Lunch Date*]. You know, he made a great student film and it won every single award possible. He was on the cover of the *New York Times*. He was in *Vanity Fair*.

There were agents certainly fighting for him. At one point, [fellow Columbia student] Greg Mottola told me that Davidson would come home after hanging out with the guys and there would be like twenty-seven answering machine messages from different agents and producers. And here it is, two or three years later, and he has yet to make a feature. He was all set up and had a big agent.

To his credit, Adam is a very level-headed guy, and I don't think it made him a jerk or anything. He was a little bit weirded out about how the feeding frenzy came to him. He maintained that "I don't know, I thought it was an okay movie" quality. His ability to tell a story visually is of a very high caliber. That, and the fact that it is a great story, is what affected people so much. You can't slight the acting or the storytelling of that movie. It was really well done.

They all wanted him. In the end Milos Forman jumped on the bandwagon and wanted to work with him and got somebody to pay them a lot of money to write a script together. Which I could never understand, because I thought if anything they would ask Adam to direct a feature, not write a feature. Nevertheless, that is what happened, and it all fell apart, unfortunately.

BOBBI THOMPSON, Agent

One way of insuring some success is finding another director who can mentor you. Phil Joanou had a mentor in Steven Spielberg. Jocelyn Moorhouse, who is not a student film-maker but who directed an Australian feature film, has found a mentor in Sydney Pollack.

Alison Maclean *(Crush)* is another New Zealand director I signed on a short film that I saw at Cannes. She's a film school student in New Zealand. She went on to write and direct a film there and she's found a mentor in Martin Scorsese. So there are directors who like to produce and like to be a voice.

So here I am, working for Trimark, writing *Whore II*. And I may even wind up directing it.

I feel like if you deal with these things truthfully, though—in a manner that portrays how human beings would behave in these situations—you don't just have to make them do fucked-up things for our amusement, which is what pornography is. Not that I'm categorically against pornography, but that's another argument, because I think it has its place. Dehumanizing and degrading people for other people's amusement, I think, is a bad thing. It leads to fascism.

Whether or not I would want my name on *Whore II* is a question I have to deal with every single day. Every time I make a character speak or decide to have sex, I think, What's that about? Am I doing this because I want to titillate? Or *solely* to titillate? Or because this is what this human being that I'm creating is really about, and it's something he or she would do?

And what do I really believe? That this is a sick thing that they're doing? And how am I, as the author of this film, showing this to the audience? Am I commenting on it? Am I saying, "Look, the author of the movie thinks this is a fucked-up thing"?

The people at Trimark are on our backs all the time. The development woman calls my partner, Tom, because I guess I'm the bad cop and he's the good cop. But they did everything they could, up until the last second. According to this contract we were supposed to deliver a treatment and get paid for that. And they wanted to see the treatment before we got paid, which is very uncool.

So through us Kanter, my agent, would not allow that. Both Tom and I were saying, "Not in this lifetime." We turned it in and got paid and had a meeting with them, all standard fare. But then after we met with them, they wanted us to give them a "beat sheet"—a revised treatment, basically. They wanted us to write two treatments. That kind of pissed us off, but we thought we would have to do that anyway before we start writing, so we agreed to do it.

Then they said okay, and started wanting us to turn in pages. That's when we finally put our foot down and said no, absolutely not. Not because we wanted to be difficult, but because we wanted to do good work, and you can't be constantly second-guessing yourself in the middle of writing a screenplay. It's a very difficult thing to pound through 110 pages of material and feel free enough to make certain kinds of decisions about what characters do and say and how the thing should be structured. We have already gone through that in great detail with them.

If they don't trust us that much, they should not have hired us. So they're not going to get pages. When we're finished with the draft—in four weeks, a very quick turnaround period—they'll have it. They can give us notes and we can proceed to the next stage. I don't think we're doing anything out of the ordinary.

I'm writing the third draft of the Western on my own, without Tom. He's trying to write a movie for himself to direct, and he and I are writing *Whore II* at the same time. We're really knocking out the pages. We switch scenes and meet every third day. We're supposed to be exclusive. But for the amount of money they're paying me they shouldn't expect me to be exclusive, because I can hardly pay my laundry bills.

I'm excited about the Western. People liked this draft a lot. And I like it a lot. Soderbergh is looking for a Western, and we did talk about that. He said, "Yeah, send me the Western." He's finishing up *King of the Hill*, and then he's going to produce Greg Mottola's movie, then he's looking for the next thing. [Mottola's film, *The Daytrippers*, was a hit at 1996's Slamdance, a renegade festival held near Park City, Utah, concurrent with Sundance.]

When I'm writing or working, I talk to my agent maybe once a week. When I'm not, that's when I start calling him up—"Hey hey hey." Every once in a while he sends me a script, I think to pretend he's doing something. He sent me a script that's set up at MPCA this morning. It's called *Mayonnaise and Margaritas*. Okay, so it's alliterative. I don't know. I'll read it.

I really want to do *The Trials of Leo*. That's the thing that's near and dear to me. Unfortunately, I think very few people really like it. There was always another way for unconventional movies to get made, but now I can't seem to find that. Even independently, it doesn't seem like it's going to get made. We're putting a cast together for it. Frank Whaley is committed to doing it for free. I want to use Steve Brill in it. Lisa Shue [Davis Guggenheim's wife, later Oscar nominated as Best Actress for *Leaving Las Vegas*] is a friend of mine. I want to put her in it.

Where am I going with this career? Some days I wake up and think, "Yeah, I should be happy." I'm working, I'm getting paid to write, but I do feel behind schedule—like, the real stuff I want to do, I haven't done. I feel like I need to make a personal, independent movie to get me to the next step. And how I'm going to do that, I don't know.

Leo needs to be rewritten. Chad Oman and I have talked about doing it through MPCA for about $300,000. And once he finishes the movie he's producing, I'm going to give it to him in a slightly reworked version and we're going to start to work through it. He's very smart, has good taste, and knows story structure. Together he and I can rework this thing into a draft for which Brad Krevoy will give us some money.

Brad likes me and believes in me and I think he will give me some money to do the movie. I told him I would direct any dopey comedy he wanted. I will direct *The Barbarian Brothers Go to Mars* if he wants, in exchange for letting me do this movie on a very small budget with people that I want to use. And he seemed to indicate that that would be okay. So I have to finish these two scripts so I can shoot these two movies.

If I got that film made I wouldn't have such a problem driving around in my shitbox car. It wouldn't matter. I would have made the movie I wanted to make. I am around guys who are doing well and making big, fat checks. I play golf with Steve Brill, who wrote one of the biggest fucking movies [*The Mighty Ducks*] and just bought a house, and it really doesn't bother me. Now he's going to write and direct *Mighty Ducks 2*. That's okay. These people are my friends and they're doing well, and they like me, obviously because of who I am, not because I'm doing really well or anything, so that makes me feel good. And I genuinely like these people, so that's a good sign. Hopefully that means that I'm in good company and I'll do well myself.

Nobody has a long-term plan for developing talent, or nurturing a younger generation. They want them to hit, and then they want to jump on the bandwagon and say, "I've always known you and believed in you." Which is frightening.

Soderbergh told me last night that some basketball player said, "You're always going to meet some guy who practiced a little harder than you, and when you meet him he's going to beat you. If you're not spending all your time looking at videos on laserdisc, studying movies and writing them and working, there are going to be people better than you, and they're going to burn you when you get there." And that's really a tough, salty attitude. I wonder if I want to have my life so consumed. And I wonder if it's the only way to make movies.

MARK KRUGER, Writer–Producer
I remember seeing Soderbergh's films in '85 or '86. He was a young kid, and had made all these short films—he had written spec scripts that were in development. You knew he had talent and it was just a matter of time before someone was gonna give him a shot.

PIETER-JANN BRUGGE, Producer
The only one of the young directors who seems to *want* to work outside the system is Steven Soderbergh.

MARCO WILLIAMS
January 21

In October 1992, Marco Williams's agency, InterTalent, had merged with big-three agency ICM. On Friday, January 15, Daily Variety carried a prominent two-page ad: "International Creative Management is pleased to congratulate our CableAce award nominees."

Following were three dozen names, including Billy Crystal, Holly

Hunter, Walter Hill—and Marco Williams, nominated as Best Director of a Dramatic Series for Showtime 30-Minute Movie: "Without a Pass."

I don't know if they have it together. They picked a bad weekend to do this, with the inauguration going on.

January 25

The following weekend, Williams wore a tuxedo and a white scarf to the nationally televised ACE Awards, which were held at Hollywood's Pantages Theatre. When his name was announced in the list of nominees, he noticed himself in the monitor and smiled broadly. Williams's competition: Gary Fleder for Tales from the Crypt: *"Seance," HBO; Brad Turner for* Kurt Vonnegut's Monkey House: *"More Stately Mansions," Showtime; and the winner, Ian Mune, for* The Ray Bradbury Theater: *"Great Wide World Over There," on the USA network. Mune, who said he came eight thousand miles from New Zealand to accept the award, thanked Bradbury, who was in the audience.*

It was kind of dull. Friday was the exciting part, arriving at the cocktail party. All the celebrities I recognized were from ESPN. I got a real gas out of that. I watch SportsCenter two or three times a week, so I recognized Robin Roberts, Peter Gammons, and Roy Firestone. Friday was more about sports programming and documentaries, it was not the star-studded night. I saw Bernard Shaw, but I don't generally walk up to someone unless I have something particularly intelligent to say.

After the picture didn't win Best Movie or Theatrical Special on Friday, I knew it wasn't going to win Best Director or Actor. Sunday was a much bigger to-do—televised, etc. But quite frankly, after my award came and went, my interest lagged because I didn't know much of the other programming. I would generally read about it like I do the Golden Globes, on the following day—I don't need to be there. So it's kind of anticlimactic. But I enjoyed myself inasmuch as it was a first for me. To use an expression of my mother's, I can "check it off my list."

The Showtime people were very generous and supportive. Friday night I sat next to Dennis Johnson, [a V.P.] who was a big supporter of my film from the very beginning. And Steve Hewitt, the Senior V.P., came over and congratulated me with no trepidation whatsoever.

I wrote a speech; I had something I wanted to say. It was a statement recognizing that the next day was Martin Luther King's birthday, and my film was about intolerance, which he fought against in his life, and I had a quote from him. I regret not having that chance, but I didn't expect I would win.

I threw out the treatment for the feature version of *In Search of Our Fathers*. We have some new meetings set up on that. I'm going younger, and I've come up with an "A" story [main plot] that has nothing to do with a guy looking for his father. It's surprising because I sort of realized or imagined a more commercial idea which will trigger the search for the protagonist's father. Right now he's not looking for his father from the very beginning.

I've got the basic arc for the first act and a half, and now I have to figure out how to integrate the highlights of the documentary into the story line. The protagonist will be twenty-five as opposed to mid-thirties. And if I go to a meeting I can say, "It's like *Crying Game*—you think it's about this, and by the end the two story lines converge." But I haven't found the convergent point yet.

The other thing is making the decision to work on this more myself as opposed to being dependent on a writer. I decided to do my homework and realized that I could write this. I don't need somebody else to develop this with. I'll sufficiently remove the documentary from the story line so it's like I'm writing something else completely.

I also have an idea for an adaptation of *On the Waterfront* that I'm ready to pitch to whoever wants to hear it. It's a way for people to see something—give them a set of glasses. I'll point it out, but I didn't buy the rights, there will be no Terry Malloy [the role played by Brando in the 1954 film], that sort of thing. It will be set in L.A., and about race and the riots. It's not inspired by waterfront crime or corruption in New York City.

> GARY ROSS, Screenwriter
>
> I think the studios buy less pitches now. There's almost an assumption that if you have an original idea you have to write it first or write it on spec if you're unknown. For some reason they think they know what makes a better movie than you do. Instead of turning to writers to generate ideas, they recycle old TV shows or something like that. It's harder now for someone breaking in than it used to be.

JOHN KEITEL
January 26–31

The only moguls in Park City, Utah, during the last two weeks in January are the bumps on the ski slopes.

Hollywood's moguls—the Eisners, Roths, Lansings—wouldn't be caught dead at that town's Sundance Film Festival, where the average budget of the films presented might *cover one of their yearly expense accounts. It's the worker bees of the next rung down, the production V.P.s and junior agents, who are all too thrilled to take five—days, that is—at Sundance.*

The setting is charming: a former mining town where you can drink the tap water or the ale made daily at the Wasatch Brewery on top of Main Street. Park City functions as a ski resort for half the year.

I didn't notice one tasseled loafer or Armani suit. Here $250 Timberland boots and L.L. Bean parkas are de rigueur. *The agents and executives wearing them scope out the restaurants, parties, premieres—and of course the slopes—on the lookout for the next Coen brothers or Soderbergh. Tough job, but somebody's got to do it.*

Robert Redford, who founded the festival in 1981, sees Sundance as more of a "film community" than a "schmoozefest." And compared to the "I'll get back to you" social and professional games played on the coasts, the festival does put the "wannabes" in the faces of the "players." It's easier to get around by public shuttle bus than private car, so it's not uncommon for the "suits" to be forced into exchanging pleasantries with the very people whose calls they wouldn't return back in the city.

"This place really jumbles the Hollywood hierarchy," says John Keitel's cinematographer, Ann Kim.

Many of the films that premiere here, such as El Norte, The Trip to Bountiful, Reservoir Dogs, and this year's Twenty Bucks, have been developed in Sundance's Screenwriters' or Filmmakers' Labs. Others are submitted, viewed, and selected to screen either in or out of competition.

There are major differences between the types of product shown at Sundance and more commercial, big-budget fare: American studio films concern themselves primarily with physical behavior, while independents tend to explore characters' emotional lives. A prime 1993 example was Victor Núñez's Grand Jury cowinner Ruby in Paradise, a $350,000 slice-of-life about a young woman's relocation to a new town.

While Hollywood pictures are promoted almost exclusively by performers who have been paid handsomely for twelve weeks of work, at Sundance the directors are the stars. Independent films are indelibly linked to their creators, the visionaries who have spent years—and often their own and/or their relatives' savings—to bring a project to fruition.

That's not to say that name performers don't "do" Sundance. Sally Kirkland, who had executive-produced and starred in a 1993 festival entry called Paper Hearts, at one point burst into "Z" Place, a central meeting area next to the Press Room. "I've just had a car accident," she breathily told a phalanx of reporters, many of whom, familiar with Kirkland's propensity for offscreen drama, were less than visibly shaken.

The reclusive Sam Shepard, surprisingly, was there too, cold-shouldering Sundance board member L. M. Kit Carson, who against Shepard's wishes got a screenwriting credit on Wim Wenders's 1984 film Paris, Texas. Redford made his customary appearance early in the festival, as did Jeff Bridges, who was publicizing the indie American Heart.

Upon arrival in Park City, John Keitel's boyfriend, Carter Bravmann, called his uncle in Salt Lake City. Bravmann had recently "come out" to him and was curious to hear his uncle's reaction to An All-American Story. (The uncle had attended the first showing, held the night before.)

Hanging up the condo phone, Bravmann said, "My uncle says the film was the best received, and got the most applause. I believe him. He wouldn't just say that. He really sounded sincere. But he did say he didn't agree with the 'lifestyle,' " Bravmann reported, rolling his eyes.

The second screening of An All-American Story—part of a quartet of short films entitled "Where the Boys Are"—was held on Tuesday night,

January 26, at 10:30. Ten minutes before show time, the smell of pungent marijuana wafted through the theatre. The cinema seemed to be filled not merely with Sundancers but with much of the gay population of Salt Lake City, hungry for what the program had to offer.

The other "Where the Boys Are" films were Billy Turner's Secret, *in which an inner-city homophobe must deal with the consequences of shunning his best friend after he comes out;* The Dead Boys Club, *a raw, darkly funny but touching memoir of the sexually liberated, disco '70s; and* Deaf Heaven, *the solemn, slickly produced story of a man coping with the inevitable AIDS death of his lover.*

I'm hypersensitive to audience reaction, so I end up revising my initial feeling based on what people say to me. I thought they were all received well, especially after going to other screenings. I was basing it on past experiences in much larger theatres. But it was somewhat of a subdued response, I thought. The audience started laughing and interacting a lot later than they normally do.

But people came up to me. Given the attendance at Sundance and the small portion who were at that screening, I was approached by approximately fifteen people over the next three days—a pretty good rate of return.

STEPHANIE ALLAIN, Studio Executive

More and more when I go to festivals, it's a personal thing, it's about just absorbing movies that are not mainstream. Because of alternative means of storytelling, a lot of movies are not made with studio intervention, so they're freer in a sense. But a lot of them are really bad, and I have a hard time sitting through them.

The good thing about the festivals is you can see the movies and meet the filmmakers and have a dialogue with them right there, and make a lot of contacts and bring the films back to the studio so your associates can see them. You can tell a filmmaker is talented, even from a small, offbeat independent movie. That's why I go—to meet the people who are making those movies.

Invitation-only sponsored events at Sundance were hosted by the Playboy Foundation, Entertainment Weekly, *Independent Feature Project (IFP), and the Samuel Goldwyn Company. The hot parties were only discovered through word of mouth, however—CAA had one, and Keva Rosenfeld and his partner Karen Murphy [*Twenty Bucks*] another, at the tony Deer Valley Lodge.*

In typical fashion, the toughest ticket to come by was for the movie with the weirdest buzz, Jennifer Lynch's Boxing Helena. *The twenty-four-year-old Lynch—David's daughter—had not only her age but her lineage against her.*

On the same day Boxing Helena *was dismissed as "tripe" in the pages of the* Hollywood Reporter, *Lynch appeared as a panelist for a seminar entitled "Twenty Somethings: The New Generation." The other participants had all directed films being shown at the festival: Tony Chan (*Combination Platter, *later awarded Best Screenplay), Leslie Harris (*Just Another Girl on the I.R.T., *later cited for "outstanding achievement in a first feature" by the Sundance jury), Rob Weiss (*Amongst Friends, *a popular favorite), Robert Rodriguez (*El Mariachi, *a feature made for $7,000), and Bryan Singer (whose* Public Access *went on to tie with* El Mariachi *for Grand Jury Prize and who later directed* The Usual Suspects*).*

The discussion's moderator, producer John Pierson, began by reading a Kit Carson quote from a recent New York Times *article:*

" 'These filmmakers here grew up on Sesame Street *and video stores. They haven't found a style yet, a grip. The features here are a struggle for coherence and an authentic expression of where these people are. . . . We have a generation whose perceptions are unfinished because they learned it from television. In contrast, young filmmakers and films of the 1970s, while as different as Martin Scorsese and George Lucas, or* Five Easy Pieces *and* Easy Rider, *offered a coherent vision. This is the generation that somehow felt they had a grasp on the world—they thought they knew what was right and wrong.' "*

Asked to respond, the filmmakers took a breath, and then Rob Weiss—a friend of P. J. Pesce's—responded, "I don't think I'm coherent enough to answer that question." After some discussion of the deeper meaning of Carson's quote, Robert Rodriguez leaned into his mike: "Did anyone see the remake of Breathless?*" (The audience applauded; the 1983 film, from Carson's script, was a critical and box-office dud.) Tony Chan explained that, contrary to Carson's thesis, television was not at all part of his childhood.*

Jennifer Lynch responded to a comment about the absence of powerful experiences such as the Vietnam War in their own lives. The well-spoken Lynch, whose father has endured publicized divorces and rumors, observed that her generation as children of broken homes and domestic violence have faced their own wars.

All of the directors stressed the importance of short films, and some said they would continue working in that format. Regarding the merits of shorts versus features, Lynch broke up a heated debate—as well as the crowd—by declaring, "People have been saying for years that length doesn't matter."

I had a question for the group: "I don't think if this panel were held five years ago that Michael Lehmann [Heathers] ever would have predicted that he would direct a $40 million Bruce Willis movie [Hudson Hawk]. If each of you went back to your hotel rooms and Joel Silver was there with a check for $500,000 to direct Lethal Weapon 4, *would you take it—yes or no, and why?"*

Film school dropout Weiss, who wore a Cypress Hill baseball cap and spoke in the street patois of an urban black teen, said that his cinematic passions overrode his desire for material wealth. Pierson asked each of the other filmmakers to respond, and all answers were in the negative, with two exceptions: Rodriguez said he would take the money, spending a million on the movie and the other $39 million on the films he would like to make, while Leslie Harris insisted that she would never be asked to direct the hypothetical Silver movie in the first place.

KEVA ROSENFELD, Director

I would never do *Lethal Weapon 4*. I know what Michael Lehmann's experience was like on *Hudson Hawk* and I would never go through it. It's not the reason I got into the film business. I never wanted to make big movies that were just huge movies for the sake of it.

Movies I like are more personal, about relationships, more about an individual stamp from the person who made it. Most Joel Silver movies, you see the stamp of sound effects—not the personality behind it. I haven't been offered that kind of stuff and won't be.

The third screening of the "Where the Boys Are" program was held on Saturday, January 30, again at 10:30 P.M. Michael Mayson, the hetero-sexual director of Billy Turner's Secret, *opened by telling the crowd, "These are gay-themed films—not necessarily by gay filmmakers." The crowd murmured as John Keitel added, "And you get to guess which one [isn't gay]."*

Keitel then thanked the crowd for coming out on the eve of the last day of the festival, and introduced his cinematographer, Ann Kim. "As you will see, her role was very important in the making of this film, as was that of Carter, my boyfriend. Now you know I'm not the one."

Mark Christopher, director of The Dead Boys Club, *leaned into the mike and rather than introduce his film said only, "I'll keep you guessing, too."*

NEAL JIMENEZ, Writer-Director

I was in Sundance in '88 or '87 with *River's Edge*, but the festival didn't have the reputation it has now. I didn't even know the film was there. I wasn't even invited—I was just the writer. The producer and director went. We didn't win anything, and there was a lot of controversy when they were giving out the Grand Jury Prize. I mean, obviously *River's Edge* wasn't the kind of film that was going to win the Audience Award. I've heard scuttlebutt that there was a lot of controversy on the jury—it was a very divisive film, and that year *Waiting for the Moon* won the jury award.

But in '92, when [codirector] Mike Steinberg and I were there for *The Waterdance*, the festival was very exciting. We got there five days into it, so the "buzz" was already traveling about which films were the ones that were being noticed and were in contention for the award, and ours was one of them. So we were kind of the belles of the ball immediately, and the intensity of the attention we got was overwhelming.

I didn't get to see a lot of films, because we did have a distributor at that time, and had a PR person who was arranging interviews for us. There was a camplike feeling the year I was there—struggling filmmakers—a feeling that this could be the only place your film shows and that would be satisfaction enough. The people that were watching the films were average filmgoers, and very excited.

On the day of the awards, it didn't matter if we won or not. It was nice to have won. I noticed that they had built a wheelchair ramp to the stage, so I thought, "I think we won something." They also pulled us right up to the front so that it would be easy for me to get to the stage.

On January 27, John Keitel and I attended Sundance '93's independent film production seminar. Keitel was interested in exploring possible avenues of financing for Ground Zero.

The panelists represented independent companies such as Fine Line, Polygram Film Entertainment and TNT. Most stressed that—with rare exceptions—they only bought completed screenplays.

Another consensus was that elements such as name actors were important to a proposed package. Ronna Wallace, Sr. V.P. for Production and Acquisitions at LIVE Entertainment, reinforced this with her belief that it was Harvey Keitel's name that got her company to make Bad Lieutenant. *Wallace was the only panelist who said her company was open to reading unsolicited material; many in the crowd anxiously jotted down her name and that of her company.*

A week after Sundance ended, the folding of LIVE was announced in the Hollywood trade papers.

ADAM DUBOV, Director

This took a long time for me to learn—it's like Marlon Brando says in *Apocalypse Now*, like a diamond bullet hitting you right between the eyes—the brilliance of your script is not going to get it made. The brilliance of your script, plus a really good director, until it's an A-list director, is not going to get it made.

What is going to get your movie made are actors. They control all the cards. People are not buying movies, they're buying packages. The littlest guys, the independent investors, are buying packages.

Before he left Sundance, Keitel saw a documentary by Christian Blackwell on the painter Joan Mitchell, and attended a party.

Carter and I went to this party at Sundance—this gay party—and we met this guy and I asked him what he did and he told me in that tone, "Well, I'm an Executive Vice President of Development." Then he looked at us and said, "What are you all doing here?" and I told him I had a film in the gay shorts program. I already knew if he didn't recognize me that he didn't go see the film.

So he took it one step further—he said, "*Gay-themed* films? You mean there were *gay-themed* films here?" It was funny. I realized it's the last night, I was a little punchy and I could have started saying stuff.

I liked what Joan Mitchell said in the film about the distinction between being a person who paints and a "painter." Being a human being is by far the more important thing.

Sundance was the sort of thing where you have a lot of expectations and then as soon as you arrive and get the lay of the land you forget everything you expected. I've seen more films in a more compressed period of time. But I've liked ninety percent of them, unlike Hollywood, where you like ten percent. I raved to everyone and was really glad I could participate in any way I could. It made the community of filmmaking much smaller and more accessible for me. Even though I was determined before, it's now more of a reality for me. It was a rite of passage in that way, because you go and rub elbows with these people that have made films, that other people are talking about. It was like *now* I've graduated from film school. It redefined the community of filmmaking for me, very clearly, beyond film school.

BERNARD JOFFA
February 4

Yesterday I got a check in the mail, and I'm now planning to leave, probably next week, for Africa, via Philadelphia, where I'm going to meet with Sydney Maree. I've spent a lot of time with him. Greg Latter, the writer, hasn't met him and doesn't want to meet him, so that he can maintain an objective point of view.

It could become a "biopic," but biopics are so boring—you're stuck with a biography. Our film is going to say "inspired by the life of Sydney Maree" as opposed to "based on," so we have a lot more license. He's not going to be called Sydney Maree. A biopic is like going to watch a history lesson, which is important, but not what I'm about.

That's what I want to achieve with this film. It's not going to be a film about a runner. It's about someone who out of desperation *becomes* a runner because that's the only way he finds a release for his frustration and anger, and the only time he feels control in an environment that's totally out of control. Being a black in South Africa, the only way he could get control was by running.

Now I'm learning about American runners. Long distance running is a high. They run. Filmmakers take drugs. We do something that's destructive and they do something that's constructive, using the energy in that way.

In South Africa Joffa will work on the first draft of the screenplay with Greg Latter, who has written previously for Cannon and Disney.

For me the process of sitting at a typewriter is a very difficult discipline. I've always been looking for the ideal partner. I don't know if it's Greg, but it might be. I like his scripts, so it makes a lot of sense. We're going to spend the first month in Cape Town, which is one of the most awe-inspiring places I've ever been to. It's where two oceans meet, at Cape Point, and we're going to get a place on the beach and just hang out there.

I believe that you should be in the most inspirational place to write, with the least distraction. So the first month we're going to be in Cape Town, and the second month we're going to be in the game park. A friend of mine's got a house. Greg is from Johnanesburg, where he lives.

We're getting a set fee from River Communications to write, and then I'm a coproducer and have a pay-or-play deal to direct. So after it's written I'm going to help get the movie together, through all the contacts that were set up by Ronda, my agent, when she first introduced me to people. Most of them said, "Okay, great. When you've got something come back."

I've learned that these things all work on the energy of the story. For Ronda to go out shouting great things about what's coming is bullshit, because how does she know what's coming? What's interesting is that I've been working closer with Chris Silverman, who was Ronda's assistant for five years. Chris has really done the whole deal, with her guidance. But he's been the person I've spoken to the whole time. He's a young guy. It's been just wonderful to work with someone who really believes in me and has made the time for me like he has.

I'm getting a ten-thousand-dollar fee to supervise the writing. That was based on what Greg did because he's a union member. We're getting forty thousand dollars each to write the script. So they're spending eighty thousand dollars on the script, of which Greg gets twenty thousand dollars now and twenty thousand dollars on delivery. I got five thousand dollars yesterday, and will get five thousand dollars in two months, and then when this film moves into production we'll get paid the balance of our writing fees. I'll get my full forty. Greg will already have his full forty. And then over and above that, if a studio picks it up, there's more money involved.

Each of us is represented by a different agent. Greg's with ICM, I'm with Broder-Kurland. So I don't know anything about Greg's dealings, except that I know he's getting twenty and twenty, and his agent is negotiating what he would get if a studio picks it up. I knew that if I requested my forty now it would have been unrealistic. The picture wouldn't get made. I knew the most important thing was to get the script done.

My deal is very much a back-end deal. All I requested up front was ten thousand dollars to pay my expenses to write the script. I feel confident enough that when the script is done I'll get paid my full writing fees, and then also for a coproducer credit, not associate producer. Scale plus ten percent to direct. DGA scale is about one hundred seventy thousand dollars. It's not about the money. I would pay them to make this picture.

I'm hoping that Disney picks it up in the end. I want the whole family to see it. It's very important, a very entertaining film with a very strong theme. It's about the insanity of government and how government is so intrusive on our rights.

Is it strange that I'm saying I hope Disney picks it up? Everybody's expecting this big political film, but there's going to be a lot of comedy in it. I've recently been watching a lot of Chaplin—films like *The Great Dictator*. Heavy scenes, done with comedy, make it a lot more approachable for an audience. That's going to be one of my goals, to try to make it as entertaining as possible. It's a *Chariots of Fire*, an American Dream story, all about honor, and taking care of family. "Family values." Me and what's his name, the ex–vice president.

Initially when River Communications met me, they had ideas about who should play Sydney Maree. A TV actor, I don't even know his name—one of these kids [Will Smith of *Fresh Prince of Bel-Air*]. That was their dream, to get one of those people. They were looking at that level, hoping to find a TV star, and once he's tied in, they'll tie in a studio.

My first choice was Denzel Washington, who they think would be wonderful. But they don't believe there's even a chance we'll get him. I know we're going to get him. Why do I know that? I *feel* we're going to get him. It's all about the role. If there's a role that's wonderful, any actor's going to want to play it.

I'm writing 50 percent of the script. It's based on a lot of imagination. We've got all the facts, thousands of facts. We've invaded the information banks in America and South Africa. The South Africans covered Sydney like a hawk, because he was the great hope. Plus he was covered in America. But those are just the facts. What interests me is the underlying stuff, which nobody has written.

I've certainly got a take on who he is. And Greg will bring in a lot of freshness as well. He's a fucking good writer. He's used to writing on his own. I'm not a good writer and don't have the discipline of a writer. If I had to tackle it on my own, it probably would never get finished. This way I know that after two months we're going to have a first draft for sure. It's his business. It's what he does all the time. For me, that's important.

Also, when you direct films you work closely on the script, it's the closest you get to a statement of personal expression. So it makes a lot of sense to me that I'm cowriting this. I'm surrounding myself with people who are better than me, the first one being the writer. Then I'm going to surround myself with the best cinematographer I can find and the best editor.

On this first film I'm going to give jobs to the best people I can get, and that's going to exclude a lot of newcomers. For me it's important on my first film that I have the support and help of technicians. And I hope that my friends understand that if I'm in a position to help them afterward, I will.

LIZ CANE
February 8

At UCLA I have an AV-type job, taping lectures and programs. It's mostly flexible and low stress.

I've also been working for L.A. Unified Schools, in Adult Education. They're doing an ESL [English as a second language] film. I'm learning how to work a new computer, which is CMX compatible. I was working on old, backward video systems.

It looks like this editing job will be regular. The director-producer has a good thing going with the school district. He's definitely a talented guy, and he's thinking of starting a production company. He's a former UCLA student and he has friends working for him.

The editing job is twenty hours a week, and I'm also writing with my friend J. C. Bennett [who directed *China on My Mind*, seen at the DGA Screening, and played a small role in Cane's film] and my father. The feature version of my film was going well, and then we got a new idea.

The script we're working on is like *Brazil* or *Dr. Strangelove*. J.C. and I wanted to collaborate on something. We'd get together but never quite got the ball rolling. Then we took a character J.C. had in mind, and combined it with an idea I had with my dad. The three of us collaborate equally.

Cane and five other women, all UCLA film school graduates, are planning a minifestival of industry screenings which they are calling "Meet Jane Doe."

Everything's costing more, except for the facility. We're each entitled to a Monday night screening. They're all thesis films. These six women are all working their tails off. I keep saying, "Don't stress out—you're not even making a film!" Alison Anders [director of *Gas, Food, Lodging*] is hosting the first night.

Anne Thompson and Ella Taylor [writers for *L.A. Weekly*, a popular free paper] both said they would come to the screenings. This one is much more demanding. I guess we're really trying to be seen, publicly and by the industry.

I turned thirty on January twenty-fourth. I want to just step back and enjoy things, and get off the treadmill.

BOBBI THOMPSON, Agent

I don't go to student screenings that much. I used to all the time, but now other people look at the films and I get my information from them. We have agents in our office with close ties to UCLA, USC, Otis Parsons, and Cal Arts.

Tim Burton was a Cal Arts graduate, but I met him when he was already an animator at Disney. Michael Lehmann was a director whose work I saw at a USC screening. His short, *Beaver Gets a Boner*, completely cracked me up. It was very offensive, about a college student who pays for his scholarship by dealing drugs. It was hysterical.

I actually pushed people out of the aisle to get to him.

P. J. PESCE
February 9

I'm really beat. In the last three weeks Tom and I finished two scripts, *Whore II* and *The Desperate Trail*. MPCA was very happy with the Western and gave me a date in the early spring to start shooting. We'll see what happens.

I broke up with my girlfriend. It had been six months and it was just too much. My parents went to Sundance. I will never go until I have a film there. I just know myself—it would drive me crazy. I'd sit there and see great films and say to myself, "That's it! I gotta go home and fucking write!"

It's so frustrating. This woman we're dealing with at Trimark came back from Sundance, and now she wants everything to be like *Boxing Helena*. "*Boxing Helena*! *Boxing Helena*! It should be like that!"

I mean, you need to be helped and nurtured when you write, not whipped. So we wrote it in four weeks, and she basically tried to get a free rewrite in a week. She said, "I won't tell them, but why don't you just spend a week . . . ?" And then her comments were like, "Well . . . sexier." What is *that*? She went to the Peter Stark program [a graduate producing program at USC]. I don't know what they taught her, though. She's just dim.

It would be great if these people had some other things to distract them—but they don't.

JOHN KEITEL
February 9

At Sundance I met Joseph Lovitt, who has his own production company but approached me about PBS. He gave me his card and I wrote him a letter when I got back. I already submitted *An All-American Story* to *P.O.V.* [a PBS newsmagazine].

I also met Howard Cohen from Goldwyn. At another party he said, "We're still very interested," and that they were going to be asking to see what people thought of its distribution prospects. He's in acquisitions. Dan Gelfand's in advertising.

I also met Brian Schwartzman at Sundance. When you hear someone's from William Morris you're kind of like, "Uh-oh . . ."

I've heard too many stories about William Morris. I continued to run into him and he was always friendly in a way that I wasn't really used to.

Two nights ago I saw him again at a party for *Out* magazine at the Chateau Marmont. There were a lot of people there from Sundance, like Steve Levitt [director of *Deaf Heaven*, featured in the gay shorts program]. Three people went up to Carter and me and said they saw the film there and really liked it.

Alan Hergott was there, and [agent] Brad Gross . . . do you know Richard Kramer (former writer-producer of *thirtysomething*]? I sit next to him at the café every day. He's doing *Tales of the City*.

Schwartzman wants to see my script, and says to make sure I have a casting director, and that there's all sorts of things that I should do. He's not one of the bigshots, but he's more appealing because of that. He knows Gregg Araki [an acclaimed gay independent director], and he's always telling me what mistakes Gregg has made.

I'm working on the script daily. Both Carter and I met with Brooke, and she's sending me an agreement. We talked about the distribution of the short and the next project. The former could take a lot of time and energy. I'll stoke whatever fires are there and use it as a learning experience, but my priority is the next project. It's in the stage of writing itself at this point and I don't think I can do anything else until I have that done. I took what they said at the Sundance panel discussion to heart.

I'd be thrilled if a studio was interested. It may be naive but I want to get it not put into development but green-lighted, where it would not be a question of developing it further. Richard Kramer advised me of that. He knows my film and loves it—he saw it in L.A. We talk a lot and he advised me of that, too. He said even if you're an established director, a development deal's the kiss of death.

Carter and I are trying to work up a formal professional working arrangement. His participation will be crucial. Hopefully it will be shot right on the Sixth Gallery's block, and he already has all the inroads with the city of West Hollywood—he's a business owner and knows everyone. Carter has a healthy distrust of Hollywood and would ideally like to raise the money through people he knows, make the film and try to sell it. Personally, I have a feeling that Brooke, being the attorney, wishes it would go the other way because she gets money much sooner. If I could have the support of a company, that would be great.

BERNARD JOFFA
February 10

Joffa was about to leave for Cape Town when his house was burglarized.

I've just been robbed. They came in through the front door, I guess, and took my camera, my clothes, and my fax machine.

The insurance company really screwed me. They set me up—they told me they were taping the phone conversation and I said okay. Then they asked me if I ever use my camera or fax machine for work. I told them I do every once in a while—I take stills on the set for home use, and use the fax occasionally for business, but primarily it's for personal use. They said, "We won't pay for the fax machine and camera because you use them for business." I said, "I wear my clothes to work—why are you paying for those?"

LISA KLEIN
February 11

Peter and I could enter *Radio Wars* in this short film competition, but most of the films that were entered were under ten minutes long. I don't think I saw anything that even approached twenty minutes. I couldn't imagine us fitting into anything like that. But I may do it anyway just for kicks. I think we'll do okay in festivals but I really wasn't expecting anything from Sundance.

If the school likes it they'll submit your film, and you don't have to pay anything. If CINE [a major student film awards organization] likes it, it will go to other foreign festivals, so that's cool.

There are a couple we can't get into because of length—or width, the whole 16mm thing. The only one with a width requirement is Ann Arbor. Another one we couldn't enter because of length. I don't know if we could have made it a thirty-minute movie without changing the story. But I think every filmmaker says that: "God, there's no way it could have been any shorter—one frame less and it will just lose the essence of the picture." I think it could have been five minutes shorter, eight minutes shorter. But I don't know about *thirty* minutes.

This manager we're talking to, James, says, "I'm a starmaker. I don't want to do day-to-day stuff. I don't want to do the writing assignment thing, I don't want to do that little bullshit stuff. I want to do big stuff—make sales."

What I'm feeling is a lack of loyalty. Maybe I'm naive to think there's some nurturing involved in that relationship. James is also very easily swayed. He reads something, and one of his friends reads it and says it's got problems, and he says, "It's got problems." It's this fantasy about the person who's your mentor saying, "I believe in you, I'm going to fight for you." Like Suzanne dePasse with Michael Jackson or something. But that's not at all what's occurring.

I've got a script I'm finishing with my partner, and the manager is so hot on this idea that after the rough draft I had to calm him down not to send it to anybody, because I wasn't comfortable with it. I knew it could be better. He just thought it was the greatest thing and he wants it badly. I'm hoping that by the time I'm done we have other representation. He wants it to be easy and done and to be handed to him. It just doesn't seem right.

If he got me a writing assignment—you know, for twenty grand or so—that's $2,000 for him, which is better than nothing. Obviously he's better off with a $500,000 sale where he can walk away with $50,000. I guess I'm confused about why he doesn't want to do both. They're not mutually exclusive. He said, "If I take it as something that's a sample of your writing, then it's out of the spec script market." I've never heard that before in my life—is that true? [*Author's note*: More or less; with rare exceptions, scripts submitted as writing samples *are* perceived as unsold specs.]

I don't know who he represents. He represented David Mickey Evans before he did *Radio Flyer*. That's his claim to fame. If he represented Bo Goldman and Robert Towne I'd feel quite differently, I'm sure, because they're incredibly gifted writers. It's not that I don't respect Evans because of *Radio Flyer*. I heard it was a great script. It was one of the worst movies I've ever seen in my life, but I'm sure that happens.

James plays the game really well. Everyone knows who he is, and he's very much a name dropper: "I just talked to my good friend Frank Mancuso, Jr., I can show him . . ." I'm getting a little frustrated.

The attorney I'm completely fed up with, and have been for some time. I don't even call him—Peter deals with him—but he's finally at the point where he's listening to me. Now he's thinking about trying to get into a small agency and taking us in as clients, and I don't want him to represent me. He's proven how tenacious he *isn't*.

James was going to send the script to twenty-three people—and he hasn't done anything yet. I just expected him to do what he said he was going to do. His excuse was "Oh, I thought Kyle [Klein's cowriter] was going to be doing more," and he and Kyle haven't been talking at all. I realized that if they're not communicating, how are they going to know if they sent it?

MARK KRUGER, Writer-Producer

My spec script *The Apostasy* went out on a Friday to three producers. On Saturday they all called my agent and said they liked it and wanted to be part of the sale of it. Then you can go either of two ways—you can carve up the territory and give it to a different producer to bring to each studio, or each producer gets X, Y, or Z studio, which is what we ended up doing. There were three or four producers.

The different studios got the script on Monday. On Tuesday people started to indicate their interest and make bids, and by Tuesday afternoon there were real offers on the table and we closed it Tuesday night with Cynergi.

When it happens that way, it's fast and furious. You don't have time to think. It's really exciting, like winning the lottery. I didn't expect it going in. What I was hoping for was that I would get some validation as a writer, that it was a decent script and people would respond to the story, and that there would be some interest and somebody might want to option it or get involved.

Just as you're thinking about that, suddenly it's gone beyond that. It's popping faster than you can even comprehend. By the end of the week I had left my job and devoted myself to what I wanted to do, which was write full-time.

From the buyer's point of view, the advantage of spec scripts is that they're already written. You can see what you're getting, as opposed to an idea. A lot of them are bought on the basis of concept, which is not a bad reason to buy something. If you have something that is a really good concept, and it's an okay script, then hopefully you can make it better. The studios are concept-driven. So if you can write a script that fits into a concept mold that's maybe a little different, then that's a good way to strategize it.

The ratio of ones that get sold to ones that get made is low. It's who buys them—certain studios would just crank them out immediately, others would develop them endlessly. It all depends on where it ends up.

James finally sent it to Monika Skerbelis at Universal. I don't know how much power she has, but she's been incredibly helpful. I could get any script I want to that studio—she'll read it immediately—so he sent it to her. *I* could have done that! He sent it to the one person I knew at Universal. She liked it enough to give it to a production company on the lot.

I think I need one more draft of this, but James could never articulate what the situation was, or what was going on. He said, "Before you send it out you have to do one more thing. I don't know what it is . . . something with the McGuffin." I didn't even know there was such a thing as a McGuffin in anything other than Hitchcock movies! I don't even know what the McGuffin *is* in my movie, so I don't know how I'm going to fix it. It's just so absurd.

I need someone to read the script and be cruel right now. I don't want to send it out until it's perfect and I don't know anymore. I'm a cynic with an optimist trying to come out—or an optimist with a cynic trying to come out.

The thing is, it's a chicken-or-the-egg thing with agents. I'm sure not all of them are assholes. But are there those who are attracted to the idea of being an agent because they're assholes, or do they *become* assholes once they become agents?

STEPHANIE ALLAIN, Studio Executive

I don't try to deal with all the agents—I don't have time. I've developed relationships with agents who will call me on the phone and say, "Watch this." I know that if I take an hour or two to watch this it will be worth my while. That's how I get material through agents—I will not let myself be "agented."

What I find problematic with agents and directors these days is that everybody wants to be a superstar right away. So these agents call and they say, "We have this hot new talent, and if you want him it's this, this, and this"—it's so overblown. There's no reality check in terms of "Well, has that person directed anything?" or "Have they directed a movie that's made any money?" There's no sense of earning it—it's like you *win* it. All of a sudden you've got the big ticket in the lottery.

I don't think I could make *Bad Lieutenant*. I don't have it in me to make a movie that so many people would walk out of. Edge is great—but this movie I'm writing, *Fat City*, centers around fat people, and I want to make sure that any of the fat-type jokes are coming out of the mouths of overweight people. I just have to be sensitive about that, so it's tough.

James thinks we'll sell *Lovestruck* right on the heels of this, that it'll become one of those things where they'll buy anything from you. There are so many subplots in this, though—so much more going on than in *Lovestruck*. There is a romance in there we have to make sure not to clutter.

Daily Variety reported on February 4, 1993, that Marcia Lucas Rodrigues, former wife of George Lucas, was funding a unique project: a feature film developed and produced with USC students and alumni.

We're probably going to submit something to USC's feature program. However, what I think it's going to be is probably a glorified 480. The assistant dean, Jacki Woolf, is going to send me a brochure on the guidelines.

I have to decide if I want to submit something to write and direct myself, or if Peter wants to take *Lovestruck*. Working together would be good because we did on the thesis film, *Radio Wars*. But we're not in good stead politically, because I have a little too much mind of my own. Apparently what they want is to get somebody they can mold, like the 480 class—like the woman who directed that first script of mine, who was a nightmare.

What I think would be different with this is that it's not going to be in a group with ten other films—it's going to be the only one they do. So they may not go by the usual flexible standards. There is a committee and I imagine you send them a director's reel and a script. You have to have graduated within the last couple of years.

Marcia Lucas gave them the money. There'll be a stipend for the director and producer—I don't know about the writer. The editor and cameraperson will be graduates. It'll be a million-dollar deal, and between one and three percent of the budget will go toward the script.

LIZ CANE
March 1

The first of the two "Meet Jane Doe" screenings was held Monday, March 1, at UCLA's Melnitz Theatre.

Ashley McKinney, director of one of the shorts, introduced the filmmakers: Jeanne Lusignan, whose Pictures From the Floating World *is a slow meditation on the lives of the crew of a solar research vessel; McKinney herself, whose* Roundabout *is a story of two sisters from a dysfunctional family (Cane was assistant cameraperson on this film, while McKinney art-directed Cane's* That's What Women Want*); and Cane.*

McKinney then introduced director Alison Anders, whose daughter starred in Roundabout.

"I read that three percent of all filmmakers are now women—and that's supposed to be a good thing!" Anders began. "All of our mentors have been male—until now." Anders also spoke of her invaluable relationship with

Abbe Wool (a UCLA graduate best known as cowriter of Sid and Nancy*).*

After Cane's film, third on the bill, a reception was held on a soundstage where bulletin boards suspended from beams showcased press coverage of the films.

Anne Thompson, a long-respected industry reporter, devoted one of her L.A. Weekly *columns to the "Jane Doe" screenings. The article featured a still photo from* That's What Women Want, *which Thompson called "a hilarious satire." She devoted considerable space to the speculation that sexism was the reason the film was not included in a competitive screening at the DGA.*

In her Weekly *blurb on the festival, Ella Taylor described Cane's movie as "slightly undisciplined but hilariously irreverent," while the L.A.* View *called it "intermittently comic . . . episodic and gleefully tasteless . . . unfortunately veers wildly in effectiveness."*

The L.A. Reader, *another free paper, ran the only negative review. "By far the weakest work in the entire series . . ." it read, "a barely coherent sexual romp by director Liz Cane . . . [a] painfully immature screenplay . . ."*

I got a good feeling from people. It's always inspiring when they react to the comedy. Universal was not as packed and it was a bigger theatre. I.R.S. Media didn't come—a woman called us and we got her the tapes. We had three press screenings. The *Reader* was harsh—they didn't like anyone's film, except Michelle's.

LIZ GLOTZER, Producer-Executive

I still go to student screenings. I think those screenings and festivals are mostly useful for young filmmakers to hook up with agents. In some cases, film students get development deals at studios out of those screenings, but it seems like very few of those deals are productive. Naturally, there are exceptions like Phil Joanou or Kevin Reynolds.

The way my company works, and I work, is that the script comes first. A lot of times you'll see someone's movie, and the agent will say, "Well, what do you have to offer me?" I don't think we would find a young director that way. They have to come to me with a script first.

There's no more viable commodity than a good script. There are a lot of directors out there who are good, bad, and medium—but there aren't enough good scripts for them all to direct.

March 8

On Monday, March 8, again at Melnitz Theatre, the second and final night of the "Meet Jane Doe" screenings was held.

In her opening statement Ashley McKinney made a point of noting that it was International Woman's Day, then introduced the guest speaker— as "tonight's role model"—Polly Platt, production designer, writer, and producer.

From Platt's words: "Every time I go to see the work of women, I come away enriched and proud to be one of them. One of the credits you didn't mention was my ex-husband [Peter Bogdanovich], with whom I made an extremely low-budget film called Targets. *After that I realized that anyone who finishes a movie, period, has something to be proud of. Films give me a reason for living, or—if I've worked on a really bad one—for dying. Giving your work to the public is a releasing, terrifying experience. I consider myself an artist first, then comes my sexuality."*

Platt concluded with a quote from Albert Einstein: "Why are the scientist and artist at odds? Each uses symbols to explore the unknown."

Polly Platt said nice things. Barbara and Richard Marks turned us on to her [she was producing *I'll Do Anything*, which Richard Marks was working on]. She's going to take our tapes.

One thing this festival taught us all is to feel secure, and the value of relentless self-promotion. It's harder for women—we're taught to be demure. Just the way we stood up when we were introduced, you could see, we had this urgency to sit back down.

STEPHANIE ALLAIN, Studio Executive

I don't think strength and confidence are male qualities. Socially, they're associated with men, but what we have to realize is, that's just a good director doing what he or she has to do. How do women deal with "assholes"? The same way men do—direct, up front.

I think the problem is that it's mostly men in the position of power with the green-light button. Men know they are capable and assume other men are just as capable. And they sometimes assume that women are not as capable. So I think that we need to have more women in the executive ranks, and with the ability to green-light pictures, because I know I'm capable—it's not a gender thing—and I think that Darnell Martin is incredibly capable. I did not think about it when we went ahead with *I Like It Like That*.

It's all laying groundwork. But nothing will happen until I write one or two good scripts. Dan Lupovitz called me—he went to the screening. He just produced an *American Playhouse*. He seems to be into offbeat, subversive, low-budget films. He's doing something with Dennis Hopper. He offered to call Brad Gross on my behalf. Another woman approached Jeanne and me about combining our films with hers for theatrical release. She's German. She just made a documentary on *In the Line of Fire*. Clint Eastwood and John Malkovich were going to see our films, but it didn't work out.

MARK KRUGER, Writer-Producer

I attended student screenings as a production V.P. years ago. Before the screenings, you know who the "stars" were. I don't think you were going in to discover some unrecognized talent. Word of mouth had filtered down so that people knew what the good films were. Just the fact that they were being shown—especially from schools outside of L.A., NYU or Columbia specifically—and the fact that they only picked eight or ten films to show, you knew they were the best of the bunch.

Some of those filmmakers had already found representation—there was a buzz around. I went to not be out of the loop, to see what everyone was talking about, and to meet the people, because you never knew if one of them had a spec script sitting in the closet or had a good idea. I wanted to have that connection already established.

MARCO WILLIAMS
March 8

I'm getting a little sick of the up and down of the elevator—the thought that just one deal will give me the key to the kingdom.

But I've become lazy when it comes to the documentaries and the funding. I sent a memo to Sheila Nevins at HBO about the *7 Up* project and she said she needed a more substantial proposal.

I've had many meetings on the *Waterfront* update. RASTAR was very into it. Stephanie Allain passed—she was concerned that I was a first-time writer-director. I'm a smart man. So when I have something good and people aren't interested, I take it personally. Stephanie's not the only buyer in town. There are other places I could go. But I think something got lost in the translation. I don't know what her problem can be with me as a first-timer.

[Writer-producer] Daniel Petrie [Jr.] and I pitched it at two places, one being Universal. I feel comfortable as the writer of this, but have no ego problem if a better writer comes along. It seems that most places don't want to develop from a pitch—they want a script.

It's such a simple, direct sales pitch. *On the Waterfront* won every major Oscar. What black actor wouldn't want the chance to play that Brando role? It's *inspired* by *Waterfront*. At the studios, you have to give them the context.

Having something I believe in, I look forward to the meeting, displaying this ware. If I didn't believe in it, I might feel sleazy, but I strut and stride into these meetings. I'm a farmer—I tilled this land and sowed the seed.

Due to Denzel's·nomination [for *Malcolm X*], he probably doesn't want to act in my first film. But he is the premier black actor and should be made aware of the project. And I direct this one—this one is mine—at least for five days until they fire me. [Laughs]

I'm going to Paris, to a documentary festival called *Ciné de Réal.* I told them I had a lot of frequent flyer miles so they offered to put me up since I was paying my airfare. I'll be there a week or ten days, then go to London for a meeting with Channel 4. They are commissioning a film on the two Rodney King trials and now are considering hiring a black director. I did nothing last summer but study this case [for the aborted HBO project].

P. J. PESCE
March 8

Trimark wants to meet again and again and again. They say, "We have to have the *Whore II* script as soon as possible. Can you write it in four weeks?" Tom and I have done it before in five weeks, so we said yes. Then over Christmas we went out and got PowerBooks and data modems.

In the meantime, Trimark is just trying to figure out *how* they're going to fuck us. What color blanket to put us on, which position . . .

Finally, they signed the contract. We turned in the script and they said, "Wait a minute—this script looks like it was written in four weeks! Why didn't you tell us you needed more time?"

In the first draft, their problem was that the characters were too schematic. They try everything with us. "We're very disappointed with the script. . . ." I feel like Barton Fink—"We want a wrestling movie with that Barton Fink feeling"—[only it's] "We want a whore picture with eroticism and heart, but less heart and more eroticism. More plot."

I know as soon as I finish polishing the Western they will start casting. I'm in a great position with *Unforgiven* winning all these awards [Clint Eastwood had just won the DGA prize]. But if I don't act soon, I'm going to blow the whole trend in Westerns, and they'll slot something else in.

I think Westerns have been dead forever. I mean, *Pale Rider* was just bad Sergio Leone. Now, because cable can rush things out, we've got fucking Jane Seymour in designer clothes. And *Young Guns*—Sergio Valente instead of Sergio Leone.

If Robert Rodriguez made that film [*El Mariachi*] for $7,000, he didn't feed his crew. Someone should do the math and figure out if you can even *process* that much film stock for that money. I mean, what did the guy do? He made a Renny Harlin movie. A Hollywood movie. A calling card.

He's not opening things up, he's closing them down. The big twist is he's a Chicano. So now we need a Hispanic *Die Hard* or a Chinese *Lethal Weapon*? Once upon a time—in the '70s—we made different kinds of movies. Movies about human beings. There was *The Taking of Pelham One Two Three* and *Dog Day Afternoon* but there was also Warner Brothers giving John Cassavetes money to make *Minnie and Moscowitz*! Now they all want to make *Mean Streets*. God, I sound like an angry, bitter old man.

I got a call from Michael Costigan, who was an assistant to John Solomon at Witt-Thomas. Two years later, he's a creative executive at Sony/Columbia. They're interested in *The Trials of Leo*, and MPCA may do a negative pickup. Michael took me to Katsu Sushi, where we spent $250 of Sony money getting shitfaced on sake and eating sweet shrimp. Of course, he has a bigger fish at Sony who must approve the deal.

LISA KLEIN
March 15

I just finished *Fat City* with my partner Kyle, who is working on his thesis film. James is all over it. We met last week. It was the first time Kyle and he were meeting, so Kyle was quizzing him. James said, "There are five people I know who would go crazy for this."

We said, "What if they pass?" We were testing him based on what happened when he gave *Lovestruck* to someone to read and he quickly lost interest. He said, "Oh, I would keep sending it around."

He wants to produce the film, not operate as our manager and not take commission. [Unlike agents, managers are legally allowed to both produce and represent talent.] As long as there is no conflict of interest, that might be okay. Kyle asked if it would be in his best interest to get us less money if he were producing, but James said he would actually want to get us *more*. If the script is worth more, everyone makes more, he said.

I wouldn't be comfortable if James was the primary producer. He just doesn't have the clout. It's hard to know what's real and what's bullshit, who he *really* knows. If half the people he says he knows read it, it will get made. If a quarter do, who knows?

I like *Lovestruck* better, personally. I've just been through so much with *Fat City*, maybe I'm not as close to it. But sometimes it feels like this script is the Emperor's New Clothes. I don't trust anyone. James is just one guy who's going to go out and peddle this one script. But it's not arithmetic, it's a crapshoot. I can't let myself get too excited because if it doesn't work out I'll be really depressed. I am definitely trying to control these emotions, though. I mean, everything is meaningless.

Midday Thursday, after James read the script, I got five messages from him: "I'm on page twenty-three, I'm on page thirty-six, . . ." I mean, he was my wake-up call in the morning! He's either a psycho or he loves the script. It's nice that someone loves it who's not a friend, or my mother. James can certainly have impact, but he's just one person. He can't change my career single-handedly.

We did some work on the script last week. We added a couple of new scenes. My roommate threw three copies of the old draft into the recycling. When we went to drop it off, I saw the scripts. So I stand there hand-shredding 360 pages. I guess you could say I'm a little paranoid. The rest of my life is being dictated by this part of my life.

Peter and I met with a manager named Richard Glasser last week. He was interested in distributing *Radio Wars*. I gave him *Lovestruck* and *Guardian Angels*. He wanted us to make a clean break from James. Richard lives in "The House That Fievel Built." Their son was the voice of Fievel [from the animated feature *An American Tail*]. Richard was in music publishing and finally decided to go into this side of the business.

I can't wait until I can quit waiting tables. Or start spilling things on a few select customers.

LIZ CANE
March 16

Twenty million dollars was cut from the L.A. Unified budget. I was hoping the job would be steady. This was ideal, it paid well, and it was part-time.

Now I'm working on the feature adaptation of *That's What Women Want*. It's gotten a renewed life. The thriller I was writing was getting complicated and difficult. I met with an agent, Doug Brodax at Paradigm, who said it sounded dark and meek. He thought the feature version of *That's What Women Want* was something studios would be interested in. He said it's already been done in the short so it's all in my head, anyway.

Doug's assistant called me the next morning after the screening. He wanted to get my tapes for his partner to see. I told him I was advised not to move too quickly. He asked if I was going to make a decision, could I make it by next Friday? It was an interesting meeting. Brodax also approached Shelly Wagner, who did *Where Beans Grow*, and asked her to decide by Wednesday. For TV, I could see why they would be interested.

CAA called me. They want a feature script. I said I was nearing completion on one. The guy asked, "When?" I said in two to four weeks. He said, "How about if I call you in three?"

Cane was approached about having her film distributed as a feature in combination with another short.

Greg Watkins, the actor in my film, did a film called *A Little Stiff* a couple of years ago for $10,000, which was shown at Sundance. Caveh Zaheti, a friend who used to make films with Greg, directed it. He sold domestic rights for seven years but hasn't done anything with foreign. My film complements that one nicely. Both have Greg, and both are offbeat comedies.

STEPHANIE ALLAIN, Studio Executive

When I met John Singleton in 1990 he was a senior at USC, looking for a job as a reader. But someone said, "You know what? He's a really good writer."

I happened to read a script of John's, *Twilight Time*, before he came in. It was fabulous. The dialogue was great. I think it won the Jack Nicholson Award or something. So when we met I said, "Well, let's talk about you as a writer," and he told me about *Boyz N the Hood*. I said, "It sounds great, I'd love to read it," and he said, "Well, you can't, because I'm going to direct it. I'm going to get the money, and it's not going to be a studio thing, because they'll fire me."

I said, "Oh, but let me read it, let me read it." He said, "No, no, no," and I called his agent every day for two weeks. Finally I got the script, I read it, it was great, and I said that we should make it.

The thing with John Singleton was very simple—we couldn't have the script of *Boyz N the Hood* unless he directed it. That was the deal. And I wanted that script, and my people wanted it. Also, he wrote very cinematically and very much from the director's point of view. So we felt it was a vision only he had, and we couldn't get somebody else to come in and capture that vision. It was unique and had not been seen, and we just felt like he could do it.

P. J. PESCE
March 17

Brad Krevoy took me to Chinois [a high-end Santa Monica restaurant] last night to celebrate the start of preproduction on *The Desperate Trail*. My agent David Kanter came, too. It was so much like he "deigned to be there."

At one point, Krevoy said, "We can take the film to Cannes." Kanter said, "Well, it won't mean much there because P. J. is not an established director. Not yet, at least." Ha ha ha. I could have killed him.

I got home and couldn't sleep—I thought, God, I have all of this work to do. I slept two hours last night.

JOHN MCINTYRE
March 23

I got some good news and bad news last week. The bad news was that I was laid off as an assistant at Duck Soup. It's the recession backlash. They say it's good if an animation house puts together ten straight months. We're coming off of a year. The good news is that I'm going to be directing, four promotional films for the company. They think a lot of me. They see an angle from my work, and now I can put a director's reel together.

The first promo is shooting Saturday. It's going to be a parody of those '30s newsreels, set at a laboratory. The duck mascot will jump off a table into a bowl. It's live action, and we're doing it period, like the NYU film, but more condensed, with quick cuts. I've been working with my friend Joe Forte on the script—the announcer's lines, etc.

We're shooting it at a school. I called a couple of places and they wanted a $1,500 or $2,500 location fee. Finally, I started calling using the voice of, like, a thirteen-year-old kid—"Umm, yeah, I'm making a movie, it's Super 8. . . ." The principal said, "Okay, kid, just pretend we never had this conversation. Go ahead and do it."

So I have to wear the duck suit, because I built it and molded it around myself. I keep thinking of Chaplin as the chicken in *The Gold Rush*. And then on Sunday I have to wear it to the birthday party of one of the Duck Soup owners' son. It's really political. What am I going to say, no? He's having two donkeys and me in the duck suit. I said fine, as long as the kids don't ask to ride me.

I had some goals for the next four years and now they've all changed. They've been set in front of me. The short-term goals are changing. In the next year I'll be doing four or five of the promos.

Theresa and I are talking about marriage more and more. I was up for this McDonald's thing that would have paid $5,000 a week. Naturally I thought it would cover all my debts. I definitely thought there was a ring in it for her.

BOBBI THOMPSON, Agent

Tim Burton was an animator. He was given the opportunity
to do an animated short. He was also given the opportunity to
do a half-hour Disney cable channel piece, and then to direct
Frankenweenie, a short feature, which was unusual. It cost
seven or eight hundred thousand, and was supposedly going
to show ahead of *Pinocchio*, but when Disney tested it they
found that it frightened kids.

Tim was then given the opportunity to do a *Faerie Tale
Theater* by Shelley Duvall, who was in *Frankenweenie*, and
then a feature film by Warner Brothers, *Pee-wee's Big Adventure*, because one of the executives was taken down to the set
of *Frankenweenie* and was introduced to Tim.

P. J. PESCE
April I

*On the golf course with Pesce, I noticed a tattoo on his left bicep—a knife
piercing a heart. "I should have teardrops done," he said, pointing to the
corner of his eye.*

"From heartbreak?" I asked him. "Because of old girlfriends?"

*"Hell, no," Pesce laughed. "From not getting a film made. I should
have a drop for every year I don't make a feature."*

*Pesce had decided not to watch the Academy Awards telecast the previous
Monday night.*

I called all my friends, but they either weren't home or didn't pick
up the phone. So I stayed in and worked on *Whore*. [Dramatically,
like a newscaster] "Woody Allen boycotted the Oscars when he
was nominated in 1978; fifteen years later, P. J. Pesce stayed home
and wrote *Whore II*." I'm just finishing it. It's due right after taxes.

Brad Krevoy called me from Aspen. He loves the Western and
wants to start shooting immediately.

"I read part of it all the way through," Samuel Goldwyn once said of a project, inadvertently explaining the need for studio script readers. A friend slipped New Line's reader's report on The Desperate Trail *to Pesce.*

Coverage forms commonly feature a grid on the title page which grades a screenplay based on categories such as Concept, Story Line, Characters, and Dialogue. Pesce's and Tom Abrams's script was rated between "good" and "fair" in each department, with the exception of "good" under Characters.

"THE DESPERATE TRAIL is a moderately exciting offering that distinguishes itself by presenting a man-woman outlaw pairing," the comments read, after a two-page plot summary. "Throughout the work, the authors take an uncompromising approach to violence. . . . this isn't make-believe 'Cowboys and Indians' stuff.

". . . This is an above average Western that boasts several elements that set it apart from the pack—THE DESPERATE TRAIL at least deserves a look."

ROBERT BENTON, Writer-Director

I grew up on Westerns. To keep any genre alive, you have to do that complicated thing of both being true to the genre and changing it so that it feels fresh again. That's the beauty of doing genre movies—you can bend a genre, but you can never break it. It's knowing how far you can bend it.

LISA KLEIN
April 19

James, in four weeks, has given *Fat City* to exactly seven people. The problem is that he wants to produce. So he's only giving it to people he wants to work with.

One producer expressed some interest, but said he'd like it rewritten, which he would pay for. He wants the city—which we spent a long time taking out to heighten the romance—to be more of a character.

I've given myself a deadline to stop waitressing—June first. It'll be two years and I just don't think I can take any more of it beyond that.

P. J. PESCE
April 21

MPCA wants me to cut twenty pages of the script and shoot it on a twenty-four-day schedule. And what will happen is that I will say no, and they'll have to get someone else. I can't take a script that people love, in this time when every studio is doing some Western—and I've read them and they suck—and have people see this movie and say, "Oh, that was a great script, but he ruined it." I won't hang myself.

I need thirty-five days to shoot this movie. And I have got to find a movie star, which is fucking impossible now because of this Kim Basinger thing. [Basinger lost a publicized legal battle over an alleged "verbal agreement" she made—and then rescinded—to star in *Boxing Helena*.] They can't make a pay-or-play offer. They're not in that position. And a star wants a studio to guarantee a negative pickup [an arrangement in which a distributor agrees, prior to production, to pay for prints and advertising], so I'm fucked.

I read *Bad Girls* [Fox's Western about a posse of hookers]. It sucked. All of these Westerns do not help me get mine made. I think they will flood the market with shit, and people will say, "Well, this and that didn't work, so why should we make yours?" These aren't interesting projects like *Unforgiven*. These fuckers are so frightened that they think they can just take something that was made in 1963 and just do it again. But it's a different world now. You can't just do *Have Gun, Will Travel*. The studios are each going to make their one Western, dip their toes into the pool, and then when they fail say, "Oh, *Unforgiven* worked just because it was Clint Eastwood."

Unforgiven was great because it was a revisionist Western. The hero is not Clint Eastwood from 1967. But these assholes are going to make all these corny, clichéd Westerns now. I feel angry, impotent, and disappointed. My agent says, "Well, I'm not the producer, it's not my job to get a star." He's starting to get on the stick, but I think it's too little, too late. Brad Krevoy doesn't know what he has here. So here I am telling everyone I've built a better mousetrap, and thumping my own tub all over the place. But how far will it get me?

I need a godfather, someone with juice. Brad doesn't have

enough clout. They've made only shlock. MPCA's made money, but it's all been on T&A. They're on the periphery. People just don't see him as someone who's going to take a chance.

Can they pay a star? Yes. They can pay three or four hundred grand [far short of a star salary]. So they have this script they spent $25,000 on, and they say, "Let's cut it to bits, and shoot it in twenty-five days for one million." It'll make its money back and they'll presell all the rights. But it will suck.

I've thought about approaching Scorsese. I just don't know how. I mean, he's got these people . . . I approached him when I wanted him to get *Trials of Leo* to John Turturro. I sent it and spoke to an assistant, someone named Monica, who gave me a terrifically cold, nasty take on the script. I have no idea if they even mentioned it to Marty.

They just want to be close to Marty. They don't want *other people* being close to him. So nothing makes them happier than to say, "Sorry. He doesn't like it." And you say, "Did he read it?" And they say, "Sorry. He doesn't like it."

Tom and I are supposed to have a meeting with Monika Skerbelis. Kanter sent her *The Desperate Trail* and she really liked it.

LIZ CANE
April 23

It was fun to go to the Houston Worldfest film festival. It was good to get accepted, and it gave me a little perspective on what that means. I saw the other short film programs, which are less well attended and don't get as much attention. My favorite film was this inventive not-quite-a-documentary about a film historian trying to piece together one of the first films ever made. It was really funny and well done. [*Author's note:* No, it wasn't John McIntyre's *Melbridge*, but it certainly sounds like it.]

Doug Brodax, an agent from Paradigm, called me the other day. He left a message and I really got my hopes up. But then the next day I talked to him and he said, "We can't take you on right now."

BOBBI THOMPSON, Agent

Quentin Tarantino turned us on to a director, Reb Brad-dock, who made a short film called *Curdled*. It was about a woman who made a living cleaning up houses after murders. And it was sick, but it was good.

I think that which makes you feel something makes it worthy of considering representation. If it makes you feel outrageously idiotic, if it makes you feel hot, disgusted, appalled, moved. If it makes you cry. Very often I find student films soft. They don't have action, drama, or violence. They have emotion a lot of times, but they're very contained. And I think, still within the parameters of budgets of student films, there's a way to grab people and show them that you see things in a way no one else sees them. That's what I'm looking for.

The market has changed, but the desire to see new talent has not. And the market's always in flux. It's a chessboard— you go to sleep, and when you wake up, the pieces have moved, but you haven't touched them.

MARCO WILLIAMS
April 24

Williams had just returned from the Channel 4 interview in London.

It was for a documentary about the Rodney King police trials. I felt infinitely prepared due to the research I did on the HBO project. But I don't think they were crazy about my film work. The supervising producer lobbied for me, and as I was walking out the door, there seemed to be a shift. Plus, I don't think they know any other black documentary filmmakers. I've had a lot of opportunities present themselves, though, that never panned out. So I don't get too up or down about any one thing.

I was just hired to do a ten-minute film for this production company ITS, with the Independent Television Service. They're doing three one-hour films for PBS. Each hour will consist of five ten-minute pieces illustrating the U.S. Constitution.

They hooked me up with Arianna Huffington, this conservative from Santa Barbara who is married to a politician. She will write an essay on "the pursuit of happiness," and I will visualize her voice. I went to Washington to meet with her.

My film work was brought to the attention of these producers, then they found the essayist. I wanted John Edgar Wideman, or this youth from a facility in Chino that utilizes the arts. Proximity got me this job. Plus, they had a chuckle about the odd marriage of me with her. I don't have a clue as to how I'm going to visualize this. Huffington is into "giving" as part of the redefinition of the pursuit of happiness. I haven't yet taken a position on her.

I'm being paid $1,300 a week for five weeks—$6,500. It's pretty much the normal rate; I usually budget around $1,200 a week for the director.

I ask Williams about the recently delivered guilty verdict against two of the policemen in the Rodney King case.

It made perfect sense. I had no feeling of euphoria. One could say we learned from the explosion of rage last year. All four should have gone down. I agree with Eldridge Cleaver—"If you're not part of the solution, you're part of the problem."

P. J. PESCE
May 10

MPCA wants the budget lower on *The Desperate Trail*. So we had to cut the big train sequence, which sucks.

They have some pathetic casting director downstairs that they pay like $3,000 a picture. They don't even care. They haven't even called me, the assholes. Call the director? That wouldn't even occur to them.

I don't have a start date, a location, or anything.

ALAN SHAPIRO, Writer–Director

Tiger Town cost $800,000. It was a ridiculous sum of money.
Roy Scheider took scale. He always wanted to play a baseball
player, and it had a really short schedule. We legitimately
pleaded poverty. It was very thrilling and scary and everything. The scary stuff I got over pretty quick, because you're
just so overwhelmed with everything you have to do. And I
had some really good people working with me.

At the time Roy was a movie star, so I was a little nervous. But this was a great lesson I learned. I mean, I was a
complete nobody as far as he was concerned, and yet he was
so typically insecure, as most actors are. He constantly
needed my approval, and for me to say that he did great, and
I kept thinking, "What does he care what I think?" But he
did. He cared what I thought.

He had read the script and liked it—he had not seen my
student film—and Disney was making it. But I learned that
even if you have to fake it, you will command more respect.
Actors need that surehandedness and approval and all that
bullshit. For Roy in particular, he was insecure about his
baseball abilities, and I happened to know a lot about baseball. So that gave me a good in.

BERNARD JOFFA
May 14

Joffa had recently returned from South Africa.

I thought I'd be there two months and stayed two and a half. We
stayed as long as we needed to finish the screenplay, and I left the
night we completed it. I wasn't in a hurry to come back, because I
was in South Africa during such exciting times. So much is
changing there. It's becoming a country where people are getting
their dignity back.

The original plan was to work in Johannesburg, where Greg

Latter, the writer, lives. He seems to have the most ideal form of living. He lives at home, and he works out of Hollywood. It's what I have been looking to do. My dream has always been to get out of Hollywood, but on my terms, so I can live where I want to live and work there. This seems to have been achieved by a lot of foreign filmmakers. Beresford and Weir live in Sydney or Melbourne and they come here once a year and make a film, which represents the ideal for me.

We arrived in Johannesburg and it was tense. This was just prior to Hani's assassination. In three days I heard of three people who had either lost their cars or lost members of their family. There was a helluva lot of indiscriminate chaos and violence going on in the streets as the end comes closer. Johannesburg is like one huge prison. Every house has got forty-foot walls, with barbed wire fences, or fences which will electrocute you if you touch them. That's white Johannesburg. In the first three days I was there, my aunt's nephew was killed in a carjack, the wife of the friend I was staying with was held up at knifepoint on the street, and my friend's next-door neighbor was killed.

I said, "I can't write here—I'm out of here." We were going to go to one of the game parks to write, and then said, "Let's go to Cape Town immediately and get away from the violence."

In Cape Town we found paradise, a house owned by the family of a friend of mine. Ocean in front of you, mountains behind you, four-minute walk down the steps to the beach. You could swim in the Indian Ocean like a warm bath.

It took us three days to drive to Cape Town. That drive was extraordinary because we sorted out the major stuff of the screenplay. It was one of the most fruitful journeys I've ever had. We understood what the movie was about. I had never written with a cowriter before. In fact, I'd hardly written—I'd written one piece in my life. Greg's written eleven feature films that have been made. He's a madman, even a little more obsessive than I am. Friends of both of us warned us that it could turn out to be a disaster—the two of us in a house for two months.

It was one of the most extraordinary times of my life, though. I can honestly say that the past two and a half months were the most rewarding ever. If I were to get run over by a car tomorrow, I would say life has been good. It was obsessive, but it was turning my negative energy and my anger from my whole life into something positive. For the first time I understand what that is about. It was just two and a half months of positive energy going between myself and Greg in terms of this film.

We woke up at seven every morning and would go for an hour walk along the beachfront—a wonderful walk—and literally map out the day's scenes. We wouldn't come back until we were satisfied that it had been done. Then we had breakfast, wrote, had lunch around four, carried on writing through the evening, then went out to dinner to discuss the next day's scenes. We'd come back and usually write until about three in the morning, go to sleep, and wake up at seven.

This went on for two months. Every day—Saturday, Sunday. My parents live there and I saw them four times in a month and a half. They understood. When I got there, my mother said, "Bernard, this is a very important time. You must use it wisely." I'm very lucky to have such support from my parents. She tried to matchmake me with some women.

The day after I arrived there I fell in love. That is also very nice. I had this amazing relationship with a woman which was also so inspiring. She was a very busy person herself. She is deputy editor of *Playboy* magazine in South Africa, which is just starting. She's Scottish, Catholic. Interesting combination, a Catholic and a Jew.

I had met her three years prior when she came to L.A. and wrote an article on me for *Cosmopolitan*. I hadn't seen her since. I saw her the day after I arrived, then she went away for a week, to a health spa. Sometimes she would come at two o'clock in the morning and we'd meet.

Greg has a wife and three kids. So it was hard for him, too, to leave them in Johannesburg. They came up for ten days, during which time we couldn't work. Every time the children walked in, it was ridiculous. We couldn't concentrate.

The journey felt like one of those Kerouac stories, like *On the Road*. We drove down and stopped over in this little town, Peru. We were awake all night in this little motel room, him with his laptop computer. We "met" two very important characters that night. A guy called Jumbo Elliott was Sydney's mentor-trainer, his father figure. We got a take on him which I'm very happy with. It was written for Marlon Brando.

Greg's an actor, which is another nice thing, because as we would be writing he would act out the parts. He's been in a couple of movies, loves to act. We would both take on different voices. I would do Sydney, Greg would do another character. It was what jazz musicians must feel like when they jam. There was never a moment when our egos got involved. I'm going to work with Greg for the rest of my life, probably, as a lot of other filmmakers have worked with writers, like Robert Bolt and David Lean.

Also, we come from vastly different backgrounds, me from Jewish middle class, Greg from a Protestant working-class mining family.

What was interesting was the coincidence of things—Sydney, Greg, and myself were all born in 1955. We all left South Africa in one way or another, came to America. I got nominated for an Academy Award, which carries a sense of arriving. Greg wrote screenplays for Disney and Mel Brooks in the last few years. And Sydney got selected to represent the U.S. in the Olympic Games, but never ran because of a hamstring problem.

In a way, we all got a little bit of the American Dream, and we realized that this was the story of all of our lives. My parents live in a house that I bought, Greg's mother lives in a house that he built, and Sydney's life was about building a house for his mother. There were a lot of freaky coincidences and circumstances that brought this whole picture together. Why did we all tap into it?

We finished the first draft and I'm sure there will be more to follow, but I'm very happy. First thing we did was a detailed thirty-six-page treatment. That took us the first month. We kept faxing the treatment to New York, to the producers, every day. There was a certain "committee" feeling but it worked fine with the fax from Africa to New York. Once we completed the first treatment, we stopped and did another one, another thirty-six pages. The company gave us a lot of good input.

After the second treatment we started the screenplay, which took us about three weeks, because all the work had been done in the treatment. It was hard work. It was craft at that point.

I showed *Senzeni Na?* in South Africa. It had never been shown there before. The response I got was interesting. People felt uncomfortable. It's now going to be shown in the big international festival in Johannesburg in September, the main event of the calendar year.

I showed it in a couple of difference places. One was the Group Filmmakers Union, which supports mostly documentaries and politically driven stuff. So most of the people who saw it were activists—people who had been in prison or who have spent the last fifteen years of their life fighting.

The ANC [African National Congress] had a one-week conference on the role of the new government in culture, a section for film, radio, television. Some high delegates saw *Senzeni Na?* and want to show it around the world. They thought it was the most honest film to come out of South Africa, to deal with such a big thing in such a small town.

Most liberals felt uncomfortable and unsatisfied with it. They get too wrapped up in the specifics—"Oh, we don't use a truck like that in South Africa," or "That doesn't look like a railway ticket," or "The truck was driving on the wrong side of the road." Then I realized they couldn't be detached about the film, because it was about *them*.

I'll premiere it also at the *Weekly Mail* Film Festival. That's the liberal newspaper they started in South Africa. They saw the film a couple of years ago and invited me to show it.

So when we got back we gave the script to our agents. Ronda only got it on Monday. Greg's got it last Friday—David Warshafter and his assistant Amy Ferris at ICM. They faxed three lines to Greg on Monday: "We love it. We would love to package it. We can get to Denzel, and we're sure he'd love it." Which was fantastic. They get dozens of scripts every day!

However, my agent hasn't read it yet. She's going to read it this weekend. I'm anxious that she like it. If she doesn't, it's going to be something that we have to talk about, because she can't be excited about the project unless she's enthusiastic about the script.

Chris Silverman, Ronda's assistant, read it and liked it a lot. But his comment to me was that it was "too rough," and that I should do another draft before I give it to Ronda, which I had a problem with because I didn't think it was rough. It's kind of a harsh word, "rough." I'm not sure what he meant by it. I think it's in the writing style, because it's very frenetic.

I didn't resent the comments at all except that I should change it before I give it to Ronda. I thought I'd rather Ronda sees it as he saw it. I don't want to make changes for every Tom, Dick, and Harry that comes along. But he felt very strongly I should do another draft before Ronda sees it. I don't think he trusts it enough.

This is what I've learned through the writing process. If you don't trust your own material you start putting in things that don't need to be there—more emphasis on a plot point, or a character point. We kept taking out this tape of David Lean talking about his work, and he was saying, "You've got to trust it. You've got to trust the piece, and it will do its job for you." If you don't, you're going to start getting too complex in your writing style.

It's hard for anybody to read [multiple drafts]. He's not saying to change it, just "clean it up." I thought, How? I mean, every word is specific. I asked him to be more specific.

There's one scene in which Sydney arrives in Philadelphia. He's lost everything in the world. He's got nothing. His baggage, his money—everything's been stolen from him, like the country's turned on him. He finally arrives in Philadelphia, walking and running from New York, to meet Jumbo Elliott, the trainer. Finally he gets to him, and Elliott says, "I'm not going to take you on."

He's high up on these library steps. It's based on my relationship with my grandfather, my angel. So Sydney finally meets God, and Jumbo doesn't even look at him—he's got his nose buried in a book on anatomy.

Sydney says, "Excuse me, sir, I was wondering if I could approach you with the view of possibly considering the opportunity of training me." Something like that, very awkward. That's how Sydney spoke, he never learned to speak English.

Jumbo says, "I'm not training any new people."

Sydney says, "But I've walked all the way from New York."

Jumbo says, "What's your times?"

Sydney says, "3:57."

Jumbo says, "Barefoot?"

Sydney says, "Yes."

And Jumbo turns around and says, "Sydney Maree?"

That's how they meet. Sydney's feet are fucking blistered, blood spilling all over. Jumbo says, "Let me see those feet." Jumbo cradles the feet and says, "My God, boy, what have you done?" And Sydney starts sobbing. It's the first time that he is comfortable in this terribly alienating world of America, where everything has gone wrong since he got here. And this man is cradling him like a baby!

When I asked for a specific, Chris said to me, "Why does he

cry?" He said, "It's quite out of character that an eighteen-year-old boy would start crying."

I said nothing, except that I would like Ronda to read the screenplay without me making changes at this point.

Ronda must read it and either like it or not like it. I'm hoping she loves it, at which time we'll move on. It's complicated, because Greg and I have different agents. I'm hoping my agent will love it just like Greg's agency that wants to package it. No point in having your agent representing you if she doesn't like it.

Joffa was asked whether he believed he would get Ronda Gomez's honest reaction, and whether he would change to another agent if she did not respond favorably to the script.

Absolutely. I must do that. How can somebody represent my work if they don't like it? In a situation like that I would discuss it with her and I'm sure that she would understand that I need to be with another agent who does like it.

It's a first draft, which is the bones of the script. But either you're going to respond to this, or you're not. It's a very well worked-out first draft. It's the best that I can do right now.

What I'm saying to my agent is, you never quite knew who I was. Maybe *Senzeni Na?* was me at a certain point in time, but now *this* is me at this point in time. If you don't like what you see, you can use the opportunity to say you don't want to represent me anymore. In fact, we shouldn't be together. It's a very, very, very delicate line with an agent. Ronda certainly loved *Senzeni Na?* But if she doesn't care for my work now, maybe we've grown apart.

However, I don't want to presuppose that she's not going to like it. Ronda has such integrity. You don't hear that about an awful lot of agents.

River Communications read it, and they loved it. They had put up $50,000 from their own pockets. Joe Kessler from River Communications took a terrible risk but now has a property he's proud of.

We've made ICM perfectly aware that I am attached to direct. Which means fuck-all in the end, because if a studio wants to do it, they'll pay out my pay-or-play and find their own director.

> RANDA HAINES, Director
>
> It's frustrating for me sometimes that I take so long between projects, but it has to do with falling in love with material. And that doesn't happen very often. Particularly at the moment, there's a dearth of good, human material. There are a lot of films being made, but not films that people can identify with—the kind of films I like to make. Films about real people, emotions, and relationships.
>
> Most of the things I've done I have developed, some from other forms—plays, books, etc. And that takes a long time, a lot of nurturing. One of my projects I have been working on for two years now, and hopefully it's the film I will make next. I also need a certain amount of time to regenerate between movies—not necessarily two or three years, but it usually takes that long to get the next one ready.

JOHN KEITEL
May 18

On December 10 the Los Angeles Times *ran a feature story on the appointment of former agent Larry Auerbach to USC's film school as a liaison between graduating students and the industry.*

I haven't spoken to Auerbach. I think he just got there. He was a hotshot at William Morris.

The [*Marcia Rodrigues*] feature film thing at USC sounds like a big publicity stunt to me, something [Dean] Elizabeth Daley cooked up. What they need to do is succeed at distributing their short films first. Someone would be crazy to get involved with them on a feature. They have no experience whatsoever with features.

LIZ CANE
May 18

I'm working on the feature version of my film, developing the lead character and his girlfriend—making them more lead characters. I'm dealing with their relationship more in the first third. They're using a video therapy that I have actually experimented with myself. They just go into a room and no one is there but them, and they have it videotaped. I think maybe the technique could be marketed.

I feel better about where I am right now. I have a lifestyle I like, more discipline, and I'm not as stressed. I'm focused and concentrated, and not impatient. I enjoy having time for everything.

The director of the Houston Worldfest film festival recommended my film to a distributor. They are creating two packages of three films each. They just finished one, which my film was not part of.

Also, Headliners Productions, a distributor of alternate films that released [recent UCLA graduate] Edgar Bravo's film *I'll Love You Forever . . . Tonight*, are releasing a one-hour documentary about a woman with multiple personalities. They want to put it with something else.

At her apartment Cane showed me a videotape of Libido, *a short documentary she made featuring a cross-section of elderly men and women. The film consists of their comments about sex, which could be made by adults of any age—"He enjoys it more than me," "She enjoys it more than me," "It's gotten better," "It's gotten worse," etc.*

The stereotype that you lose the desire to have sex is a myth. I made the film in 1989 for a class assignment in Production Workshop. I did three films and two video projects in that class. One of the big advantages at UCLA is that the students pay for their films and own the rights. USC pays for and owns the rights or doesn't pay for and owns the rights. Either way, though, they'll make you a print but they always keep the negative.

I found participants for the film by calling the Gray Panthers. One woman was really great and invited me on a hike with senior members of the Sierra Club. I went and took a camera and got them hiking, and then filmed a couple dancing in their living room. I've thought about using the film to get a longer one financed.

My roommate Laura and I are trying to get *Libido* distributed. It's a good discussion film for classes, about the continuing pleasures of romance among older people. It was part of "Aging: The Process of Perception," an exhibit which has toured East Coast galleries, and also in an exhibit called "Love & Death" in San Francisco. The University of Hawaii is putting together a thirteen-part series on aging. They bought the rights to broadcast it for $3,000, and PBS paid $600 to air it on a series called *The 90s: Getting Older.*

LISA KLEIN
May 19

We got *Radio Wars* into Houston, the Worldfest. We sent it in, got into the festival—and had to pull it because we only have one print.

This was incredibly frustrating. We had also sent it to the Student Academy Awards, which we were going to pull it from because we thought: There's no chance, we're not going to get a Student Academy Award, they look for message pictures and that's not what *Radio Wars* is. Then we got a tip from someone at school who said it looked like we were going to get into the regional competition, and we thought, "Oh God, we have *one* print!" And it would cost another thousand dollars to get another print within three days.

I thought about calling my mother. I talked to her afterward and she said, "Why didn't you call me? I would have given it to you."

So we had to make a decision, and had to pull it, and we're very bummed about that.

I don't expect to necessarily get to the next level of the Student Academy Awards. It's not *Panama Deception* [a recent Academy Award-winning documentary] . . . but who knows?

First they pick out of a certain number in the country. Each region chooses—out of, say, ninety, they choose nine or ten. So we were chosen in our region, and they showed them at Loyola, and out of those they chose a Narrative, a Documentary, and an Experimental. So we got through that level. Now we've gone from the regionals to the nationals, and from that, they choose three in the country. They have some kind of ceremony, and then they go down to one.

We got into CINE and got a Golden Eagle, so they send it to various festivals in the country. A really good friend of my sister is involved with the Colorado Springs film festival, and she called me. I have a problem sending it to Colorado [due to recent anti-gay political referendums]. She said, "If we have you come and speak, you could talk about the issue. It could be contingent on that." I told her that either way I would show her the film, and sent it to her.

USC owns half of the film—I think it's fifty-fifty. They have the negative and copyright. Any money we get for the film is going back into the film, to make a print, to pay people back, but we'll never get enough. If the film were to sell to HBO, that would be split fifty-fifty.

There are two ways to do a thesis film. One way is to use school equipment and shoot on school property, and the school owns the negative. The other option is you take it as a class, but you do everything independently, you shoot wherever, and use your own equipment. You get student status, but I think you own the film. We chose the first way so we could shoot on a soundstage.

There are one or two festivals we did not get into. Peter's paying the entry fees right now, because I can't. I still owe a lot from the film and stuff. I still have friends I owe who I can't call because I'm too embarrassed. The one I really wanted to enter was Ann Arbor because I went to school there, but we had the 35mm problem. I don't know if we would still be eligible next year, but I would definitely shrink it down to 16mm to enter.

I have the first act basically done on an idea Peter and I thought of together. We pitched it and got a great response, but I ended up doing another draft of *Lovestruck*. I got paralyzed two days ago after talking to James about this. I also have this other idea I'm totally stoked about. This one that we started is a romantic comedy—my third—so I'm romantic-comedied to death. And this other one is not a straight comedy; it's darker, different. It's a total challenge. I'm totally excited. (I've been out here too long, with all these "totallys"!)

Plus, I've started a book. It's a biography of seven different people, and how they like construction work. It's really interesting, though. [Laughs]

No, actually, it's more like a journal, quasi-autobiographical, *Postcards From the Edge*-ish. Stream of consciousness stuff—situations, me rambling. It's a great outlet. I get on these kicks where I'll paint, or do a crossword puzzle. So now this is my thing. It's much more amorphous and dense.

I hit this brick wall, and ran and called USC to see if I could teach. I'm suddenly going off in fifty thousand different directions. I don't know what to do right now. But I have to make a decision, I can't not do *anything*. For two days I've been on the phone trying to figure out what my job is going to be to support my writing, instead of writing. I can't afford to do that. If I have a great day of writing, I can go to work and not think about anything. But if I have a bad day, it'll affect me, too much.

I'm going through a career crisis right now—I'm just incredibly frustrated.

James was really excited about *Fat City* and started sending it out, and Kyle, in the process, sort of ended up alienating himself from him. They had a big blowout that I was sort of in the middle of. The biggest problem was that I was supposed to be the voice of reason. But I wasn't *raised* to be the voice of reason. I was raised to be neurotic. So I found myself in this role that just wasn't me.

I think *Fat City* had gone to ten or twelve people. Out of that there were a couple of friendly passes. A couple of people thought the fat issue was too tough. There was one guy who absolutely loved it and wanted to do it, but it's the usual bullshit-type stuff. The bottom line is no one said, "Here's a check right now."

So suddenly it's "Let's get *Lovestruck* going—that'll be the one!"

I say, "Why stop this [*Fat City*]?"

He says, "I don't know, it just isn't selling as fast as I thought it would." And I know that wasn't the reason. I'm not stupid. It was because of Kyle. That's what I think.

We talked about it a little yesterday. James doesn't want to get two scripts going at once. So I said, "Fine, but I think we should get this one done first, and see where that can go."

He had read *Lovestruck* before. The biggest thing was that the characters and dialogue were great. You've got to get the magic working in the beginning. So I got that to work, and then he starts talking about this other stuff that's been in there when he's read it two other times, and I'm just insulted by that. So I say, "Do you have any idea what it's like to go through a rewrite?" I mean, I realize a script goes through seventeen or eighteen rewrites, but that's when someone is getting paid, which makes something of a difference.

June first is my self-imposed deadline to quit my job, and it's really creeping up on me. So lately I've been trying to figure out what the hell to do. I can't continue to do this, I know that. This will be a year since the movie's been done, and I will have been waitressing for two years. One year I was working on the movie and writing a little, and the other only writing.

I realize it takes some people ten years, but I'm not going to draw any comparisons. If you ever want to totally lower your self-esteem, start waitressing. It's fine in the beginning, but now I have my master's degree, and I want to come up with something better than this.

But I don't want a development job, or a reader job. I just don't like the business. I want to write, and that's it, as crazy as that sounds.

I may extend my quitting deadline. I mean, June first, I don't know if I can walk away. There are trips and things I want to do this summer. I thought I could maybe find some way to get fired [Laughs] for disorderly conduct or something.

JOHN MCINTYRE
May 20

I was breakfasting with McIntyre when my friend Adam Nimoy approached our table. Nimoy, son of actor Leonard Nimoy, had just directed his second episode of Star Trek: The Next Generation, *and explained in some detail how difficult the experience was for him.*

Boy! If they give Leonard Nimoy's son a hard time on *Star Trek*, I can imagine what directing is going to be like for me.

Duck Soup is helping me build a reel. They have a live-action division. They'll give my tape to reps, and agents will get ahold of it. It's a great opportunity. Usually a production company doesn't give you money to make a reel. They think I'm funny enough and have "got it" enough to pull this off over the next six, eight months.

Right now I'm on unemployment. Perhaps in a month, or five or six weeks, there will be more assistant work at Duck Soup to get back to just paying the bills. I can always do boards or layout.

I'd like to do four thirty-second spots for the reel. It could take a year or eight months. They're pulling favors, from cameramen, etc. If another production company was interested in me, right now my loyalty is with Duck Soup. But if nothing was going on and I wasn't making any money, my loyalty would dwindle.

I want to do broad-based products. I have an idea for Junior Mints, for Crest, for Nike. General national ads. The idea comes to me, I see that first, then I plug it into a product. I realize I don't need to know everything.

P. J. PESCE
May 21

I had this ugly fight with Tom. He's got this other gig—a Paint-ball movie [Paintball is a simulated war game played on an open field between teams with paint-pellet guns]—and he doesn't think he wants me to write it with him.

He says he didn't have a good experience on *Whore II*. I think it's about money, ego, or both. He's going to go to New York to teach. I don't know, I just need to find a way to survive.

May 26

I had lunch with Tom. He was apologetic. He knew he was being a jerk. We had this big psychological talk and he said he just doesn't like to confront things.

He said that during *Whore II* I was so preoccupied with the Western that he had to do the lion's share of the work. Which was kind of true. The Western *was* my number-one concern.

So now he's doing the Paintball script with another guy I know. And the agreement is that if the Western falls apart, I'll come back in as a partner.

Speaking of *The Desperate Trail*, I went in yesterday. I called the meeting. It was me, the unit production manager, and some woman. Maybe she was the cashier. (Laughs) We tried to trim the budget of 2.5 million to 1.1. At first the mood was bitter and angry, and then it became friendly and cool. Like, when the script says, "The camera swings high and wide," they said, "Sorry. No crane."

I explained that there are ways I can shoot things. I mean, John Ford had them. And "Eisenstein 101" is that you see one guy with a gun and then cut to another clutching his chest with blood spurting out. There are ways to use film. It doesn't have to be Paul Verhoeven. They were, like, "Ohhh—I see."

So in the middle of the meeting Chad Oman, the coproducer, came in. He said that this V.P. at Miramax read the script and loved it. She's giving it to the others to read, and maybe they'll put money into it. Who knows? The train scene could be back in.

Chad and I went out to Smalls last night and I got really drunk. I met this cute girl, but she's twenty-three years old.

MARCO WILLIAMS
May 27

Williams edited his segment of "Declarations of Independence" in a small room at Midtown Video in West Hollywood. He worked with Yamana Demissi (also a friend of Liz Cane), who served as production manager and then assisted Williams in postproduction.

On this day they were running dailies and doing a "paper edit," in which cuts are discussed and notated rather than actually made. The images on the monitors were of Arianna Huffington, a conservative Santa Barbara–based writer, preparing for a lecture. Huffington is the author of biographies of Maria Callas and Pablo Picasso (Creator and Destroyer), and is now writing The Fourth Instinct—*which she considers Giving, after Power, Sex, and Survival. (In later months she gained notoriety as the driving force behind her husband Michael's losing senatorial campaign.)*

Other images in Williams's footage are from the studio of photographer Richard Ross, who paid homeless people five dollars each for signs they held asking for money and/or food. Ross photographed the signs en masse and Williams tracked him down after seeing them reproduced in the L.A. Times. "Tired of beans, will work for peanuts," one read.

The three hours in the show are divided among "Freedom of Expression," "Equality," and "Life, Liberty and the Pursuit of

Happiness." Each hour is comprised of five segments, each made by a filmmaker and an essayist.

The dynamic that people might have expected between me and Arianna didn't quite pan out. It was never well defined how the relationship would work. The essayist, I guess, was supposed to be the engineer, and the filmmaker the facilitator. But there was definitely an imbalance in the dynamic with us. There was just no real exchange of ideas. She definitely wanted to avoid conflict, as opposed to a conservative who relished conflict.

We do have different opinions, for example, on the subject of whether money should be given to the NEA, or other places. That she is a wealthy Republican and I'm a Democrat who doesn't have a lot of money is a sidebar. The point is this: there are those who help by doing and those who help by giving. I would say she is the latter, not the type to get her hands dirty.

The Huffington piece doesn't feel quite sincere—no, that's not right. It's exterior to a reality. Nothing was staged but, for Arianna, "walking the walk" is to talk about these things. Ideas, in order to reach people, have to be dissected and questioned, challenged, and proven to hold weight. To me, the frustration is that this piece did not permit that sort of discourse.

I, in fact, believe the premise here. The pursuit of happiness is more than just the pursuit of pleasure or material things, and could in fact be defined as the pursuit of service to others. I think that's a very genuine idea but, to me, for that to really reach people and be meaningful, it must be questioned. I couldn't do that in the production phase. Whether or not the editing allows for some kind of challenge, or presentation that the idea holds up, I don't know.

It became a gig. Perhaps to their credit, they did not know what this would yield or what this would be about. The whole idea was to create new TV, getting filmmakers and other people to collaborate.

I don't know anybody else's story. There may have been other instances of differences like I had, but at a certain point I found that it was not a two-way street. In production I suppressed my own ideas, and whatever Arianna asked me to shoot, I shot. I did it cinematically, so I wasn't totally compromised creatively, but it wasn't necessarily the things I would have shot.

Quite honestly, with Arianna, I think these *are* her convictions. But if she would have been more willing to risk and not be so concerned about how she looked or how this would impact her husband as a politician, it would have been even better. They were concerned that she had been mistreated in the media. But my opinion is that if you're willing to be a little more vulnerable, so much more can be gained. We only touched the surface. There was so much more that could have been done.

I think about the other filmmakers in this program, whether it's Orlando Blackwell, who's a very renowned documentary film-maker, Renee Tajima, Nigel Noble, the senior producer on the show. That kind of stature means somebody else may be able to [do more].

The week after next I'm going with Chris Gerolmo to the Kobe festival near Osaka, Japan. The festival has twenty films. Three are American, mine [*Without a Pass*], Chris's [*The Witness,* also a Dis-covery Program short for Showtime], and someone's from AFI.

I had a couple of meetings in the past two weeks with Dawn Steel. Gay Hirsch is a Touchstone executive who apparently is a fan of mine, though I've never met her. She may have suggested me. They have seen a lot of Afro-American directors for this proj-ect, which is called *The Power of No.* It's a modernization of Aristo-phanes's *Lysistrata,* in which the women of a Greek town tell the men they will no longer continue to have sex with them if the men continue their warring ways. It's been updated and now set in urban America, where the warring is gang activity.

I like the story. It's about empowerment and choices. Tina Andrews wrote the script. I told Dawn, "I could see how you would want a black woman to direct this." She said, "All I know is that I definitely don't want a white man."

At the second meeting I met her partner, Tim Reid from Black Entertainment Television. The meetings have been at Dawn's offices on Maple Drive in Beverly Hills. I walked in. There were two men [in the waiting area], and I sat and bullshitted with them, about my tough weekend in Santa Barbara with all these conserva-tives. Dawn came out and shook hands with the men and said, "This way, guys." They got up and I didn't. Then they said, "You too, Marco." These were the guys I was meeting with! We went into another room and suddenly I was in a meeting with five other people who work for Dawn.

Barbara Dreyfus is my agent at ICM on this. It's her territory. [At the major agencies, the studios and networks are divided up and assigned to specific agents.] I read the script three times, and outlined five or six sections in terms of what my cinematic treatment would be. I have to say I felt like I was doing a good job.

Dawn had opened the meeting by saying, "I want you, Tim, to know how much I like Marco, and that I believe he is right for this project."

They said to me, "This is a comedy—how do you feel about doing comedy?" Now, people will tell you that I am about as serious as a heart attack. But I *am* sensitive to comedy. I made an analogy that I got from Richard Marks at UCLA. He said that the key to directing is having an emotional connection to the material.

Of course, they asked, "Who do you see in the film?" I told them I know that there is a plethora of black talent on television now, but that the only thing I watch is basketball. The usual names came up, *Different World* people, Will Smith, Halle Berry, Rosie Perez.

As I was leaving, Dawn said she would call me later, but I really didn't expect her to. When I got home, five minutes later the phone rang, and she said, "You're our guy. We'll set up a meeting with the Touchstone people."

I dropped two prints of my film at ICM for David Hoberman and the other Touchstone executives to see.

BOBBI THOMPSON, Agent

In convincing a studio executive that a director of a short feature film, or even feature-length student film, is ready to direct a studio feature, you only want to be in business with that client on a picture that has a producer who's going to help it, and that has a studio executive who has worked with first-time directors before.

In the room with a producer and a studio executive, the director and the director's talent ultimately seals the deal. Also, the agency's recommendation and support of the talent—either by virtue of supporting the picture with casting or a writer, or by a track record of knowing from experience, the same way producers working with first-time directors know how to do that. So somebody's got to have a past track record, even if the director doesn't. But ultimately the director's talent and presentation is going to get him or her the job.

Tracey Kemble, like each of the other creative executives at Hollywood Pictures (a division of the Walt Disney Company, as is Touchstone), was given $75,000 in discretionary money in an experimental attempt to acquire and generate new material. Production executives—one level up—were given a spending limit of $150,000 each.

Tracey told Chris Moore she wanted to find something for me. "Information is the coin of the realm," Chris Gerolmo told me about Hollywood. So I haven't told Dawn about this other deal.

Tracey had an idea, about the world of high-class strippers and dancers. I had been to a thirtieth-birthday party at the Hollywood Tropicana. She had two educated women friends who danced. We're clarifying the money now. I think it could be like an *Alice in Wonderland*. I told Tracey I thought this was a little fleshy for Disney. She said, "Wait until you see *What's Love Got to Do With It*."

PIETER-JANN BRUGGE, Producer

There are talented directors who are put up to tasks that they have not quite mastered yet. However, I think that if a producer hires a director who is up to the task, he or she might find a formidable opponent in that director, which may not be in the producer's best interests.

I mean, the producer may decide that he or she wants to exercise a certain amount of control along with the star or just by himself, and basically have somebody who may be "kick-aroundable." I don't think that they codirect, because I think that on a set there can only be one director, otherwise it becomes messy. Some of these pictures might become messy, as clearly there is not one guiding voice.

June 4

The Power of No is moving along. We had a meeting with Disney on Wednesday—with Hoberman, Donald DeLine and Gay Hirsch. They saw both *Without a Pass* and *In Search of Our Fathers*.

Last week I had a meeting with Dawn and Tim Reid. I felt good about the meeting. I've been prepared, thinking a lot about this story, doing my homework. I read the script a lot. Prior to every meeting I reread the script so that I didn't have to go on memory.

The meeting opened with Dawn saying something like, "Tim and I are really inspired by Marco, we think he's great," and then it was me. And I probably wasn't as organized as I could have been. I learned something about preparation for these meetings.

I should have gone to the meeting by myself, driving in my own car. For one thing, I don't have a radio in my car. I know what happens is, if I'm by myself, I will think and rehearse the first five minutes. I drove with Tim Reid, which was absolutely great because I hadn't had a chance to talk with him at all, so I was learning some things about him, and some background about how this script evolved—that sort of thing. I didn't feel one hundred percent prepared, the way Bill Walsh would be with the first forty-one plays. For a meeting I'll usually have the first two or three things that I'll say very clearly mapped out.

So I didn't quite have that, but I was all set. I had had a pre-meeting with Dawn and Tim, and actually had a breakfast with Gay Hirsch in the morning and talked with her about it. Wednesday night I just wanted to watch a basketball game. I couldn't function.

I laid out all of my thoughts about the script. I talked about how much I liked it, why I wanted to make this movie, the way I would treat it, the way I would direct the actors, things that needed improvement in the script, and I talked about tone. I covered everything.

I told them that the real key here is that this has a fablelike quality which needs to be emphasized. I mentioned *Do the Right Thing* as a paradigm of a fable—reality-based issues set against a backdrop that's sort of hyperreal. I don't think there was one question asked during the course of the meeting, but I laid everything out, I was funny and having a good time.

Two things were said. I told them, "I have another hundred things I could talk about, but I've been talking for a good forty minutes, so maybe you have some questions." David Hoberman said, "I understand what you're saying about the way you'll treat it, but it sounds like maybe you have too much emphasis on *this*, and might want to do *that* . . . and maybe it's going to be a little too much—" And I interrupted and said, "Wait a second—all those things will integrate very well, and in no way will they intrude upon the story. I'm just giving you a palette." He acknowledged that and then asked the one question I knew would be asked, and it was my one mistake. I should have started with this—which I thought would be the one perception of my shortcomings.

Hoberman said, "Looking at your films, you come across as being very earnest, and this is a humorous story, it's a 'dramedy.' If someone were to talk about you and your work in terms of humor, they would probably talk about the absence of it." I should have said that wasn't exactly true. *In Search of Our Fathers* is very serious but the commentary is full of wry thoughts.

So he said, "What about that?" and I had a response, because Dawn had asked me that and everyone is going to ask me that. I had had this conversation with Richard Marx, the editor, about whether or not someone called him up and said, "Richard, we're looking for a great comedy editor," or "Richard, we're looking for a dramatic editor," and he said they look for a good *editor*. A good editor can do that sort of thing.

Although I'm not yet a director in Richard Marx's league as an editor, I do believe I am a good director. And I know I can handle the comedy. I cited a couple of examples of how I would approach that.

And that was it—the one question that left me feeling like I got "stumped" when I left. It was the single biggest challenge. That question colored the whole meeting, because there I was trying to convince them that I was capable and qualified. It was a little frustrating.

Dawn told me afterwards, "Although I can tell you what they're going to think, you were great." Tim put it perfectly, "If this is a business run by money, it's more about power." I am very confident about my vision, and as a result, throughout the meeting, I was kind of in control. It was me. And this was the one moment for them to let me know that *they* were in control.

It's also a legitimate question. I mean, I knew that would come up, and it's not unreasonable to ask. If I had said something like, "Oh, you're right. I'm afraid of comedy," the deal would have been blown. I may not be a stand-up comedian. But I pointed out to them I'm actually a closet comedian—most people don't get to see that in me, but it's there.

Afterwards, as I thought about it, I understood that that was just one iota. I was really "on" at the meeting. Afterwards I got a few calls. Dawn called and said, "You knocked them dead, they loved you, they're really into you—it's great." Gay Hirsch called the next day and said much the same.

What this was all about, I think, was that they may require me to take a director's test. And I had made it clear to Dawn that I wasn't real keen on that. It's not like I'm a first-time director. I've made some movies, so it's not like I'm a nobody. That's assurance enough that this is going to get done. So it seems to me that the comedy question was if they want to have a reason for me to do a director's test.

Averaging budgets between $80,000 and $125,000, director's tests are a fairly common practice for studios considering working with new directors. As with screen tests for actors, the full deal for the director's services on the feature must be negotiated before the test is done.

Right now everybody's in my camp fighting against the director's test. They are presenting it to Katzenberg, and he just has to look at my films. Nobody's really discussed what it entails. But it's not like I've never made a film. With a writer, it's "What's he going to be like on the set?" I've done a number of movies. I can direct a movie. So I don't need to prove that I can direct a movie. Just let me make the movie. That's how I'm approaching it.

I'm going to have to do it if it comes down to "You either do the director's test or you don't make this movie." My feeling is that

Dawn and [agents] Bill Block and Barbara Dreyfus are going to make it clear that they don't think it's necessary. If they prevail, I don't know. I wouldn't be surprised, if nothing else, if it's a way to hedge Jeffrey Katzenberg's response. He may say, "Well, can the kid do comedy?"

The fact of the matter is that this story is a "dramedy"—comedy that grows out of the interactions and situations. Maybe that makes it harder, but it's really a dramatic story which will say things, as opposed to Steve Martin comedy or Robin Williams comedy. We'll see. I mean, I don't have enough clout to say, "You want me to make this movie? I don't do the test." They have that clout. It's probably a ten- or twelve-million-dollar picture, so that may be what will have to happen. So I'll do it, but I don't *want* to do it.

I'm sure I would get whatever the minimum salary is. If it were $50,000 I would probably be insulted. I'd like to get as much as I can.

In May, Williams's agent, Chris Moore, had left ICM.

I knew about Chris Moore quitting before he did it because he told me. I was a client, and he wants to produce, and there's one project of mine that he's very into. It's too bad. I like him, as my agent. So now I have to deal with the next agent, whether it's Barbara Dreyfus, or whomever. And obviously due to the fact that I'm up for a movie, it's been very interesting to me. I don't know if it's sucking up, but people are calling. I have to decide. Somebody gets to represent me, and now it's a question of who.

I mentioned it to Bill Block. "What's going to happen? Whose lap do I fall in?" He said, "For right now, you're in *my* lap." Whatever that means. He's also concerned that other agencies will start calling. I have gotten a phone call from another agency. I was shocked that I got a call, even before it was officially in the trades that Chris was leaving. I just have a gentlemen's agreement [no contract] with ICM.

ADAM DUBOV, Director

An agent at a "boutique" agency advised me to sign with CAA.

The typical story—the big agency. "We have all the power. We have all the connections. You will have the benefit of all of our clout, all of our resources, and we have the leverage over the people you will be dealing with. If they want to sign some big movie star of ours to a deal— if they have treated you unfairly, we can clobber them on your behalf. That is part of the service we can provide to you."

Not true. It's not the way it works. A big company has a vested interest in dealing with a big company. The fate of the little guy doesn't figure into that. But I believed it. I was also twenty-seven years old. I had grown up in the entertainment business—my parents were screenwriters—but still, it's a learning experience when you go through it yourself. I liked some of the people. But for me, I was acutely attuned to whether people understood my film and liked it for what I considered the right reasons. Or were they merely trying to scoop up somebody who, for fifteen seconds, is the hot commodity?

On the stripper project, technically the contract just needs to be signed. A couple of things seem to be happening with that. I'm waiting on Disney finalizing the deal with the two young women whose story this will be inspired by. I guess they want to make sure they have their rights in case they become an integral part of the script.

I basically accepted the deal they offered me, which was no money: it was $41,000 if I brought them the story versus $27,000 if they brought me the story. So it's kind of a ripoff, but better to be in the game. I like Tracey a lot and she's showed faith in me, and she introduced the idea to me. That's the reality—it's an idea, not a story. I mean, I could make a story out of it, but under the circumstances, I'm one of the "little people."

There may be a problem with doing the stripper project and *The Power of No*. Dawn Steel does not know about the project to my knowledge. Nor does Tracey know about the other deal, even though it's with the same studio. I don't understand what's going on—I'm just waiting. Obviously I'd rather direct than write the script. The best of all worlds would be that I can do both. The directing thing wouldn't go into production until September or October.

I got a call yesterday from another agent at ICM, who says that there's a script that Marty Brest [director of *Beverly Hills Cop* and *Midnight Run*] is associated with, and thought I might be a good person for. The agent had a conversation with Marty. He's sending my tapes over to him, and said, "By the way, I know there's a lot of energy going around the agency with you and *The Power of No*, but I'd love to send you this script."

Well, that confused me completely, because that's how inexperienced I am. There's all this energy, they're all trying to get me this one job, and now they're dangling something else completely.

Of course, this can be pushed back, but it seems so bizarre to me. Although I do understand that the best time to sell somebody is when there's the perception that they're hot. So, I guess they say to Brest, "This guy's about to have a deal at Disney, we gotta get him." But it just seems funny to me.

Williams had recently seen the controversial film Menace II Society.

I'm frustrated by yet another sort of gang film and teenage black film. My concern is that most blue-eyed, white-skinned people in the United States have a perception that there are only two types of black people: there are black men in gangs in the "South Centrals" of the United States, and there are those who play basketball. That's it. And the reality is that both of those communities are the small ends of the big spectrum of who black men are.

So it frustrates me that by and large the movies—the arena in which our perceptions and understanding of things occurs—show only these types of stories. It's time for there to be other types. And yet the ones that get made, more often than not, are gang-oriented or violence-oriented things.

My ultimate theory is that in the movie business, there is a real possibility for there to be less black people in movies because of the saturation of one type of style. So, hey, let's have more Charles Burnett–style films, even if they don't make tons of money, because then there are other types of stories out there.

The Power of No has got history behind it, being a remake of Aristophanes, so that's in its favor—Aristophanes was about war and gang fighting and stuff. Not that this film remakes *Do the Right Thing*, but that's one of the things I look forward to with this piece. To find that balance, where for part of the time you realize that you're being told a story. It's make-believe, it's fable, it's once-upon-a-time. And yet at the same time you realize that these things are aspects of reality. This is a story that has a spectrum of people.

The other thing is that the majority of the primary characters are women. So it's no *Girlz N The Hood*, but you're going to get a view of black life from a female perspective. I think that's where it has a chance to be different. On some level this film is light, but what I like is that it reminds you that you have a lot of choices. So if there's some idea that I'm trying to get across if I make this film, it's that, but it's using the form to do that.

My argument is this: The situation is close to untenable in many urban black neighborhoods in the United States. And yet I think that if we point out to young black people, and assure them, that there are opportunities for them, they start to aspire to that. So film is a myth-making apparatus. If you start showing black people in a lot of different things, they start wanting to be like them.

I didn't grow up watching TV, but I hear these stories all the time. "I saw such and such on TV or in the movies and I wanted to be like that." Well, if you only show those realities and not what is possible, then who dreams of anything else?

That's part of it. Then the governments and societies and cities have a responsibility as well to do more. I don't have an answer at all. It is grim, isn't it?

People need to be made aware of the problem, but also need to be part of presenting a solution. For all of the criticism of the *Cosby Show*, not only was it funny but there *are* people who are married to black doctors.

The Kobe festival in Japan is paying airfare, hotel, and food. I don't even know how much spending money to take with me. It's someplace I've never been, so it's this feeling of entering into a whole new world.

STEPHANIE ALLAIN, Studio Executive

I don't think minority filmmaking is a trend. I think that in the last fifteen years kids have grown up with the notion of video cameras and the abilities to make movies at hand, and I think that the media the way it is, kids are exposed to TV and film to a large degree. People like Spike Lee have definitely paved the way, so there are role models out there. You know, "I could do that."

So I think it's not so much a trend as an evolution, and I think that it will continue. And I think that the Latino filmmakers will also start to make more movies. There's always a danger that not enough will surface, or not enough *successful* ones. For every successful movie there's always five others that can get made afterward. *Menace II Society* was a great example of a film none of the studios wanted to touch, and New Line did a great job on it. And *Boyz N the Hood* definitely helped.

BERNARD JOFFA
June 7

My agent, Ronda Gomez, read *Home Free*, the Sydney Maree story, and said it's going to be a hard one to sell. Because right now, the trend in Hollywood is to put money into box office more than anything. I understand that. She likes the writing a lot, with a few changes, she says. No suggestions yet.

We're going to get it out. She has a list of names, and so does ICM.

We gave it to Sidney Poitier's company, which has a deal at TriStar/Columbia. They got it and loved it, and called us into a meeting on Friday, and they were the first people to get it. Poitier's company wants to give it to Sidney, who has already seen *Senzeni Na?* and apparently likes it a lot. They said, "Let's give it first to Denzel Washington, who has an office down the drag from him."

We had the meeting at ICM in the afternoon, and they said

they'll call Denzel and ask him to read it. So he will get it from two sides.

The ridiculous conclusion, the dream, is that they love it and go to Columbia and say this is the movie they want to make, and we've got Denzel Washington interested. Then we wouldn't have to look for financing, nothing. It just happens. That would be the dream! We're not thinking of anything less than that at the moment. But we're going to send it out to other companies.

PIETER-JANN BRUGGE, Producer

I don't think material necessarily has to be set in the present or has to be domestic. I think Hollywood has always been interested in any new trend. People have tried to do a picture about genetic engineering—suddenly there are two pictures, that are essentially based on a very well-written article in a magazine that catches Hollywood's attention.

The thing that has changed since the '70s—at that particular time a director like Alan Pakula was able to make a picture like *The Parallax View*, and he made *All the President's Men*—there was still an element of innocence which made it possible to corrupt with hard-hitting material. That innocence has long been lost. So when you come with a piece of material that deals with corruption, people have already seen it. And in that sense one is not surprised.

After David Puttnam makes a film like *The Killing Fields*, you don't have to make a story about the extraordinary atrocities in Bosnia, when you can see it every single night on the news. It was the same issue with projects about South Africa. When *Nightline* broadcasts stories week after week, stories about South Africa, the public becomes educated. It creates a perception that we have seen this already. Whether they have or not is secondary.

P. J. PESCE
June 7

We're on draft number nine of *The Desperate Trail*. They want ninety-five pages and no train. That means the minor characters are cut out.

If it's 1.1 million, I'm ready to go. But the waiting . . .

Some other jokers are reading it. New Line is also back in, they're reading it again to consider partnering up. HBO is considering it as well. I can't read these people. They're in a whole world I'm not able to play in.

‖‖‖

SUMMER 1993–SUMMER 1994

My sister Karen is no wizard, but she is family. Married, divorced, went to NYU Film School. Made a three-hour film of *her*, just sitting on a kitchen chair, called *Loneliness*.

—Neil Simon, *Jake's Women*

The people who make pictures are not all idiots. They just behave as if they were.

—Raymond Chandler, in a letter to Alex Barris, March 18, 1949

Hollywood is high school with money.

—Anonymous

MARCO WILLIAMS
June 22

Williams had just returned from Japan's Kobe Film Festival

We were kind of shocked when the two winners of the [Kobe] festival's big prizes, $50,000 and $20,000, were pretty weak films—but were Japanese. No prize was given for Best Japanese Film. But two Japanese films won Best Overall! Let's just say it was "political."

I got what I wanted, though, which was to go to Japan. It was the first festival where I actually saw every film. There was a great divergence of people, Czech films, Slovenian films. An Irish film-maker and Chris Gerolmo and I went to a baseball game together.

Without a Pass was received well by the people there but not the other filmmakers. Through an interpreter, the head of the festival said it was his favorite, I think because of the music and the interest in America's racial problems.

The first cut of my PBS Arianna Huffington documentary was hated by everybody. I told the producers they gummed up the works by not getting behind me. I was the hands on the body, not the brains. But I just got back from New York, where I met with them with the new cut. Now they love it.

On the Disney project, I'm doing the director's test. I'd rather not, but Jeffrey Katzenberg said to Dawn Steel, "Don't ask me to do something [take a risk on Williams without a test] you wouldn't want me to ask you to." So I'll do it in the next two or three weeks. It's no problem. I'm not nervous about passing the test. And Dawn is so committed to me that she will produce the test. We're already having casting meetings.

If the deal comes through, I will supervise a rewrite and hopefully be pay-or-play. I said I really didn't want a straight development deal. I don't want the ideas I create to be used by another director.

LISA KLEIN
June 28

Everything's going okay and disastrous at the same time. This whole *Fat City* thing with my writing partner, Kyle, and my manager, James, has become a big sort of brouhaha.

The bottom line now is that I can't really work with either one of them, just because the way that everything was handled was pretty disgusting. James has ceased everything with this script even though he said he wasn't going to, so I'm a little perturbed about that. Because Kyle is involved, he just stopped doing anything with it, so I don't want to work with James anymore.

James has no idea I've decided not to work with him anymore. I want to wait and see what else is going to happen.

I can understand, in a way, that he wouldn't want to do anything that would benefit Kyle after their personality clash. Kyle wanted James to call him and stuff like that, and he basically went through me. Kyle didn't want to hear things secondhand. It was that kind of thing. Pride and ego and all that stuff stood in the way.

At first I was just in the middle and it was frustrating, but I didn't think that everything would stop. Then when it did and I thought about it, I thought, "Well, James totally screwed me," because even though he said he was still going to pursue the script, human nature would have it that he wouldn't want to do anything to further Kyle's career. But rather than saying that to me, he just stopped. And *that* pissed me off.

And then James totally screwed me over just by handling it the way that he did. So I don't have any plans in the near future to work with Kyle. I just think they handled it pretty unprofessionally. I'm not happy about that. So that's kind of put a crimp in things.

To me, the most frustrating thing that could be happening is nothing. If the script were going around and people didn't like it, that would be upsetting, but at least there would be some movement. Now it's like, okay, I've wasted all this time writing this stuff and it's just sitting there. I'm not good at the business end of things, like sending stuff out. I'm not going to do some mass mailing to agents. I don't want to go through that.

So there's no movement in any direction on anything, except I sent *Lovestruck* to a couple of agents, so we'll see what happens with that. But *Fat City*'s just sort of sitting on a shelf now.

I spoke with Monika Skerbelis, and she's talked to a few people, and I've sent my stuff to them. One at the Susan Smith Agency, a smaller place, and the Maggie Field Agency. The other one is not so small, United Talent.

I also got a little bit coerced into sending a script to the Marcia Lucas USC feature project. I had no interest in doing it, and then they picked a couple of scripts and weren't happy with them, so they sent out scripts to the potential directors. Peter got one, and immediately called to tell me they are soliciting more scripts because they're not happy with the ones they have so far, though they did choose about three from which they're going to select one. If something else comes in that they like better, I don't know what they're going to do with those three.

I sent *Lovestruck*. It's cheap, that's the main reason. *Guardian Angels* and *Fat City* are pretty expensive. So Peter really handled the whole thing because I went to Washington. The other reason I did it was that I can get out of it at any time, like if they choose a director I don't really want to work with. We'll see what happens. They probably won't decide until July.

I'm ready to leave the job at any time. I'm on alert. I've been thinking about pursuing teaching. I've talked to a couple of people at USC. UCLA has some kind of freeze. I talked to someone at Loyola. It would be an adjunct thing, a couple of nights a week. It's not such an easy thing to do, either, but that's a possibility. I just want to do something at night, not in the industry, that isn't waitressing. I don't think anything will happen until the fall.

But hopefully something will happen agentwise so I can at least start getting the script out. I really liked *Sleepless in Seattle,* so the timing could be either good or bad. There were definitely some parallels to *Lovestruck,* which is frustrating. It's a tough sell, though—not a big movie.

I'm definitely at a frustrating point right now, a non-movement point, which is killing me. And having to sell yourself is not fun.

STEPHANIE ALLAIN, Studio Executive

We need to get a lot more women directing. I think that they're just like the guys—they gotta go out and get their own opportunities. They have to write their own stories— they can't wait around for someone to hand them a script. They've got to bring their movies in on time, and they have to be good and look good, and they have to know their craft. But it's no different from what the guys are doing.

Women are a huge part of the moviegoing population. Look at *Sleepless*—$17 million, opening weekend—incredible! No guns, no action. A girl's story.

It's interesting being a woman in the studio system. It's interesting being a minority in the studio system. To be both wears me out sometimes.

JOHN MCINTYRE
June 29

A few things are changing at work. I was doing more creative stuff with a spot a few weeks ago, doing gags and boards for "Pup-a-Roni," which is like beef jerky for dogs. They did the first spot at Duck Soup a few years ago. It was very funny. The characters are kind of English in design.

In our spot, the dog will do anything for this product. He'll pick his fat owner up in his chair, vacuum under the chair, stuff a pipe into his mouth and leap onto his stomach until smoke comes out like a bellows. All these extremely quick gags.

We were working these up, and they were all bashed to bits by the client in about five hours. Tore the whole thing apart. It will still be funny, but not what we were hoping for. But it was good to work with the owner of Duck Soup directly and pitch this out.

In the middle of doing it he asked if I wanted to start directing animation there soon, because I think they're getting a lot of work, or hoping to, and they might not have all the staff they wanted. So I said, "Sure, great," and he said when the spots come in he's going to look for something for me to direct. That would be nice. It would probably be freelance directing, so it would open me up to a better creative experience. I wouldn't be feeling like I'm just a scribe, that's for sure.

I've got a few things I want to do that I think they'll be open to. Something for Fossil watches with a very Populux kind of feel to it, with Super 8 clips from the '50s. I feel like I'm leading myself into a sort of nostalgia angle as a director.

Freelancing is better than working there every day, which is exhausting. Now I have plenty of time, and when I take a job from them every few weeks it pays for everything else. But I'm still getting used to the on-off-on-off deal. It takes a day to shift gears. But ultimately it would be the best way to get something done that's longer, like two hours.

Theresa is doing "cleanup," animation assisting at Rich Entertainment. We're happy, but we don't see each other enough. Just Sunday and Wednesday night. We're going to Cape Cod in a couple of weeks. My parents have a place there.

JOHN KEITEL
July 2

Last week Jeff Kurtz from Miramax called for the *Ground Zero* script. Then he called a week later. It wasn't ready either time, so I sent him a pound of coffee with the label "GROUND ZERO—COMING SOON," and a roll of pennies, which features prominently in the script. I sent him the script this morning.

MARCO WILLIAMS
July 11

I'm sort of surviving. The director's test hasn't happened yet and I don't really have a concrete idea of when it's going to, although in the next two to three weeks it should happen. We're probably going to have a table read of the script next Saturday. I'm hoping that soon—if not immediately—thereafter, we'll be doing the rest.

It's been fairly nebulous and I don't know why. Nobody's really keeping me informed. It's a little vague. I think it's due to the fact that a deal needs to be created before they do a test. And it wasn't until Friday that my agent worked out a deal. So I suspect that as soon as we say yes to the deal, things will accelerate a little bit. I had a four-and-a-half-hour meeting with the writer and a couple of producers and the development people from Dawn's company on the script last Wednesday, so the script is being rewritten to my specifications at the moment. Things are moving, but I'm a little frustrated because of all the time waiting and wondering.

Even though I don't have anything else going on, this is still my *life*, I still have a life, and I like to know when I should expect to start worrying [Laughs] and what-have-you. It's nerve-wracking to be unclear about things and want to make plans to go away or take a weekend off, or anything like that.

It's funny, I'm not fully comfortable wearing the jacket that says, "I'm the director," although I'm being introduced by Dawn Steel as the director of the film.

It's fascinating too, the phone calls I've received from people I haven't heard from in a while. "Congratulations. I hear you're directing this picture for Disney!" My response is, "It's a little premature." But I do understand. Just because I'm out of the loop doesn't mean everybody else is.

I've moved over to Tom Strickler at ICM. I had a meeting a few weeks ago where six agents sat across from me and I talked a lot. From that I had some discussions with Chris Moore, and then decided on a person to be my point man. I had lunch with Tom—a lot of people said he was "good people," that sort of thing—so I'll give it a try. He's a Harvard kid.

I'm done with the documentary.

I hated the experience. I did a fine cut that was different than what you saw. I had a couple of conversations with Arianna, she had some questions, and now I'm out of the loop.

Her things were petty, relating to her vanity and not to the nuances of making a documentary. But because she's accustomed to having control, she can wrestle with the production company about whether she had final cut or not. I basically said to them, as far as I'm concerned, if they want to change anything in the piece they're welcome to it. I'd like the courtesy of hearing what they want to do, but I have no desire to get my hands dirty with it.

So that's done, thankfully. It was one of those experiences where I went at it thinking it was going to be fun to make a piece, and realized at the end it was simply a job.

There are still agents making me aware of projects. I also had a meeting Friday at New Line. So I met with them about a script. My sense about what I'm doing is that since Disney still had not made a commitment there's no reason not to look for another project. So I met with a couple of creative executives and may have a meeting this week with Mike DeLuca about a script that they want to shoot in October. They're desperately looking for a director. I liked it, it was a parable set against the world of high school basketball, called *Above the Rim*. [The film was subsequently made, directed by Jeff Pollack.]

So things are moving at a pace. Not necessarily *my* pace. They say *The Power of No* will be budgeted at eight to ten million, and if they're going to do a test, they'll spend fifty or a hundred thousand. There is a chance that a Halle Berry would play the lead. There are a few great small parts. I had a wonderful experience with John Amos [on *Without a Pass*] and would like to ask him to do one. But it's not too substantial. I would embellish the role if he were interested.

PIETER-JANN BRUGGE, Producer

I think the biggest problem is that too few people are in a position to develop their craft. It is a failure of the system to the extent that it used to be that people in television could make an easy transition to theatrical pictures. Or they started in B pictures and graduated to A pictures.

I'm not talking about the genuine masters of cinema, but even people like Steven Spielberg started in television, and were able to graduate from television, where their talents were recognized. These days you have to have someone out of film school who has directed one short, and out of that short they're suddenly in a position to direct a major picture. And whether the budget is $10 million, $12 million—or $3 million or $40 million—is not necessarily an issue. The pressures surrounding somebody are so intense. And why would someone expect a person like this to succeed?

P. J. PESCE
July 11

Brad Krevoy called me up and asked me to go see *The Searchers* with him, and I thought, "Well, isn't that nice. He's taking an interest in a classic Western."

My biggest fear, of course, was that he would see it and think, "Oh, all Westerns have to be just like that." I mean, there has been another entire genre since *The Searchers*. At least one, with *Butch Cassidy* and the Sergio Leone Westerns. But I thought he would say after seeing it, "We have to make a Western just like that. You can't be funny in a Western."

So the only thing the guy said the whole time we were watching was, "Look at that, we can shoot the whole thing inside—look at that, that's definitely on a set! We'll save a lot of money that way!" Which was a little disturbing. When we came out of there all he tried to do was tell me we could shoot in L.A. and then go away for three days to get—as he put it—"vistas."

In his defense, for my birthday he gave me three very, very nice books on Westerns, which was a really nice gesture, and then we went out to dinner. We talked about a lot of things.

He said, "So what do you think this movie will be rated?" And I thought about it for a moment, and I thought maybe it should be rated PG, but then I figured I should just cover my ass and say R. So I said, "Well, I think probably an R," and he thought for about a third of a second before he said, "Okay. Great. The lead actress has got to do nudity."

I said, "What?" and he said, "Absolutely. You can't talk me out of it, don't bother talking to your agent, don't bother talking to Chad, the lead actress has got to do nudity. We'll find some unknown. She'll do nudity."

I was like, "Well, wait a minute, wait a minute, why are you taking such a hard line?"

He says, "No, no, the more you play with me—we have to do it, I'm totally convinced. There's no discussion. We'll have to shoot it the first thing. Get it out of the way."

I said, "Oh, that'll have a really great effect on the actress and her ability to trust her director. She'll feel real comfortable, I'll get lots of great performances out of the actors after that kind of a first day."

Brad said, "Doesn't matter. You're a good director. You can figure that out."

So I figured the best thing to do then was to back off, and just not even talk about it. Maybe he would forget about it.

Then we were talking about something else, and he told me a very interesting story. He said, "Look. You want me to do a movie, you want me to not have nudity in it, you want me to be an artist. How much is your rent?" I told him it's $820 a month. And he says, "Well, imagine you've only got nine hundred dollars in the bank, and I come up to you and say, 'Listen. Don't worry about paying the rent. If you'll buy this painting for nine hundred dollars, I guarantee in three months' time it'll be so great that you'll sell it for ten times that amount, because it's really a great work of art.' Or, should you put nine hundred dollars into a sure investment and get back eighteen hundred so you can pay the rent for the next two months?"

I saw the guy's point, having the rent due at the end of the month, which it was.

Then he says to me, "Well, what are your favorite movies?" So I say, "Well, let's see. *Badlands, Apocalypse Now, McCabe & Mrs. Miller* . . ." I also said *Star Wars*, and he said, "Really? You really like *Star Wars*?" And I said, "Yeah, it's an amazing movie, I mean it's a great story." And I also said *E.T.*, and he didn't believe me, and I said, "I really do like *E.T.*, it would be on my top-ten list." It's a really moving story, and really well made, and the acting is great, and the script is great. Not that I like everything Spielberg does, but it's probably the guy's best film.

Then I mentioned *Scarecrow* and he said "What's that?" So I go through the whole thing. "*Scarecrow* is this wonderful movie, it's incredible. Al Pacino playing someone other than Al Pacino, and Gene Hackman giving this great performance, and it's about these two drifters, and it's so funny," and I acted out all the parts and told him the story in great detail.

Brad was watching me, and his eyes were lighting up, and he was very interested, and finally I got to the end, and I told him about this terrifically sad scene where Pacino comes back and talks to his wife on the phone and she tells him that their child is dead. The little kid is standing there right next to her—he looks just like Al Pacino—and Pacino's on the phone and just sort of loses his mind, and hangs up the phone, and drags himself away.

I told him this whole thing, and at the end of it he said, "What happens at the end?" and I said, "Well, Al Pacino kind of goes crazy from that phone conversation, and he dies." I couldn't remember if he dies or just gets hauled away to the clink, or the loony bin. I told Brad this and he said, "Huh," and he thought for a minute and said, "I hate movies like that. I believe movies should uplift the human spirit, and you should feel good when you walk away at the end." I said, "Does the lead actress still have to do nudity?"

September 13 is the start date. I'm driving out to Tucson tomorrow night, I think. I still might go out there to shoot the Western, depending on how cheap I can get everything. I gotta get out of here, push this thing along and make it appear something is happening, and start spending his money. How far is Tucson from here, do you know?

ALAN SHAPIRO, Writer-Director

As Jeffrey Katzenberg said in his memo, there has for a while been a blockbuster mentality. Mainly I think it's a shame that there aren't smarter people in charge who are interested not just in developing, but nurturing young talent along, investing in people, and having foresight. That requires talent in itself, to recognize talent.

If they made, for every giant film, five or six smaller films, the profit margin would be just as big. There's just that mentality of going after the big killer movie—so many sequels and remakes, and it's really a shame. The last great era was the Coppola-Scorsese-Spielberg generation of the early- to mid-'70s—Hal Ashby, and Friedkin, and all those people. The films that I would sit through the credits and then watch again—like *One Flew Over the Cuckoo's Nest* and *Midnight Cowboy*, all those great movies of that era—would not be made now.

As those films attest to—because they were all commercial hits as well as artistic successes—the two are not mutually exclusive. Somehow, there's a feeling now that they are. You either do *The Last Action Hero* or you do some art film.

PIETER-JANN BRUGGE, Producer

The Culture of Youth has permeated the studio system, and the age of the executives. There are a lot of executives who are Ivy League-educated Harvard MBAs, who are not necessarily film fans. So it's very difficult for them to function at the filmmaking level.

Now people go back to the examples of yesterday that worked so well and say, "Why can't we hit with that particular formula?" That's a direct function of people who might all genuinely love film, but in the end may not understand film, because they have not received an education.

JOHN KEITEL
July 12

Keitel had taken a position at Midtown Video, a postproduction house (where, coincidentally, Marco Williams had just cut his Huffington film).

Midtown does music videos and industrials and commercials. They did trailers for *Ruby in Paradise* and *Chain of Desire*. And lots of those "making of . . ." shows. I never realized what a huge industry that is.

They wanted someone who could work ten to three, during their busy time. Someone, actually, who did *not* know the various quirks of the systems. Within four weeks they said, "We'll pay you fifteen dollars an hour, and you can be one of us." The owners are all USC people. I went to film school with one, and another is the ex-boyfriend of a woman I went to film school with.

I have mixed feelings. On one hand, video is becoming so big. You have to know about everything that's coming out. It's an electronic medium, like computers. I'm a strong believer in knowing all of the angles of one's craft. But I'm not a "techie." It's never been part of my persona. So I don't know if this is something I'll be great at.

I couldn't have a better home base. It's not a desk job, there is a social component to it. And I like the dub bay. My favorite part of the process is postproduction. My anal side says this is where I can control everything. The USC faction is also strong. So I'm the new USC kid, like an extension of school. It's a good way to keep in contact.

Jeff Kurtz from Miramax called me and said, "I missed your film at Sundance." I told him I would call him if I didn't hear from him, and after I sent my film I didn't. He was out of town and apologized. He said he liked the film and asked if I wanted to come in and talk to him.

I had breakfast and prepared for our meeting last Wednesday. I had my two-sentence thing down, which I subsequently flubbed. So I pitched two versions of what the poster would be like, as well as the story.

When I got there the receptionist asked me, "What have you

done? Have you written a script or something?" It really threw me off! Then the assistant came out and offered me a drink, and I thought it was Jeff. I thought, "This is *not* who I am here to meet." But it wasn't him.

His office had a panoramic view of the L.A. basin. I was curious how the meeting would unfold. But he just said, "Tell me about the movie you want to make." Boom!

So I did the pitch. When you write and semi-memorize, and then don't get it exactly, you say to yourself, "Fuck. I said 'was' instead of 'is.' "

I said, "It's called *Ground Zero*. When the diverse struggles of a diverse group of people throw them into the same location, the unlikeliest of friends becomes the unlikeliest of families, and everyone finds themselves at Ground Zero." At USC you had to do that, and were always critiqued against your original intent.

Jeff didn't say he was gay, but he lives in Silverlake. He was saying how the next gay film had to do more than *Swoon* or *The Living End* did. People want more than just a "gay film." It's no longer about the quantity of gay films but the quality.

I told him that since I came out my agenda has changed. I could see not marketing *Ground Zero* as a gay film. I acknowledged that there is a fine line between being expeditious and practical. But then, I'm not going to alter my vision.

I remembered that panel at Sundance and asked Jeff what he thought made a film merit a theatrical release. He said he would have to read the script. He told me they just bought a film they saw at a festival in Santa Fe.

I was working on my script, and wondering how I was going to write this major character, this black woman who moves to L.A. A couple of people told me, "Black people don't move to L.A." But I found someone who did. I went to Girl Bar on a Friday night, when it's a real scene, and researched the character by asking black women these questions. And I realized that there really are no differences. That's the humanity of it. I realized, *of course* I can write this character. Everyone has fears, desires, and needs. It's just the context in which it's placed that changes.

> ### KEVA ROSENFELD, Director
> You only get to make your first film once, and I kept thinking this when I was making mine. So the first time, you better make something you personally like, not something for other people. Because the rest of your career, you're going to be making films for other people, or you might have to. So your first film better be about who you are.

MARCO WILLIAMS
July 22

We did a table read at Disney on Saturday. That was great fun. A full house, everybody. Dawn, all the producers, Disney executives, Gay Hirsch was there, and a whole cast of characters. It was a lot of fun, and showed what the script was about, and how funny it is.

Robbie Read [a feature casting director] selected the actors for this. She cast it and brought actors in. I wasn't involved in auditioning for a table read. There was no purpose in that at all. None of these actors are necessarily going to be in the film. I'll audition. We're still trying to look for the best person for each role, even for a table read. But I didn't offer any input. It was just a question of, can you get twenty-five actors in a room willing to read for free on a Saturday afternoon?

We read the script in about an hour and a half, mostly to hear it and get a sense of what was working and what wasn't. The writer was there. We also wanted to select a few scenes for the director's test, and in many ways it demonstrated to Disney that this is a great piece, and definitely something to do.

After Dawn introduced herself and me as the director, I said a few words. I said that I was happy everyone made themselves available, I talked about what I thought the script was about, and what I wanted from the reading, which was to explore the humor in the script and have fun with it. Then I read the scene descriptions, etc., and the actors read their dialogue.

Afterward they got up and left me, Dawn, Tim Reid, Earl, Susan Landau—the creative team—to sit around and chat a little bit. We felt very good about it. We talked about the four scenes that we like for the director's test, and we'll probably do two of them and modify one, a big scene which we'll probably try to simplify a little bit. That way we can do two if not three scenes in a day, probably two to three weeks from now.

I came home and passed out. I was so exhausted, from just the adrenaline of it.

I'll meet in the next week with some possible crew people for it. We talked about casting—which actors from the table read would be good for this, or if there is someone else we should meet with.

The contract says the test cannot run more than two days, but we're looking to do it in one long day. The real objective here is to highlight the humor. I'm going to look to be creative directing-wise, but I'm going to be primarily concerned with directing the actors for the comedic timing of the piece. I think all of us are being tested—Steel Pictures because they are going to be producing it, so getting the best or right people is their objective as much as it is mine. Were the director's test tomorrow, I'd be ready.

We're moving along on the actual *Power of No* script as well, revising it. That's the other thing I've been doing. We have the rewrite outlined and Tina Andrews, the writer, is pretty much ready to go. We'll probably have the next draft of the script right after the test is done, and can almost be in preproduction. I don't think Tina's doing it for free. Whatever her deal was, was probably for a couple of drafts of the script.

When it rains it pours. I'm still taking meetings about other scripts. This is not guaranteed.

P. J. PESCE
July 23

I just drove down to Tucson and met some people, crew people. Some of them are working on *Tombstone*. It seemed like they were having a lot of trouble. They had fired the director [Kevin Jarre]. Everyone said the script sucked, it was dumb, that kind of shit. What a good way to kill the Western, by making it more and more gimmicky and idiotic.

We found places. Old Tucson is where we're going to go.

MPCA is still trying to get me to shoot it here. The start date is not official. Nothing's official with these jokers.

They're trying to push me now to sign this release form, and Kanter's taking his sweet time about looking at it. So it's been three days, and they're calling me three times a day saying, "You gotta sign this, you gotta sign this, so we can get the money from the bank, we need the money from the bank. . . ."

Basically the contract is "in perpetuity for all time, throughout the universe." I am reamed. Anything I write is theirs, forever and ever. My lawyer is supposedly looking at it as well. And of course they're putting in it, "There must be nudity. Director acknowledges there must be nudity in the film." It's kind of lame. I mean, if they would stop making it such an issue, it might not be so bad. But it just becomes embarrassing, the whole focus of the movie.

They keep telling me I have to wait for them to finish reshoots on some other movie before I can bust their chops and start casting and everything. Krevoy told me yesterday he thinks he can get more money. It's endless. But I'm planning on going ahead in September. This coming week I'm going to start storyboarding.

ROBERT BENTON, Writer-Director

The Western just sort of disappeared overnight and then has come back. You'll always see Westerns and genre movies. They may not have the place they once had in American culture but they will always be there. They speak to a certain kind of American notion of a lawless past, of a rural past with rigorous Protestant belief on one hand and outlaw subtext on the other. That conflict between good and evil is so clear-cut in a Western. All genre movies are about value systems, underneath.

JOHN MCINTYRE
August 9

I'm not really with Duck Soup anymore. There was just no work coming in. So people have been bailing.

I'm starting Wednesday at a place called FilmRoman. They do *The Simpsons* and now they're doing *The Critic*, with Jon Lovitz.

I'm doing timing. I take the storyboards and divide up where the action goes. They do the animation in Korea, and often they miss the jokes or little pieces of business.

As for the director's reel, Duck Soup says there's no money to do it, although they claim they're committed to the Fossil watch campaign, which I spent a month and a half on. But they only have one director left, so they're obviously in trouble.

I just submitted a thirty-second piece to an MTV contest. The contest was to do something about bigotry or gender prejudice. It was a good thing to do, and I'll find out in September how I did. Either way it's good for my book. Who knows? If *Beavis and Butt-head* can get on the air, anything's possible.

LIZ CANE
August 10

I'm writing a new script, about a mother and daughter. I'm writing it alone—sort of—but talking to my father about it a lot. I'm trying to finish the script by next month.

I sent *That's What Women Want* to the festival in Montreal and should hear about that in the fall. I may submit my new script to the Sundance workshop, although I hear it's real competitive.

My friend Rory Kelly just got a million-dollar film. It's called *Sleep With Me*. He got all of his poker friends, including Mike Steinberg [director of *Bodies, Rest & Motion*], to each write a scene, and it will take place in "real time." Neal Jimenez is involved, too. Eric Stoltz, Meg Tilly, and Adrienne Shelly are in it.

MARCO WILLIAMS
August 11

The director's test was postponed. It was supposed to be two weeks ago, but one of the actors had a couple of other screen tests. So now it's supposed to happen next Wednesday, in one day. One exhausting, nerve-wracking day.

LISA KLEIN
August 20

Lovestruck has not gone out.

We got a new agent, Cindy Turtle at the Turtle Agency. They're big in TV. Peter and I had a good feeling with them immediately. We just clicked, and signed with them last week.

We wanted to send it out with me as writer and Peter as director, but we're not naive enough to insist on that. One will eventually have to do something to the exclusion of the other.

Cindy loves *Radio Wars* and likes *Lovestruck*. And the fact that she didn't love *Fat City* was actually a plus for me, because *I* don't love *Fat City*. They thought it showed accomplished writing, but it's not my best calling card.

P. J. PESCE
August 23

They have given me a start date of October 11 for *The Desperate Trail*. But they've given me dates before.

I saw *Amongst Friends* about five months ago, because I got to know Mike Bonvillain, the D.P. I thought it looked great, and told Brad Krevoy and Chad that I really wanted him to shoot the Western. They said, "No, we want so-and-so," etc. I took Brad with me to the screening, and there were stars around and everything. I introduced him to Mike, and Brad took me aside and said, "I wonder if he'd be interested in shooting your film." He totally forgot that I already had this conversation with him.

For The Desperate Trail, MPCA wanted to make an offer to Eric Roberts—$50,000–$75,000 for three weeks—as the marshal, Bill Speakes. Pesce lobbied for James Coburn. In the leads, Pesce sought Dylan McDermott and Elisabeth Shue, a friend, while MPCA suggested Patsy Kensit.

"She's expensive and she can't act, but she's HOT!" Krevoy told me.

MARCO WILLIAMS
August 23

I did the test last Wednesday. I would say it went very well.

It was a long day, but that was to be expected. We did three scenes, which were about ten script pages. It was a couple of days' worth of work. If it was really a movie it would have been a week's worth of work. But we did it in one day, and we had a lot of fun.

I've been looking at dailies, wishing I had done some things differently, or done retakes from the top. Cutting it, I wish there was some more coverage. But overall I think it was a success.

I had a little trouble with the lead actress. It wasn't that she wasn't as good as we thought she would be, as much as that she didn't come with her "game face" on. She hadn't quite taken it seriously, wasn't really committed, and didn't take direction very well. That was kind of a letdown. It was frustrating. She would have to show me a whole lot for me to use her for the film. In my estimation, if this was a test for my sake, she failed it. It's too bad, because she's talented. But perhaps she didn't have enough experience as a film actress.

I feel that it reflects on me that she didn't take it quite seriously, but this test is not a screen test for actors, it's much more about directing. So sometimes you might wonder why the actor isn't as good, but I have editing to work it out and she was surrounded by some great people. The scenes will stand up despite my frustration with her.

I think it could have been better. For instance, she didn't quite know any of her lines. She got so enamored with ad-libbing stuff that she never read any of her lines verbatim. That made it very hard to say, "Okay, I want this action to happen now," because she wasn't saying the line that would trigger the action.

Quite honestly, if I was directing this and she had been "on" and it wasn't one day, I would have had a different tack. But I wasn't in a position to say, "Either get it together or you don't have a job," because the job was just that one day. So you figure out ways of doing it.

RANDA HAINES, Director

One thing I think anyone who wants to direct should do is take acting classes, if only to develop compassion for the actors. There are a lot of directors who treat actors very badly, and I think it's often because they don't understand what the actors do. And they're afraid of them, because we're dependent on them in a way. They have a lot of power. The more you can understand what they're doing and have compassion and respect for them, the better the communication will be, and the better the work will be.

We dressed a set on Disney's back lot, and then we did an interior on a stage. Dawn was there with all the producers. It was funny. In the morning, as it was their wont to observe since they are the producers, they were there in full force. But after a couple of hours I was just making movies, I wasn't paying attention to them. In the beginning I was, "Here, there, what do you think of this?"—soliciting their input and involving them, but after a certain point I was just making a movie. I consider it a movie, even though it was just scenes.

The Disney people showed up later, Gay Hirsch, Donald DeLine, and Alex Schwartz, who is a friend of mine but not associated with this particular project. They may have been there earlier but I was so involved I never saw them.

The editor started on Friday and hopefully at the end of today or tomorrow he'll have a cut to show me. And then by the end of this week I should have a director's cut, and we'll show it to Dawn. From what I understand, Disney is going to look at it on September eighth. So that gives us sixteen days or so.

It'll be in the neighborhood of ten minutes long, like a short film. We rehearsed on the seventeenth and shot on August eighteenth. It was about an eighteen-hour day.

Disney has a little more time than I would have liked to make a decision. It boils down to fifteen business days, so three weeks under an exclusive thing, and then thirty days with a preempt status, if I had something else. So it's effectively two months, a curious thing to me.

My feeling just from conversations all along is that Dawn is committed to making this movie, and I know she was very pleased with my work and is still committed to me as director. If Disney didn't want to do it, I have a sense that Dawn would like to take it somewhere else. I don't know how she is bound contractually or anything.

I really feel, in some sense, that this was as much a test of me as it was of the material. It's not obvious Touchstone or Disney material. I mean, there are enough references to female and male body parts that—I mean, the number of times people said "dick" or "pussy" just in the test is enough to make you think, "There's no way Disney is going to do this."

What's Love Got to Do With It was clearly an R movie, and I felt early on that Disney would have liked this to be PG-13. There's no nudity in it, and the violence will be minimal, but you couldn't do this story with "dork," you know, or something that sounds so stupid there would be no point in doing it. But we'll see.

I guess it's the way the movie business is, but I staked my whole summer on this thing, and at the rate we're going, if they were to say yes on September ninth, we wouldn't be shooting it until the beginning of the new year. So that's just six months of sitting around, as far as I'm concerned.

Although not really. This was great for me. If they don't want it, I'll certainly have a copy of this, and add something to my reel that shows that I can do comedy. Nobody else can now say, "Well, can you do comedy?" because I can say, "Well, here you go."

I guess I just want to do this already. It's like deep-sea fishing, and you've got a big one on the line. You don't want to get it practically to the boat and have it get off the hook.

ADAM DUBOV, Director

I think the main thing people are worried about is, are you going to have a nervous breakdown when the shit hits the fan? Are you going to crack? Are you going to run? These are very good questions—I'd ask them, too. Can you handle the budget and the pressure, and make really difficult choices on the spot? Because that's what you're going to have to do.

When it came down to the point where I was actually going to get the chance to direct a feature, I wondered about it myself. It worried me, because you don't know. You really don't know until you do it.

JOHN KEITEL
September 1

Carter and I broke up.

Things were not like they seemed between us. We broke up July fifth and since then have slept in separate bedrooms.

He got a $30,000 trust fund check and didn't tell me, and that was the last straw. I just said, "That is the last time I am going to emotionally support you through anything. I will never again make myself emotionally available for your problems."

I want to be "married," and have kids. I know a couple of lesbians who are candidates. We've danced around the subject.

I met with my thesis advisor at USC, Doe Mayer. I agreed with all of her suggestions about the script. They were all right, especially that the female lead character needs changing. Another person thinks she should be eradicated.

One way that people criticize the script is that they rip it, constructively. It's hard to hear but it's really okay. I need it.

I haven't heard from Miramax yet.

BERNARD JOFFA
September 15

I went to South Africa to take care of my father. He's got cancer, so the doctors felt I should come. Fortunately, he's now on very good medication, and he's stable.

Workwise, zero. I've put all my energy into my dad's health right now. I was there two months.

I'm seeing my agent today and getting back to everyone now.

LIZ CANE
September 23

I just finished my script and sent it to Sundance. I guess it takes a while to hear from them. I feel pretty good about it. It's called *Tripping with Mom*. It's a mother-daughter road trip.

Now I'm in a strange place. I know there are some weaknesses. I guess I need to work on it a little bit and get it out to friends. It feels good. I've never finished a feature, so it's "doable." It makes it more real, somehow, to have done it.

I have to just keep thinking about it and exploring other possibilities. But I think overall the structure is pretty good. It's kind of a drama with some humor.

You remember about a year ago I was talking about expanding *That's What Women Want* into a feature, and I kept trying to, off and on? In a way, this has elements and deals with some of the issues that the short film did. The short film was kind of a leaping-off point to writing this one. But there's a lot more character, which the short didn't have at all. So that was kind of new to me.

The script could be commercial, but it's written more as an independent, with unconventional structure. It might be a little harder for a Hollywood-type person to read. So I'm not sure what to do on that. It has a couple of good roles for women. I'll get it to a few friends and see what they think.

I've been looking at the computer so much my eyes are burning. It's all I was doing for two weeks at the end. I wasn't letting myself read the paper or anything.

I've shown it to three people who liked it. They thought it was really good. But those are people that are close to me.

That's What Women Want is going to be screened at Montreal. I may go. It depends upon my work situation, but I'd like to.

I was just assistant-editing for Caveh Zahedi. He did a feature, *A Little Stiff,* and he's doing another called *I Don't Hate Las Vegas Anymore.* He hired me for a while to put away trims and stuff. It was fun.

My other little part-time job, which goes on during the academic year, has started up again. I'm kind of looking, kind of not looking. I'm not desperate yet.

P. J. PESCE
September 24

The last two weeks have been crucial. We got the extra money, dependent on Sam Elliott's involvement.

He read the script and said, "Not interested. Don't want to play a bad guy—not the kind of Western I want to make. The kind I want to make is like *Conagher.* I care about how real it is. It's the difference between *McCabe & Mrs. Miller* and the Leone films."

So we're kind of blown out of the water. We made him a very substantial offer, and he blew it off. So we started looking around for other things.

We were losing the location, meanwhile, and all of these people that wanted to work for us were getting other job offers. It's all been kind of fucked up. So we went back to Trimark—"Skidmark"—and they took two or three days and came back with a list of people who they would okay. After three more days they said, "Forget it—nobody will work, for us, except Sam Elliott. If you don't get him, we don't want to make the movie."

So we went back yesterday afternoon with double the money and an offer to let him make another movie of his choice at MPCA, because they realize that Sam Elliott is the big draw here. And now Elliott is like, "Well . . . what's this guy done? If he's such a great director and he knows Marty Scorsese, what's he done that I can look at?" So they're going to give him my short film. I told them *not* to let him see *Body Waves.* And now we'll see.

And I've got to write him a letter saying that I think he's great. I mean, he is good, he's definitely good, but that's never meant anything to anyone in the past. I don't know why he means money. I can't image why. Apparently they believe he has foreign appeal. And definitely television.

From Pesce's letter to Sam Elliott:
Dear Sam:
First off, I'd like to tell you in what high esteem I hold your production of *Conagher*. I've watched it several times on laser disc. . . . Your performance is simple, direct, and truthful. . . .

The type of movie I want to make is a kind of hybrid between *Conagher* and *McCabe & Mrs. Miller* on the one side, and *The Good, the Bad, and the Ugly* on the other. . . .

When Speakes dies at the end of the movie, the audience shouldn't cheer or feel relieved—I will have failed if that is the case—I would like them to feel sadness and inevitability, as in Greek tragedy, where a strong and heroic man has been brought down by the forces of fate and his tenacious allegiance to his family, right or wrong. . . .

My teachers in film school, Martin Scorsese and Milos Forman, always taught me to have the utmost respect for my actors, who are above all my collaborators in creating a world, a universe, on screen. I would attempt to address any questions, problems, suggestions or ideas you have concerning our movie, because I know of no other way to do the best work possible.

With Kind Regards,
(signed)
Paul Pesce Jr.

GARY ROSS, Screenwriter

There was a moment at which we could have cast another actor in *Big*—not Tom Hanks—and been the first [boy-man body switch movie], or waited for Tom and been last. And I argued vociferously to wait for Tom and be last. I just wanted to see my movie done right.

It turned out to be a savvy decision, but there was nothing savvy about my reasoning. I didn't know when I was going to get another movie made, and I just wanted to see the right guy in the part. And if we didn't make any money, at least I would have this piece of film that would have been realized right. It turns out to be the wisest thing I could have done—but I had no idea at the time.

MARCO WILLIAMS
September 27

I was in Amsterdam, and then a couple of days in Berlin. I had actually planned to stay a little longer in Europe. I was going to go to Munich, but I had to come back for a meeting.

The *Power of No* saga is becoming epic, sort of like "development hell." I know they liked the test. They liked it a lot, and now, before deciding to green-light the picture, they want to see another draft of the script. So I was called back to begin supervising that.

And that's kind of where we are. I got some notes from Steel Pictures personnel, and I had my own notes, and a couple of notes from Disney people. All along they paid me a small fee, but it's so absurd. By the time this is all done, I should have worked at McDonald's. They are getting so much for so little, it's killing me. I like to gamble, but I don't like to have my chain yanked.

It's fine. It's part of the game, and I understand that. I'd just like it to be a little clearer and occasionally on terms that are more to my satisfaction than to other people's.

I'm sure it couldn't hurt if *Cool Runnings* [Dawn Steel's production] opens huge. I suspect that some of the delay is also related to *Cool Runnings*—that if it does very well, Dawn at least has leverage, and if it does poorly then they will have a reason to sort of say, "Well, we don't think so."

These films are not at all the same. Initially *The Power of No* was much more a comedy, but after doing the test it became clear that it needs to be less comedy and more dramedy. But I think *Cool Runnings* will help some, in that there will be some corollary one way or the other, I really do. I'm going to a screening of it tonight, so I'll decide if it can be a barometer. I hear it's funny, and good.

The preview stuff has been great. It's just whether audiences will want to spend the money. [*Cool Runnings* was, ultimately, a modest hit.]

In August, Dawn Steel, on tour promoting her autobiography, They Can Kill You, But They Can't Eat You, *had announced* The Power of No *as her follow-up to* Cool Runnings *in both the* New York Times *and the* Los Angeles Times.

Dawn is all over the place talking about her next picture as *The Power of No*, on the book tour. Whether that's the Power of Determination at work, I don't know.

I haven't read Dawn's book. I don't read books like that in general. I've been meaning to get a copy so she can sign it, just for the sake of it. I read the introduction. She has a wonderful quote from Emerson in the beginning. [The source of the quote is actually unknown.] It was something to the effect that only those who are willing to risk something stand to achieve greatness. I don't remember exactly what it is, but I was very touched by it.

BERNARD JOFFA
October 6

Joffa fills in the events of the previous three months:

My dad was having some problem with his stomach. Nobody could sort out what the problem was, so they ran a series of tests and found a blockage in his stomach and opened him up and operated. My mother called, crying, and said, "Bernard, terrible news. Our worst fears are true. Dad's got cancer, it's all over his stomach, liver, and kidneys." She gave me the doctor's number. I phoned him and he said, "You should come home."

They removed a major cancer from his stomach, whatever they could, and closed up his stomach. Whether it's going to be a month or two months, they didn't know.

So we all got into the plane—me, my sisters, fourteen of us. Within twelve hours of the phone call, we were all on the flight, my two sisters from San Diego, their husbands, their five kids, my brother from Johannesburg and his kids. We all arrived within twenty-four hours of the surgery. We all stayed in the same place, upstairs and downstairs.

When we got home he had just come around from his surgery. My sister had bought him a little Sony Discman, and I went to Tower Records and bought twenty comedy CDs. Woody Allen, Lenny Bruce, Monty Python.

Supposedly, we went home for a funeral. It was a shocking thing in my life. People don't die, friends and family don't die.

He started getting into the CDs, the power of positivity and humor. If you can laugh you can get through crisis.

We got literature and started becoming experts in cancer. There were about one hundred twelve items Adelle Davis recommended for diet which we had to run around and get and mix into this concoction.

A friend of the family put us in touch with Dick Block of H&R Block. Fifteen years ago he got stomach and lung cancer. He sold his business and put all of his money into cancer research, opened a hospital in Texas, another one somewhere else. He goes around lecturing and writes books. He said we needed to get [Dad] on a new drug called leucovorin, which was developed for leukemia, but they found, when using it in chemotherapy, that it flushes out the dead cancer cells. He said, "If you can't get the drug in South Africa, I will personally pay for your father to come and get the drug in America." A helluva thing to say to a stranger!

Anyway, we found out that it had just arrived at a teaching hospital, but it's experimental. It had just been passed by the FDA in America, not so in South Africa. Every country has its own FDA procedure. So we went to an oncologist, and he said he was willing to put him on this every two or three weeks, and we'll see how it goes.

My dad had a lot of little skin lesions. The top of his head had lots and lots of bumps. Within two weeks of the first treatment, all of these bumps started falling off of his head! And every mark disappeared. We thought, if this is what's happening outside, we wonder what it's doing inside. He put on three and one-half kilos—a man who is meant be losing weight and dying—and last week he climbed Table Mountain. We all took an airplane to a little town for my nephew's bar mitzvah. My dad is well on his way to recovery now.

It's an unbelievable story. What I have just witnessed says never, ever, listen to a doctor who says there is nothing that can be done, because all that means is, "I can't do anything."

My nephew, a two-year-old kid, was in a way the most amazing contribution to my dad's remarkable recovery—because he wasn't walking on eggshells, but being very real. We all left in a lot better shape than when we arrived. We all went for a funeral, and we ended up having a party for two and a half months. It was the party of my life. I have never yet been on such a high.

When I came back to California, I crashed. I was alone, and my home was empty. I had seemingly no purpose, no mission, and because of my addictive personality I had become addicted to taking care of a dying man. So regarding my film work, I threw it out the window. But I'm sure this will make me stronger and wiser.

The feedback on the *Home Free* script was that a lot of people love the writing, but everybody who has read it said, "We would like to consider you for another project. Obviously we cannot make this film, because it is not commercial." And I said, "What do you mean, 'obviously'?" I never saw it as being uncommercial. For me, this was a big reality in Hollywood, understanding that "commercial" means precisely that. It's got to be sold before you even begin to make it. It's got to be a product, a book, a Snapple, or something. That's what "commercial" means.

I was terribly upset at first. Paramount came back and said, "Thank you for the experience, I really loved reading this screen-play, great work, bring us something that's commercial." And that upset me. I thought it would make a really nice film.

Cool Runnings is a cool movie. I haven't seen it, but when I read about the bobsled team from Jamaica that went to the winter Olympics, for me that was enough of an idea to make a successful film. It's wonderful, it's glorious. But will it have any effect on my film? No, I don't think so. Who knows? Doctors don't know about cancer, and studios don't know about films.

My agent, Ronda Gomez, loved the first two acts of *Home Free*. She loved all the South African stuff. She didn't like the American stuff at all, and said that if the whole film was about the South African stuff, she could get behind it. But even then, it's difficult. She thinks it's going to be a tough sell, a virtually impossible sell. It's put a bit of a damper on things.

Ronda is a very busy lady. And she'll be there when it's right for her to be there. She can't spend a lot of time getting me to rewrite my screenplay. If we want to get it to any name, Ronda will do it in a second. But she feels it's going to be a very difficult sell. And she knows. This is what she does, all the time.

Ronda will help us, but she's saying there's a certain amount of work we have to do as well, like get a budget together. And until we get a budget, she can't start taking it to producers, because it makes a fool of her. She said, "I'll give you all the help that's available when you're more focused as to the way this picture's going."

Another problem that came back is, "Who the hell is Sydney Maree, that we should make a film about his life?" I never thought about that. You go to the movie and you find out about this guy. But the Hollywood system seems to say, "No, you can't make a film about an unknown. If it's going to be about a real person, we have to know about him beforehand." Which is bullshit, right? It's a marketing ploy. They're looking for an angle to sell it.

What I've realized is that you can't trash Hollywood. You need them, they need you. The fact that I'm not getting my first screenplay made into a movie is nothing to get depressed about. I must continue, and not only work with this one film. I must look at more screenplays, because Hollywood is about having a number of screenplays, especially when you're an unknown. You keep pitching.

Greg is upset because he's written ten produced features, and he feels this is the best work he's ever done. So what he perceives as his best work turns out to be the only one that can't get made.

Next, I want to write something that will get made. I don't think it's a matter of relearning about screenplays, it's about writing a screenplay that's commercial. It's not the execution of a screenplay that makes it commercial. I don't think I could write the Sydney Maree story and make it necessarily more commercial. It will always be "Who's Sydney Maree?"

But I mustn't be bitter, and I'm not bitter with this system. I'm going to find my little spot within it. I was floored for a period when I got back—the reality of coming back to Hollywood and thinking, "Fuck, what am I going to do for the rest of my life?" Now is the time to get onto welfare. It's very hard, I know it, but that's the way it is, and what it is and who I am. I've just got to get through the hard periods, and can't abuse myself with chemicals, which is what I used to do.

We've spoken about my alcoholism before? It's not a big deal. Everybody's an alcoholic in this business! I would have gone back into that.

Cedric Scott, who's Poitier's partner, loved the screenplay and said, "Please, can we give it to Denzel?" He knows him. He asked if we could keep it away from other people until Denzel has read it. We were very excited about that, and that's what we did—we kept it away while I was in South Africa, for two and a half months, because Denzel won't read anything until he finishes shooting *The Pelican Brief.*

Denzel eventually got to read it about two weeks ago, and he loved it. He liked it a lot. He said he doesn't think he can play an athlete, especially at the age of eighteen or nineteen years old. And secondly, he said he doesn't want to play real people anymore after *Malcolm X.* He doesn't want to portray a legend. It's too difficult to match up. He has his reasons, and I respect that. He did like it. But the moment he said he's not interested is when Poitier and Cedric Scott lost interest as well. For them, it was a vehicle to make a film with Denzel.

So it's not going to be a big studio picture. More than likely, if it gets made it will be a low-budget independent, or maybe on HBO or Showtime. That would be realistic for an unknown director and unknown everything. I looked too big at first.

Alfre Woodard was in *Bopha!* I was blown away. I had never seen her, I don't know her work . . . or do I? She's great. She would be Susan, Sydney's mother. In *Bopha!* she played an African woman, from Soweto, which is really hard, because everyone thinks they can do an African accent, but it's very difficult. She played this role unbelievably. I think she would be better than almost any South African actress.

I was talking to an agent this morning, and said maybe this is a way to go, to get people attached. It's being sent now to Wesley Snipes. I don't see Wesley as being the right actor for the job. Sydney's more like a victim role, and Wesley's not a victim. His characters are always big and strong. But I must at least give him the opportunity to read it. If that's what makes it commercial, that's not such a compromise. I mean, he's a damn good actor, but he's not the guy I saw as Sydney Maree. I'm sure he could do a very good job. It's arrogant of me not to entertain the thought of sending it to him. Maybe that's what I've learned. That's what commercialism is.

Now I'll go the second route, taking it to other people. The fact that Denzel isn't doing it doesn't mean it's not going to get made. It's not a terrible script, I know that. There are nice qualities to it. It's a first draft. With a few rewrites it could get better. It can be a low-budget film. Route B is not the ideal situation, which would have been a studio, with Denzel. But that's not going to happen.

I woke up yesterday and suddenly have all of this power and energy back that I had lost. In this business of Hollywood, you can lose it completely. It happens to people all the time. I lost it. I came back from Africa and for two weeks I was terribly, terribly depressed. I was in a really, really dark place. Yesterday I woke up and started smelling the beautiful fragrance of plants outside my window. I thought, "This is a sign—this is amazing!"

I'm not getting this energy out of any indication from Hollywood that I am making a film. It's just an indication from myself that I'm okay, happy to be alive. Being in South Africa for two and a half months with a so-called "dying man" put me in touch with life more than anything. I had my little death for two weeks, then woke up.

STEVEN STARR, Director

Look how many attempts were made to duplicate the success of *Rocky*. You can't shake a stick at the lightning-in-a-bottle quality of this business. We can all sit here and try to replicate the $800,000 fairy tale versus the $75 million windfall, but that's the nature of the business. I'm certainly a strong believer in that idea "Nobody knows anything" [usually attributed to screenwriter William Goldman]. If they did, we would be churning them out as we speak.

It does come down to the audience, and that's what makes it such a joy and a nightmare. I made a movie that's very heartfelt to me. Is the audience going to respond? Who knows?—That's the reality. Stallone made a movie that was very heartfelt to him. I do not believe that he sat in his bed at night going, "This is going to spawn a career where I'll be making sequels, and ten million dollars a movie." No way. It came from the heart.

JOHN KEITEL
October 11

I went to a festival in Florida and my father was there to see *An All-American Story*. I hadn't seen him in three years. He remarried, and it was so weird, the wife was telling me about her son—he's gay and forty-six and not dealing with it very well—and she said, "He needs a community like that [the people in the film]."

There was a street fair on Sunday, and my Dad said, "Yeah, we have to go down there and see more films." We had passes, and they saw the Gay Men's Chorus. They loved it—they were giving them standing ovations. It just was a *trip*, for me to observe this in my family. I've been incredibly lucky with my family, if that's the right word. I mean, people can't believe it isn't an issue in my family that I'm gay.

The film screened at the Tampa Theatre, which is an incredibly beautiful, ornate old theatre that was renovated. I introduced my father, and he stood up before the film.

He lives in Republicanville, he's a member of a country club. A golfer. He's showing all of his friends my film on video. He's like that, he's a character.

My relationship with him was pretty much nonexistent, on the surface as opposed to interactive. I don't think it's unusual, even for people who don't have divorced parents. Father relationships are bizarre.

I held it against him for not coming to my college graduation and lying about the reasons. He just didn't want to be bothered with coming out there. Then when I confronted him, he went nuts over it, and I just said, "That's it, I can't be bothered with this." So I have sort of been punishing him by being inaccessible.

He's been pretty tenacious at times, and finally called the café recently looking for me.

I told my parents about me and Carter, but they both seem to think it's all going to work out. Carter and I are still living together. We're very civil. There's a level of communication that wasn't there before. I'm reticent, though, to get back together. Things are working in a way they hadn't before, given the context we're now "living broken up," if that makes sense.

He has an impetus. He's in therapy. I'm not. He definitely wants things to continue, but I'm not sold. Because when I start getting sold, something happens. I think the key here—as with a lot of relationships—is the financial end. I'm pretty firm in my belief that he uses money as a controlling mechanism, and he doesn't quite realize it, in the way his father used money with him.

I'm seeing life clearly, in a way that I haven't. My peripheral vision is operating. I couldn't tell you what destiny holds for the two of us. We're both pretty strong in our convictions and stubbornness, and we're both independent and want to steer. It's less obvious how I try to manipulate, so I may be more difficult to deal with. What can I say? It's life.

I'm also trying to find the fire to get back into this project. Jeff Kurtz from Miramax wants to see what I do now. He said *Ground Zero* is hard to pull off and I should focus on the two main characters, and then somewhere down the line I can be Robert Altman and make my *Nashville*. But he really likes it and wants to see what I do. He was the last person I talked to who emphasized the focusing thing. So I'm getting the message, to go with these two characters.

I went up to the Notre Dame game when I was back at Stanford recently, so I was back on campus, and I thought to myself, "Think of these two characters as Stanford students, which is what you know. Think about where they would live, who they would be, *here*. Forget a school you're not familiar with." And as soon as I started doing that I started to really feel it, it started pumping in a way. I was thinking, this is where she'd live and that's where he'd live, and this is the geography of their lives. It made it all seem a lot simpler to me. So maybe I should think of it in terms of if it

happened on that campus, even if it doesn't, for the sake of this
rewrite.

KEVA ROSENFELD, Director

The first big lesson I learned was, never sink your own
money into a project. Because two years after I started
making my first film, I was still borrowing $2,000 here,
$1,000 there, trying to finish the movie. Once you put your
own money into a movie, the buyer on the other end has no
vested interest—there's no reason for them to help you out.

Somehow I piecemealed the thing together. I got a
$20,000 grant. It cost $40,000 or $50,000. It was an hour
long. I broke even. If I made anything, it was $1,000. But
that's not why I made it.

P. J. PESCE
October 15

Sam Elliott just backed out.

This afternoon I called him, because he called me yesterday and
said, "Where's the script? I want the new script, I'm really excited.
I want to get to work." I sent over the script last night. This
morning I called him to see if he got the script and read it. He's like
"Yeah . . ." I thought, "Uh-oh, that didn't sound good." He said,
"I don't know . . . I'm going to have to back out of this. I'm not
into it, and I really gotta get into it, and I feel terrible about it," and
blah-blah-blah, and then he gave me, like, fifteen different excuses.

We'd had breakfast together, which was great, a mutual appreciation society. Sam loved my short film, he saw my long hair and
said, "I can tell we're going to get along." He said he had some
troubles with the character and how mean he was, and I said I
would gladly go over that and adjust it, sit down with him and
rework it. He said that was fine.

MPCA told me at about eleven this morning, and I just kept it
to myself until I spoke to the agents this evening, and then told
them. Kanter was freaked—like, "What?!?" Patrick Whitesall, the

agent who has been dealing with Sam and bringing him along the whole way, is in Boston, unfortunately, so I got this other agent to deal with it.

When I spoke to Sam I left it, "Why don't you just think about it some more?" and he told me he would read the script again and call me later today. Well, he never called back and I didn't expect that he would. When I spoke to the agent she basically said that he said, "You have to tell him that I'm not going to make the movie."

GARY ROSS, Screenwriter

In terms of moral ambiguity, and rooting interests, I think everyone's always advocated a strong hero, and heroes winning. Ironically, I know that people think I make very mainstream movies, but I had a lot of conversations about the end of *Big* being disappointing. "Could the woman become a little kid at the end in order to stay with him?" and all sorts of nonsense. I mean, it is a sad ending. But I would argue with the studio that so was *Casablanca*'s and it kind of worked.

An audience doesn't necessarily want a "happy" ending. That's the biggest misnomer in the world. An audience wants a satisfying ending—you just want to understand the reason for it, feel the behavior is motivated, and take something out of it. If what they take out is bittersweet, that's as satisfying an ending as a happy ending.

He got real wimpy. It's a drag, but Whitesall, who's also at UTA [Pesce's agency], seems to think we can make a last attempt here. I'm going to write another one of my famous letters.

Kanter got Sam involved as much as anyone can. He spoke to the agent and really got behind me and said how great I was, and how great the script was, and got the agent to submit it to him, with an offer from MPCA [$225,000].

Whitesall was really bummed with this all. Now what he suggested is that I write Sam another letter and address each one of his concerns. He thinks there's a chance. We've already been through this once—Sam said no, then he said yes, now he's saying no again.

And even when he said no today, and I said, "C'mon, we should work on this," he said, "I'll read it again."

You just have to remember that no matter what the guy appears like, and no matter how cool he seems when I sit down with him, he still is an actor, with all of the mammoth insecurities that every actor has. Otherwise he wouldn't be doing what he does for a living, going out in front of the cameras and wanting everyone to like him.

Pesce did write the letter to Sam Elliott—a longer one than his first— which said, in part:

> Dear Sam:
>
> You know I hold your talent and seriousness about your work in the highest regard. It's for that reason that I have all along insisted on having you play the role of Bill Speakes, and no one else. . . .
>
> Our agreement was that you and I would stick together on this thing and make the movie that *we, you and I*, want to make. . . .
>
> As the director, as the leader, I'm here to serve the production, to serve you and everyone else. . . .
>
> Are you worried about the script, about your character? . . .
>
> I'm a filmmaker, not some hack, and not some green naive writer getting my first crack at directing. Shit, I've been making movies since I was a kid, since I was *fifteen*. I know what it's like to be in the heat of battle with not enough money. I did a feature for Roger Corman for $200,000 that looks better than a lot of three million dollar pictures. . . .
>
> Harvey Keitel did *Reservoir Dogs* because he believed in Quentin Tarantino, the film's writer and director. . . . You can be my Harvey Keitel—help me make this film—make this film *with* me—and I promise you you won't ever be ashamed or embarrassed of the work you do for me. . . .
>
> I'm asking you man to man to do me the courtesy of sitting down with myself and Chad Oman, the producer, and allowing us to talk with you about the budget and the films [MPCA] made on a shoestring, and how we plan to do this one; talk to us about any concerns you have with the script.

One meeting. Let us attempt to address any reservations you have.

> Most Sincerely and Respectfully,
> (signed)
> P. J. Pesce

I've got to somehow turn this around. I just don't know what I'm going to do. If this doesn't work, it's really dead, at least for this year. We're totally backed against the wall now in terms of time. We're scheduled for November seventeenth. So I don't know what the hell to do. It's really hard to get it up again. I've done this so many times at this point, I just feel like, what's the fucking point?

Of course, you read about guys who go through this shit all the time—Steve McQueen was in, then he was out, then he was in again, then he was out again, then he wound up doing the movie and it was great. I mean, Jesus Christ.

I was driving home and thinking, what else can I do? I only know how to direct movies. I don't know how to do anything else. I could be a haberdasher. I know this is what I want to do and I know that I'm good at it but, Christ, what it takes to do it is unbelievable. Just unbelievable.

FRANK DARABONT, Writer-Director

Tom Cruise was interested in playing the Andy Dufresne role in *The Shawshank Redemption* for a time. I met with him a number of times. He struck me as a particularly nice, down-to-earth guy—surprisingly so, given his circumstances. A feet-on-the-ground sort of guy who cares very much about what he does.

Ultimately he passed, and I can guess what his reasons were. My feeling was that he had a natural reticence about working with a first-time [theatrical feature] director. Let's face it—he's Tom Cruise. Can you blame him? I can't. He's got a fifteen-million-dollars-per-picture career to protect.

I ultimately didn't try to talk him into it. I respected his decision and, in a way, afterwards, thought this is probably for the best, because it is a quirky character piece, more of an ensemble piece than anything, and I suspected that having a star of that caliber—he's a very good actor, but he is also a star of an extraordinary caliber—in one of these roles would probably throw a certain imbalance into the film. It would not really be a movie about these guys in this prison and their friendship. It would be "the Tom Cruise movie."

The fact that Tom was interested kind of got out, and was mentioned in the trades, and suddenly I could sense it gearing up. I could already feel *Premiere* magazine tunneling under the prison to get inside the wall to find out what was going on moment to moment on the set.

When Tom declined to do the movie I thought, well, at least I won't have to deal with that kind of pressure. If you're a first-time director and Tom Cruise does your movie, the eyes of the world are upon you. If he doesn't, the eyes of the world are not upon you, you're just off doing your movie in relative anonymity, just going about your job. I'm sort of glad I didn't have helicopters flying over the prison with *Entertainment Tonight* cameras pointing at me.

MARCO WILLIAMS
October 18

Nothing's happened on *The Power of No.*

We did a rewrite on the script, and got notes from the Steel Pictures people. We wanted to ground the script more, find out what's at the core. Not make it quite as broad but more situational. Decisions about characters—what are the consequences of the plan to these men and women? We wrote a scene that we realized should be between the hero and heroine. I'll get the pages tomorrow.

Disney is uninvolved right now. What they do will depend on

their reaction to the material. [The successful opening of] *Cool Runnings* is there, but it really depends on the material.

The stripper project never panned out. There were some legal problems with the two women. They had huge demands and Disney was unwilling to work with them.

ICM set me up with Marty Brest but that didn't pan out. I think that until the Disney situation is resolved, no one really wants to get involved with me.

LISA KLEIN
October 25

I just wrote a *Seinfeld* I'm really excited about. It took me no time.

My agent says I should write a *Northern Exposure* or *Picket Fences* instead.

JOHN MCINTYRE
October 26

I'm doing animation timing at FilmRoman on *The Critic*, which is scheduled for January, so they're rushing to complete thirteen shows.

It's a different genre than commercial work, and a lot more exciting. The money is better—$1,000 a week.

P. J. PESCE
OCTOBER 26

There's been a lot of drama. Sam's back.

It was the letter I wrote him, the second one. After waiting a week or ten days I finally called him yesterday and said, "Hey— how's it going?" He said, "P.J., man—I gotta talk to you. I'm really sorry about everything." I said, "Oh, it's all right, don't worry about it." He said, "No, no, I just wanted to tell you, I really like you a lot, and I wish you all the best of luck, and I'd really like to work with you on something at some point." I said, "Yeah, okay, you know, we'll do it. I just wanted to see how you were, and see if you read my letter and what you thought of it."

He said, "I didn't get a letter. I only got a letter from the producer."

I said, "Really? That's fucked up. Why don't you just let me print it out and send it to you again? There are couple of things in it I wanted to just say and know that you knew it." It was a pretty long, impassioned plea. I think it was really well done.

So then I printed it out again [and arranged to have] some guy pick it up and bring it over to him. This morning I was woken up by my buzzer. I ran out and there was this messenger ready to leave, and he said, "Oh, P.J., you're here—what happened to the letter?" and I said, "Oh, man, here it is." It somehow got pushed through the mail slot back into my house. So I gave him the letter and he took off, and I figured that would be it, I would just give him the letter, and it would be as it was.

Today I met with these managers. I thought maybe I'll hire a manager and try to start moving something else along. So I puttered around the house a little bit because my meeting with them wasn't until noon, and then I had some breakfast and got into the shower. While I was in the shower, I was listening to Howard Stern really loudly, and I thought I heard the phone ring but I wasn't sure. So I just ignored it. And then I thought I heard it again, and I ignored it again and figured, fuck it. Then I got out of the shower and there were two messages on the machine.

The first was Sam—he said, "P.J., it's Sam. Why don't you give me a call?"—and the second was from Kanter, and he said, "Don't do anything. Don't call Chad, don't call Patrick Whitesall, just sit tight and wait for my call and say some more of your novenas."

I thought, huh, this is kind of interesting.

I dicked around and cleaned up a little, and forty-five minutes later there was a call. It was Kanter, and he said Sam was back in. He was all happy, but I just said, "Okay." I couldn't even get that excited. It was like, okay, that's another thing. Good, now keep moving along.

I went in, I called Chad just to get preproduction really going, and we got the U.P.M. [Unit Production Manager] moving and scheduling us to leave.

Then I called Sam later on and he said, "Hey, I really apologize for making us waste ten days," and I said, "Don't even think about it, let's just get to work," and he said, "You're a helluva personality." I said, "Oh, you just hold onto that letter. Maybe some day it'll be worth something." And he said, "Well, it couldn't be worth anything more than it means to me right now." It was cool. It was very cool.

November seventeenth is the start date. Twenty-four days. I come home for Christmas—in a box, probably. Kanter said [to MPCA], "Ink the fucking deal and announce it in the trades, if you please." So Chad and Patrick were dealing with that today. We hired a casting director today, and there is so much minutiae. Should I hire Sam a costume guy? He really wants him and I want to please him, and I can't back down as regards money. He was so worried about the money to make the movie, and being able to do a good job, and how committed they are to that. In fact, I'd rather use his costume guy and spend a little money.

Right at this moment these guys are going behind Trimark's back in Milan to the Miramax guys, going back to them and trying to get them to cough up $3 million instead of $2 million to do the movie, and kind of leaving Trimark cold.

Sam doesn't know who the fuck MPCA are.

At this moment I'm a little terrified because I have so much to do and so little time to do it. I met with Lara Flynn Boyle's mom and agent tonight. She's really hot for it, but she has also been offered a very small role in an Alan Parker movie [*The Road to Wellville*].

KEVA ROSENFELD, Director

A good trick for a first-time director is to ask really good actors to do something that they've never done. You get them to work a lot cheaper.

Everyone gets typecast. Like I was typecast as a guy who couldn't work with actors—I was a documentary filmmaker who couldn't work with actors. Chris Lloyd is always the mad scientist. I wanted him to do a normal guy in *Twenty Bucks*, and he loved it. He never gets offered the normal guy. Linda Hunt always plays authoritarians. She loved playing a character who had no control over her life. I did it by default. I didn't know this, but it's a good thing to know.

LIZ CANE
November 2

I did some post work on Caveh Zahedi's film, *I Don't Hate Las Vegas Anymore*, and then brought the print to the L.A. Sundance offices. It felt good to handle the film and do something like this. Caveh was out of town and couldn't do it.

I submitted my script and the short film to Sundance, and wrote a letter to [festival programming director] Geoff Gilmore. I think I will hear in a couple of weeks.

That's What Women Want was in competition at the Montreal International Festival of New Cinema—I think that's what it's called. It screened twice and there was lots of press. It was also accepted at the Bilbao Festival in Spain, and they're looking at it for the Hof Festival in Munich.

It's hard to get back to the rewrite. Things are happening, it's just slow.

A group of us from film school had a few regular meetings. Then one guy's father died, another got an assistant director job in Ethiopia, and two are going to Oklahoma to do paid research.

P. J. PESCE
November 4

Everything is sort of falling part. It's falling apart, falling together, it's crazy. I'm shooting in ten days. But it's definitely happening. During preproduction, I'll be very crazed.

I'm casting locals. We're talking to Craig Sheffer. He'd be good. I'm dealing with Elliott's best friend, this old cowboy R. L. Tolbert. I got a fifteen-page fax with his credits. He's a stunt man–wrangler. Sam sort of leaned on me. Sometimes people do that and the guy they want you to hire doesn't know anything, but this guy's great. He knows his shit. He's cool and helpful and respectful, a pleasure.

MPCA is doing their best. Trimark are the real boneheads. They're putting up two million bucks, doing a negative pickup with MPCA. I met the head, Mark Amin, once when I wrote a script for him.

We got the locations [in Santa Fe]. We're now casting, and

trying to find an effects person. I'm dealing with the little things. Unfortunately, I keep getting called away from my real intended gig, which is that I need to be working on the script, finalizing everything, and I fucking well need to be storyboarding.

Abrams is not really involved. He's my cowriter, and I'm going to put him in it [as an actor], but he's not really doing anything at this point. He's very excited, he's been really helpful. A couple of times he sat down with me—when I was up against the wall and I didn't know what I was doing, he worked on some rewrites with me for no money at all.

Elisabeth Shue is not into it. She's like, "Oh, P.J.'s movie." To other people I'm a big deal. To her, it's just P.J. Go figure.

I'm trying to get Frank Whaley out, he really wants to do a role. I think I'm going to have him play Walter, which I think would be very good.

What would help me? Another million bucks, another three days of shooting. Kanter's trying.

MARCO WILLIAMS
November 9

I've been supervising the editing of *Nana* [the South Africa documentary Williams has been producing] for the last few weeks, for three or four hours a day. They've changed the name. The latest is *Uncommon Ground*, with some long subtitle. They're trying to get it submitted to Sundance. It's a good thing for me to put my energies into. The director and I hadn't been seeing eye to eye, and now they need a fresh perspective. I'm the producer.

On November 3 a cover story in Daily Variety *reported, "Dawn Steel is expected to close a deal this week to head Turner Pictures."*

I had a meeting with Dawn last Friday. I called the meeting because it's always good to touch base and keep in contact. I tell her I need fifteen minutes.

I had two questions. One was that I had heard rumors that she was going to Turner and I wanted to know how that would affect the movie. She said she was amazed at what people wrote in the papers, and would not confirm or deny anything.

The other question was this. There was a fashion spread in the *New York Times* last week, and Dawn talked about how she only wears Armani underwear. So she happened to be wearing an Armani suit that day, and I asked her if she was wearing Armani underwear. She laughed and said that might constitute sexual harassment, and threatened to throw me out of the office.

I honestly don't know how she does everything she does—the book tour, the movies. What concerned me was what will happen if she becomes an executive. Then who produces the movie?

We just got the official revised first act, which was where the problems were. I've made a policy that the producers must submit script notes in writing, and it's amazing how tough it is for them. By doing that it forces them to commit to them. Disney has still not seen the new draft, and coupled with Dawn's movement there is pressure not to let this window of opportunity slip away. But it is frustrating because I'm not the writer, so there's only so much I can do.

Trey Ellis did a director's test for Touchstone on a project called *The Inkwell*. And John Payson did one for *Joe's Apartment*. He was a student of mine at Harvard. Neither of these projects got made. So I have heard that it's a convenient way for them to say no sometimes. They often have their mind made up already.

The Inkwell was subsequently directed by Matty Rich for Touchstone. Trey Ellis, the writer, asked that his name be removed from the script. Joe's Apartment, *a feature based on a one-minute film Payson did for MTV, was directed by Payson for Warner Brothers in 1995.*

P. J. PESCE
November 16

Though half of the people in the movie business claim they want to move to Santa Fe, I can tell you there will be no mass exodus until they get an airport. When they do, of course, the town won't be the same, and no one will want to move there anymore.

I flew to Albuquerque and drove to Santa Fe on the Tuesday before The Desperate Trail's *official start date.*

At 9:15 that night I walked into P. J. Pesce's suite at the Pichaco Plaza Hotel. Chain-smoking inexpensive cigars, he occasionally punched the keys of a PowerBook set up on a catering table. In the corner of the room stood Pesce's guitar case, bearing a bumper sticker reading EVIL GENIUS. *On couches across the room, several makeup and costume crew members conversed.*

At 9:30 Craig Sheffer and Linda Fiorentino, the film's leads, arrived. Sheffer has acted in sixteen films including Some Kind of Wonderful *and* The Program, *and the previous year made his most notable appearance to date, opposite Brad Pitt in Robert Redford's* A River Runs Through It. *Fiorentino first came to attention in* Vision Quest, *as the older love interest of Matthew Modine's high school wrestler. Since then her films have included Martin Scorsese's* After Hours *and Alan Rudolph's* The Moderns. *She has often played supporting roles which fit her natural demeanor—tough-on-the-outside, tender-on-the-inside urban Italian-American.*

Fiorentino was in good spirits, munching from a box of Cheez-Its. Sheffer, whose first two days of work would require several scenes on horseback, had a pinched nerve in his neck and shuffled around awkwardly. Lying down on Pesce's bed, he groaned, "I'm going to be great on the horse tomorrow, man." Sheffer did not want to try on his wardrobe. Pesce was agreeable but insisted that Sheffer's hair be cut that evening.

His costar consulted with the makeup people. "I usually use rice powder and Clinique—everything else makes my face break out," she warned them.

Fiorentino told me, "They called me last Thursday with the offer. I knew about the script. But, I mean, I've never done one this crazy, on such short notice. I've just been listening to the locals, trying to get the accent. They all talk the right way."

On the other side of the suite, Sheffer's coiffure began as Pesce looked on intently, puffing and pacing. "So," asked the actor of his director, "is this a Western or a parody of a Western?" "A parody? No way," Pesce replied brusquely. A few minutes later the Coen brothers were mentioned and Sheffer asked Pesce if he liked their work. "I love the Coen brothers," Pesce stated flatly, through a cloud of smoke.

Despite Pesce's conviction that Sheffer's mustache was inappropriate for the character of Jack Cooper, described in the shooting script as "open and gregarious, welcoming, intelligent," everyone in the room agreed that the mustache looked great. Sheffer said that several hairs had not grown in, however, and suggested that a brown eyebrow pencil be used the following morning, the first day of the shoot.

In the production office set up on the hotel's third floor, D.P. Mike Bonvillain offered me his perspective: "It's four times the budget of Amongst Friends *[Bonvillain's first feature], but I get the same money, and it's the same bullshit, squashed schedule."*

November 17

At 7:00 A.M. a crew of fifty had begun driving trucks and hauling equipment in freezing temperatures to the Bonanza Creek Ranch, sixteen miles south of Santa Fe. The Desperate Trail *was not the first Western to shoot exterior scenes here:* Wyatt Earp, Silverado *and* City Slickers, *among dozens of others, had used the location.*

There are reasons that journalists are not ordinarily invited to movie sets on the first day of shooting. In seven years covering the movie business, I never thought about what they might be. Then I observed the first day of The Desperate Trail.

It was more what I felt than what I saw. For one thing, I felt cold—really cold—as I'm sure the crew did, having underdressed in baseball jackets, many of which were souvenirs of various locally filmed "shows" they had worked on, like Sam Raimi's Army of Darkness *and the Western-themed* Back to the Future III.

The other palpable feeling was one of fear. After three weeks, a film crew is like a family, for better or worse. On the first day of shooting, the chain of command is being established, personalities are emerging, and responsibilities get dictated.

These things don't happen formally, of course—they just happen. And underneath it all is the knowledge that if something goes wrong early on, even on a low-budget picture, heads will roll.

When I arrived, the crew was positioned for the first shot at the precipice of a deep arroyo bisecting the hundreds of acres of the ranch. Sheffer's and Fiorentino's doubles, Ramon and Arizona, would ride together on horseback down into the arroyo. In the script, the scene followed the first action sequence, in which Fiorentino's character, Sarah, escapes a stagecoach robbery with Jack (Sheffer). This shot would precede a heated exchange in which the two blame one another for almost costing them their lives.

It was a long shot, and the doubles were able to face the camera because it was so far away. The sequence required the assistance of R. L. Tolbert,

Sam Elliott's friend and the production's horse wrangler. Tolbert would truck in several horses each day as they were needed and coach the actors as well as the animals they were handling.

Pesce had dressed for his part as director. "We went and bought new boots," said Chad Oman, the film's coproducer. "But P.J. panicked and wore his old ones today. He hated the idea of what it would look like if he showed up in brand-new boots." Completing Pesce's rather severe look was a full mustache and beard, a weathered Stetson, and a lined suede jacket like the one Dennis Weaver wore in McCloud.

As with most movie shoots, there are very few people for whom the experience is terribly interesting. Tessa Rodriguez, from Bronxville, New York, was a film loader. "I'm a schlepper," she says. "I just really, really want to be a D.P."

Then there was the guy from Pittsburgh who worked for the catering company, which would serve two meals daily—breakfast at around 5:15 A.M. and lunch at 11:00. "I came out here to be with my girlfriend and just sort of fell into this," he told me. "Movie people can be really strange. I worked on Natural Born Killers, the Oliver Stone movie. One day at lunch, Stone is sitting there about to eat, and he snaps at me, 'Craft Services!'—that's what he calls me. He says, 'Mustard!' Now the funny thing is, there were at least five different kinds of mustard on the table right in front of him. Dijon, French's, you name it."

Several takes of the opening shot were unusable. In one, the actors got caught in a bush on the way down the side of the arroyo; in another, the horse looked a bit too much like an unsteady burro toting tourists to the bottom of the Grand Canyon. Each take required between ten and fifteen minutes of setup. The crew became visibly antsy. On the sixth try, the horse and doubles bounded down the hill perfectly. "Cut—print!" Pesce shouted.

The next shot was a close-up of Jack (Sheffer) hiding under a ridge and scanning the horizon for his and Sarah's pursuers. Bonvillain moved the crew to the other side of the arroyo for this P.O.V. [point of view], which would be used as a reverse angle. Fitted with a harness, Bonvillain was tethered to a crew member above in case he slipped down the hill. "Have you ever worn one of these before?" asked the techie. "Best sex I ever had," Bonvillain coolly responded.

Between takes Pesce shared some of his feelings with me:

Sheffer and I had a major blowout. I really wanted him to shave the mustache. I mean, his character is described as "open and gregarious," and the mustache looked unfriendly. He said no. I said, "Think about it, I'll think about it."

I didn't sleep all night thinking about this fucking mustache. This morning I saw him, and I said, "Listen, I got bad news. The mustache has to go." He said, "Forget it." I said, "Excuse me?" He said he wasn't shaving it. He said, "Look, this is my seventeenth movie. It's your *first*." I said, "I don't care, that mustache is wrong for the character." He said, "Fine. Get another actor. I'm walking." I said, "Fine. I don't know how I can direct you if you won't give me what I want."

It was a real Mexican standoff. He's just a brat, a fucking arrogant brat.

Pesce rehearsed Sheffer and Fiorentino at the bottom of the arroyo, then climbed up to the ridge where Bonvillain had set up the camera. Satisfied with the composition, he called the actor. Sheffer got into position for his first closeup. The mustache—and he—had won.

Soon afterward, Pesce noticed that a P.A. had spelled his name wrong— "Pesh"—on the clapboard. "Spell my name right," he muttered without irony and annoyed by what the transgression might have represented.

Pesce's First A.D. was Chris Edmonds, an imposingly large Brit. On day one this was what he needed, someone to literally throw his weight around. Edmonds did not merely ask for silence before a take but would snap, "Folks, do I have to spell it out for you?!?"

Edmonds's rapport with Pesce was total. He was there to serve his master, though continuously harangued on his walkie-talkie by anyone and everyone else in the crew. Some of the pagers were temporarily put off; most were merely ignored until they interrupted again. Edmonds's main job was managing production triage.

As do virtually all feature-length motion pictures, The Desperate Trail *cost tens of thousands of dollars a day, an average of thirty-five thousand, according to producer Chad Oman, a twenty-eight-year-old SMU Finance major from Wichita Falls, Texas. Oman would be on the set for the shoot's duration.*

"Pesce's passion is what comes through—he just convinces you," Oman whispered, out of camera range. "A month ago, I was consoling him, telling him that if this wasn't happening, we would definitely find another project. But that meant nothing to him. He really wasn't thinking about anything else."

Oman described his relationship with Pesce as brotherly. "One day we were driving back after scouting a location. P. J. was doing this fake-hitting thing, where he would pretend to hit me in the face. On the third time he knocked my glasses off. I slapped him across the face and his glasses went flying. Then we got each other into a half-nelson, and had about a twenty-minute wrestling match in a car full of people."

At lunchtime Pesce and I ate in the trailer.

The shit that's gone down in the last two weeks has been unbelievable. This was a $1.1 million movie a month ago, and we were telling MPCA there was no way to do it. They wanted to cut the train stuff and the bank robbery. Everyone said we needed $1.6 million to do it. Then we got Sam Elliott, and everything changed. We went to Trimark. TNT offered $2.5 million, and we took it and just walked on Trimark.

I okayed Craig and Linda over the phone. Then I called Craig, and he didn't return my calls for a day and a half. I scheduled dinner with him here the first night and he blew me off. He had dinner with Linda instead.

So now we have this extra money and they asked me what I want to spend it on. "Well, I want an extra day for the stagecoach stuff, an extra day for the bank robbery, and more money for effects," I told them. This is after one day of shooting. They say, "How would you feel about replacing the lead actress?" The problem is that she only hits it when the camera is going, not in rehearsal. So that means I have to roll, roll, roll a lot of film. I'll have to pull a performance out of her.

Pesce wrapped the first day's shoot at 5:15, which frustrated him.

I didn't realize the days would be so short here. We blocked out a scene and then couldn't remember what we had done, so it was a washout.

If we had a chance to work together for a week before the shoot, none of that shit with the mustache would have happened. Sheffer and I didn't trust each other. We were like dogs, sniffing each other out. It was a pissing contest, and we were each afraid that the other would make us look bad. It's very hard to shoot a dramatic scene not having read the whole script together, because everything is out of context.

That night, when Chad Oman called Pesce in his room, Pesce asked him, "Can we give Frank Whaley some more money? It doesn't have to be a lot, just something." He also said, "Kanter didn't send me a telegram for the first day, for congratulations—nothing. . . . I'm a little surprised." He hung up.

Working in that arroyo was fucking hell, and that was an easy day. Wait until you see the stagecoach stuff.

ROBERT BENTON, Writer-Director

You have to pace yourself so carefully when you're shooting. It took me years of directing to learn that I have to have a kind of cool-down time between the time I see dailies and do business and have dinner with people. I have to have some time utterly alone.

I sit and shine my shoes every night. Twenty minutes when my mind is utterly blank. My eyes are open but nothing else is functioning. Then I'll sit and read, and take myself to some other world—remind myself there *is* another world out there.

I make sure that I am in bed between 9:30 and 10:00 and I am up at 4:30. I'll get up early and exercise for thirty minutes, and put myself together and go. I try very carefully to live a very disciplined and quiet life when I'm making pictures. Because from the time that car picks you up in the morning until the time that car drops you off in the evening, you're at a dead run. There's always something to be done, and it's seven days a week. It doesn't stop. And it requires an enormous amount of focus and energy and diplomatic skills and determination and flexibility.

November 18

At lunch on the second shooting day Pesce told me, "Things are going well. I think things will work out with Sheffer."

There did seem to be slightly more rapport. The two spent some time discussing Orson Welles's work. Sheffer also joked with Pesce: "People are going to say that the only reason you got to direct is that you're Joe Pesci's son."

Sheffer became more casual with the rest of the crew as well, to mixed results. Atop his horse at one point he told Bonvillain, "That is about the ugliest way you could possibly light me." Self-conscious about his small eyes and crow's feet, later Sheffer was told that his hair needed to be fixed, which he did himself. "Sheff, you do hair, you do lighting, you do it all," Pesce needled him.

At the end of the day, Sam Elliott arrived on the set, wearing a mustache that would have given Yosemite Sam a run for his money. Sheffer and he exchanged compliments about each other's work, as did Elliott and Fiorentino. Pesce and Elliott bear-hugged. When Fiorentino's stunt double Arizona introduced herself, Elliott quipped in his trademark mumble, "Well, I don't have to ask where you're from."

"P. J.'s the reason I'm here," Elliott told me. "It wasn't what he said in his letter but the way he said it. It's all about execution, you know what I mean?"

FRANK DARABONT, Writer-Director

In one scene in *The Shawshank Redemption* Morgan Freeman's character goes to a wide open field, finds a rock he has been given directions to, and removes a small tin box filled with money. When we shot the scene Morgan walked into the field and was looking around, both ways. I thought, "What is he doing? Why is he looking around?" Then, when he opened the box and it was full of money, he looked around again. I did not really understand the choice.

Then we screened the film for audiences. When he first walks into the field and looks around, they loved it—*loved* it. When he opens the box, sees the money, and looks around again, they roared.

LISA KLEIN
November 30

My agent thought my *Seinfeld* was really funny. But *Seinfeld* buys nothing. So they haven't done shit with it. Now, I have three other *Seinfeld* ideas I could do in a second. But what's the point?

I also have about half of a *Murphy Brown* idea. I'm not ready to face the blank page yet, but part of it excites me. I'm just not sure about the other part.

I also finished rewriting a script called *Waltzing Matilda*. I got it down from 134 pages to 122. So now the Turtle Agency has three finished screenplays. I gave them that one a week before Thanksgiving. How much time do you think is a reasonable amount for them to take to read it?

JOHN MCINTYRE
December 6

I'm still working on *The Critic*. We're waiting to get some color footage back, maybe next week. That'll be exciting. We saw ten seconds of a test, but now we'll see an actual show, I think, just before the video edit. So we'll have an idea of what it looks like.

The air date is January 13 on ABC. I'm timing the acting scenes. I might see five scenes that I'm able to do, plan out motions, gestures, whatever happens. This is the most normal-paced of all the time I've been here. I was working on a show that had really hectic and uneven hours. We were working until two in the morning a couple of days, and then seven hours the next day. It was very inconsistent but we were just getting started. Everything was behind schedule. Now everything's behind schedule, but acceptably so.

I read the script. We'll do an animatic to the script for me to use as a storyboard. Disney is credited for having started to use animatics in the late '30s. It's a film version of the storyboard, with more specific poses indicating acting. So it's a storyboard in time. If there's a gesture or important bit, a pose will be drawn for it that may not have been in the storyboard. It's a little more specific.

That animatic, with the soundtrack, will be shown to the show's two creators, and they will maybe change the acting, eliminate lines or put in new lines—whatever they see fit. "Timing" will be my credit. There's four of us doing that.

I've missed a couple of creative meetings and James Brooks [whose company produces *The Critic*] may have been there. Al and Jean are the two *Simpsons* writers who created this. They just keep saying "Al and Jean." I don't remember their last names. I want to meet them. [*Author's note:* The creators' names are actually Al Jean and Mike Reiss.]

I think it's going to be funny. The first show I was working on, I wasn't laughing too much and everyone else was. I thought I would keep my mouth shut and learn this whole thing, maybe it would get funnier as it goes. But there have been later shows—there are thirteen in all—and some of those seem to be funnier.

I get paid weekly with overtime. The pay is good.

I made a point of letting Duck Soup know how happy I am, and that I'm really getting a lot out of it and enjoying entertainment more than commercials. I had meetings with them about developing ideas for Nickelodeon, and I developed a little concept for a show and they sent it to a friend at Nickelodeon, and I'm waiting to hear what she thought. But I want to have it as an ongoing thing, that when shows come to me and I develop them, I send them things. If that ever developed into any kind of viable project, Duck Soup wanted to be the production company. So we informally discussed that possibility.

After I hadn't been working there for a few months, they called me to have me come back and do those commercials. By that time, I didn't want to put the time into it, and I didn't think we had the time to do them justice. And they were talking about doing them on the weekends, and I knew there was no way weekends would be enough. And I got the sense that there would also be no money in it. So without going any further I just said, "Forget this." It was kind of abrupt but I just said, "Look, this is what I'd rather work toward—Nickelodeon or some series, entertainment thing."

I got invited to their Christmas party, which was conciliatory. There are no hard feelings.

I definitely like doing this, and I feel like I'm seeing more of the industry and more of the core of people that are out here but I wasn't really seeing. Once I saw someone from NYU, but a lot have stayed in New York or done other things besides animation.

I'm going home for the holidays for about a week. My father

was really sick a while ago, and I went home the next day. He nearly died from this freak flare-up of spinal meningitis. He had been treated for something else with steroids and this one steroid they gave him just blew up his bacteria. So I flew home, and they didn't know if he was going to survive, and a couple of days later he was better. Now he's home and he's okay.

Theresa is working on *Swan Lake*, now called *Swan Princess*, for Rich Animation.

I was over at Disney last week. They showed their four features in progress to animators in the union. They're trying to get people. They don't have enough animators for all the projects they're trying to do. They showed animatronics and line drawings, and the trailer for *The Lion King*. The camera moves and perspective look beautiful, but you can't tell much about the movie.

It was nice to be wined and dined by Disney. I walked down Dopey Drive. It's funny, you can always feel Disney behind it. Although it's a really fun atmosphere, just behind those bushes you see two security guards. You really see the boundary.

KAREY KIRKPATRICK, Screenwriter

More than anything, writing for animation taught me how to rely on visuals to communicate a thought or idea, and to be a member of a creative team. On *The Rescuers Down Under* I was one of four writers credited. But there were nine storyboard artists, thirty animators, two directors and a producer—all of whom contributed to the story, too. This has helped me tremendously in pitch meetings and on other scripts I have written, because they are all highly collaborative ventures.

P. J. PESCE
December 21

The announcement of The Desperate Trail *to the Hollywood business community was oddly fitting, given its wobbly production history. A* Variety *headline on November 30 read: "Trimark on Lawsuit 'Trail'."*

The accompanying story reported, "In a suit filed in L.A. Superior Court Nov. 23, Trimark claimed it made a handshake deal to pay Civilizations (Prods.) and MPCA 30 percent of the net receipts from distributing the $2 million pic, which is likely headed for homevid and cable."

Pesce and I spoke shortly after he returned to L.A.

I'm fucking glad it's over.

It was a difficult shoot. The production was very, very disorganized, and we were constantly waiting on props and wardrobe. The scheduling was very bad. We wound up being put in situations where we had almost no time to shoot something that should have taken twice the time, and then given a day where we shot for half a day and then didn't have anything else to shoot. We couldn't just go off and shoot something.

So it was very frustrating for the actors and they tended to blame me for it. It's not my fault. It's the First A.D.'s and the producer's fault.

This came up immediately. Since "the mustache incident," as it has become known to scholars, we had a huge, all-out battle and then things were kind of okay.

Craig was not good about learning his lines. You'd think that for the amount of money he was paid [$115,000] he would have been shamed into it, but the fact is, he wasn't. And he made it a point of honor, almost, that he wanted to change the lines. I'm the sort of writer who's not very precious about his words. I'm very, very open to change. But to come in, not know any of his lines, and just improvise the scene is very difficult for the other actor. It wastes a lot of time, and we're not on that kind of show where we have time to jerk off like that. It was just lack of discipline.

Craig did, however, want to direct the movie. I was constantly having to say, "No, we're going to do it this way." And he would get upset about things that I would get Linda to do. He was trying to get his hands on everything. So it was like a pitched battle from day one.

The guy's father is a prison guard. Maybe he's got a problem with authority—I don't know.

Linda was professional in that sense, but she tended to be more difficult when Craig was around. If he wasn't there and I was doing something with her, she was much easier to deal with, much more agreeable.

The first night set the tone. Here I hired this guy to do this movie, who fought with his agent and with the company to get an extra $15,000 on a movie that could ill afford to blow that kind of money. Then he came out late—they [Sheffer and Fiorentino] refused to come even a day earlier—they came out there two nights before the shoot. I told them both I want to meet them for dinner that night so that we could start talking, and they blew me off. Unbelievable.

I mean, just personally for another human being, a person who has written this work and is going to direct it, it's very disrespectful. It shows no concern for that person. It's like, "Well, we don't give a shit, we'll just do this movie and take the money, and I don't care what you say about it." It's like they're not interested.

Elliott was great. If he was going to change one word he would come to me and ask if that was okay with me. Nine times out of ten I would say, "Absolutely fine." And in the one case where I would say no, that would not be a problem. He would do it my way.

Once we were waiting on Craig, who maintains to this day that he was not told we were waiting for him. I have no idea what the truth is. Anyway, all I know is that Sam was under the impression that we were waiting for Craig, who was consistently late to the set by between twenty and twenty-five minutes. Near the end he got better. He understood that we were under time constraints and he was really on time and he made an effort. It's like he took a lesson from Sam, who was on the set all the time.

One day Sam fucking got in his face—got right in his shit— and they were yelling at each other, and I said, "Okay, boys, all right . . ." But if they would have thrown it down, I don't know if I would have gotten in the middle. [Laughs]

The mustache was kind of a joke after that. In fact, the next day Craig said to me, "You know, now that I've got it, I wish I could have shaved it off." He turned around and said, "Maybe we can do something where he's a con man—he could take the mustache off, and it's a fake mustache, something like that."

I got back last night. I think Trimark and MPCA are going to make a deal. No one's called me [about appearing at trial]. As far as I'm concerned I'm going to Miami for Christmas instead of court. My family asked whether they should come to the set, and I told them, "It would probably be better if you don't go," because it was so high-pressure.

For Thanksgiving I went to dinner with Sam and Katharine [Ross, Elliott's wife] and R. L. Tolbert, the stunt coordinator.

The first couple of days with Craig and Linda I felt like I could do nothing right. Everything I did was wrong. Any way I tried to direct her she just stormed off. She never wanted any direction. Didn't want to rehearse, which made it difficult for the other actor, because she didn't really want to work until the camera was on. Once the camera was on she was great. She did some really wonderful stuff. But that became a problem because Craig didn't know the lines and she didn't want to do it until the camera was running. So trying to block the thing out before I shot it was a fucking nightmare. And when I started shooting they would want to change it. Which drove the camera people insane.

We shot the stagecoach in four days. I think it's going to look really good. Dailies looked great. The problem was we could only see dailies on film every fifth or sixth day, which was horrible. We had to look at them on video. I was pissed off that I couldn't see them on film all the time.

Mike Bonvillain, the cinematographer, did a very good job. They wanted to fire him at one point, though. The First A.D., Chris Edmonds, was scapegoating him for all the problems.

It was really *their* problem. Chris, because of the lack of preproduction, had great difficulty anticipating things that would happen. Admittedly, we all had that problem and things would change. But he didn't make it his business to find out the information from me and Mike the night before. He would be sitting in the bar hanging out with his wife [the Second A.D.].

It wasn't that he was unavailable. He just didn't come to me on a daily basis to find out information. Usually I wound up telling him that morning. Which is fine, but it's not so good for a long schedule. He never sat down once before we shot the movie and made me say to him, "This day's going to be too big, this day's going to be too small." We sat down and tried to do that but I was getting pulled in eighty-five directions. It was his responsibility because he needs that information to do his job properly. "What's this day like? Is it good, or is it bad?"

It never became this efficient fighting machine. Chris continued to try to scapegoat Mike until the very end. The second week everyone was pushing me hard to fire Mike. Chad, Steve Stabler, and the First A.D. were all pushing me to fire him. He got wind of it, he just felt it. I tried to tell him, "Look, there's some bad shit blowing in the wind, and just make sure we make our days and that everything cuts real good for a little while here. And just make sure that we're really efficient together."

And he did, and Mike and I *were* efficient. And we just kept track of how many times it was production we were waiting on. We never waited on camera, we fucking never waited on camera. We waited on actors, wardrobe, costumes, and props. And we got fucked over in scheduling. We had to much to do on some days and not enough on others.

If they would have fired Mike they would have destroyed the movie. At the moment it was happening I didn't know that. I considered, for a split second, firing him. Then, it was purely personal loyalty that held me to him. Because I really started to believe for a second. And then I talked to him, and he said, "Wait a second! We never waited on camera."

And then I went through another day with him and I really watched what happened. We never waited on camera. He would say "Fifteen minutes," and it would be fifteen minutes. And then he'd say, "Okay, Chris, fifteen minutes and the camera's ready," and Chris would say, "Okay, bringing in the actors," and that would take ten minutes. So Mike would keep working, like any driven, artistic person would. He's not going to sit there and smoke a cigarette, waiting, sitting on his ass.

I knew Mike long before Rob Weiss ever met him. Rob Weiss was shown my student film, *The Afterlife of Grandpa*, as one of the tapes Mike had done. I had no doubts about Mike's ability, he's like the Nestor Almendros of our generation. He was the gaffer on my student film. Over the past eight months or so I've become very good friends with Mike. We've talked extensively about the movie, we've gone to see movies together, and I knew that he was the man for the job.

There was definitely tension between Mike and me. Mike would probably argue with me about this, but he always thinks about the image and composition. Often I would have to go, "Mike, that's great but it doesn't tell the story. This is what I need." His visual imagination just takes off and he disregards what the picture is supposed to be doing in the service of the story. So I just have to keep coming back to that. The problem is that I can get taken in by that, too, and forget.

It's like you're driving one of these stagecoaches with six horses, you know? You have to deal with each one of them and keep them in line. Craig Sheffer's one of them, Mike Bonvillain's another one, Linda Fiorentino's another one, Steve Stabler's another one, the script itself is the lead horse, right up there, and they're all running in different directions.

I don't know if we met budget. We came in on schedule.

Chad was inexperienced, dealing with a lot of the problems the actors had. He was great for working on the script together. Tom Abrams [Pesce's co-writer] came the second or third week. Chad and I split the cost. I asked him to do some work. Tom was a great friend and partner.

Some things got lost by the wayside. Little details. But I think the essence of the story is there. Frank Whaley was fantastic—fucking great. And it was just so welcome to see him there, after dealing with these people who were so difficult and didn't even seem to want to hear my direction. Somebody who is respectful, and knows his lines, and is interested in collaborating.

The first night he was here, we had this heavy acting scene between Frank and Craig. For Frank's close-up, Craig wasn't there. That's a perfect example. I'm not sure what Craig wants to be. Never hire actors without meeting them first. They think you're not serious about it if you hire them like that. Live and learn. I learned a lot. I would insist on more preproduction, and a more organized production machine.

A lot of my friends came through and did roles, like Peter Gregory, who is amazingly talented. He won a Dramalogue Award. He just came in and did two days. Whaley came in for seven or eight days and was amazing. I felt like Craig was jealous of him or something. Frank had just won an Obie award.

The crew, in general, didn't take to Craig too well. They loved Whaley. Linda and Craig were both very condescending. Everything that was wrong was my fault—everything was me not protecting the actors enough. It got old.

Kanter came on the set for two or three days. I didn't even have enough time to go out to dinner with him, though. But it was nice of him to come.

I will be in there every single day for every single edit. It's my favorite part of the whole process.

I told Pesce that Variety *reported that* The Desperate Trail *would probably end up as a TV movie.*

They did? Oh, those fucks. That's not what I was told. You compromise your frame, you can't frame for two different aspect ratios, so I was the one going, "Fuck it, man. Fuck television."

It should be seen in a theatre, where Mike and I intended it to be seen. That's the way we designed it, it's the way we conceived of the shots—not for television. We didn't shoot it with close-ups. There's too much beautiful scenery, and people are dressed. You want to see this stuff, it's got to be big. You put it on a little fucking TV screen, you might as well have not made the movie. You might as well have made a movie about people in a room back in L.A.

Cannes is the only festival that's coming up when we're done. It would be perfect for Sundance, but that's going to be a year away when we finish editing. Maybe New York [Film Festival]. If we finish it in May and bring it to Cannes, they'll hold onto it another couple of months for New York. They know that would mean money.

Steve Stabler [an MPCA producer] was actually really good. Helpful, supportive, attentive. Not the greatest taste in certain things, but I would say in general he would bow to my needs in those areas. But when the extra money came in he came to me and said, "What do you need?" That's all you could ask from a producer. That's great, that's wonderful. What do you need? Do you need more days? Do you want to fire the actress and hire another one? Do you need more equipment? What do you need to do your job? Unfortunately, in general, the production machine didn't have that attitude.

I'm thinking of one day in particular where there's, like, a two-and-a-half-page scene of dialogue that takes place at night where they're riding on a horse. We had learned by the second week that dealing with horses in any way is hell. You can't predict anything. And these two [Sheffer and Fiorentino] were barely capable of doing a pony ride. Especially while I'm trying to cover it in any reasonable way with the camera. It's just incredibly difficult. You can't light it at night. What are you going to do while they're moving, fucking haul the camera along? It's really difficult. The whole thing became a nightmare.

My idea, to make it more simple, was do a "Woody Allen"—put the camera in one position, have them ride toward us, and radio mike them. So you hear the whole scene played out, and when they finally get there, you see them.

That worked out well. However, Chris never bothered to ask me that until the day of the shoot. And that's his job, to ask me. That's information that he needs. It's not my responsibility to give him that information—it's my responsibility not to *not* give it to him, but it's his to get the information he needs to do his job properly. For him to assume I'm going to cover something a certain way, and schedule a half a day to do it, was incorrect and wound up wasting a lot of time. We wound up going home early that day. That's a sin on a twenty-five-day shooting schedule.

Craig and Linda's lack of riding experience was a problem a couple of times. Like when they had to ride up to somewhere, stop, and ride off. They were both very cautious. No one wanted to get hurt, nobody wanted to extend themselves. So they walked up, stopped, and walked off. It was a highly dramatic scene. They're supposed to rise up there, see that their farmhouse is being destroyed, and fucking tear off the other way.

I felt like John Landis—"Lower the helicopters more!" You know, "Can't they just move a little faster?" "No, no, no." They didn't want to.

ROB MINKOFF, Director

I act differently with every person that I'm working with. Probably more based on who they are, as an instinctive response to who they are. I would find myself talking to people differently, approaching them differently, asking them differently, everything. From choice of words to tone of voice to body language. You build a relationship with people over the course of making a film, and hopefully find what works with each person.

FRANK DARABONT, Writer-Director

Shooting my first film—a TV movie called *Buried Alive*—was miserable, horrible, the worst. Every day was like a fight for survival, a struggle for existence, because you have only so much time in the day, and you have to get so much material in the can, and you're always wondering if you're getting enough coverage of any given thing.

On that schedule, it averaged out to five and a half, five and three-quarters pages a day. Some days you'd shoot eight pages, and others, when it was tricky, only four. But on average, you take the number of pages and the number of days and do the math and you get five and a half. And that's fucking brutal, man. I was exhausted by the end.

It was a toughy, and when I was done I was convinced my directing career was over, that I had screwed up from one end to the other and it would never cut together. But we got great reviews and it was like the second highest rated cable movie of all time—we had really nice success with it. I was offered a few other things. But frankly, I was so worn to a frazzle by the experience, I thought, "Whatever I've needed to learn I've learned from this experience—I don't need to do another one just to do it."

JOHN KEITEL
January 6

I'm moving to "WeHo" [West Hollywood] next week. I looked and looked, and finally put my life in God's hands and found a single on Hacienda.

I wanted to get going with my life and this project. I mean, I have more money in the bank than Robert Rodriguez [director of *El Mariachi*] did. It's weird, through. I'm paying $600 for this place. When I was twenty-one, I had hardwood floors and a view of Lake Michigan for $375.

My thesis advisor has allowed me to finish school with the *Ground Zero* screenplay. I have a friend who is a manager and he's really into helping me with this. I think I would start by casting it, and having "my people" ready to go. The rewrite is much more able to have a low budget, like a Cassavetes film. The draft before required really well-shot scenes. Now there's an *emotional* energy. But I feel like I'm way behind schedule. I create these deadlines for myself.

I'll tell you a funny one. I used to always say that when I turned thirty, the Academy Awards would fall on my birthday—because they're always around then, you know?—and that I would win one that night. Well, this year March twenty-first is my thirtieth, and Oscar night! It's more ironic than anything else.

I was contacted by this man and woman who were referred to me by the school. The Gay Men's Chorus toured Europe and they shot High 8. They need it cut into a documentary. So I put together my reel. They said they would pay enough to live on, and that it would take two or three months to cut.

The woman is forty-five years old. She went to film school after years as a journalist.

The school told me they said $800 a week was a ballpark figure, which I thought was great because I was thinking it might be like $500 a week. Then I found out people make anywhere from $1,200 to $1,500 on these things, so I felt pretty comfortable coming back with $1,000 a week.

Well, when I met with [her partner] he said, "Look, the bottom line is that we really don't have any money to pay you right now. But we can pay you a little on good faith, and defer the rest. We do have some money coming in soon from the Geffen Foundation."

Then he did something really sleazy. There was a movie theatre marquee behind me, where we met, and he pointed to it and said, "Look, we're going to get there, and we're going to win awards," and blah, blah, blah. I thought, you know, I can't be exploited like this, I'm not fresh out of film school. And besides, I have my *own* labor of love.

I mean, everyone's a producer in this town! God love him, on some level I'm sure he believed it. I wanted to say, "Guess what? I had a film at Sundance that was submitted for an Academy Award and almost got distributed."

But the bottom line is that this is a documentary about a trip to Europe. And the "gay" novelty has worn off. So that was that— Merry Christmas. He called again this week. Look, the editor will ultimately make this film work. So they would be smarter to develop a trusting relationship. As for me, I heard this "great sucking sound," as Ross Perot would say. This project might be interesting, but the people are more important.

I came up with a name for my production company. Wrong Way Productions. Like the sign "Wrong Way." It works on many levels, going against the tide, going against the traffic, breaking rules.

MARCO WILLIAMS
January 7

Disney passed on *The Power of No*. Dawn had a little tantrum. But the fact was that somewhere, after September, the momentum had been lost. The script was always a challenge, and they just didn't feel it could be worked out.

I found out by calling when I just had a feeling it wasn't happening. Then I got three messages on my machine, from Dawn, my agent, and Gay Hirsch.

I went to Europe for three weeks after *The Power of No* fell apart. Berlin, Munich, Siena, Pamplona, San Sebastian, Madrid, Paris, Amsterdam.

I was disappointed, but not devastated. I needed to take stock from this and see what I could learn. I mean, "no" means "no" and "yes" means "yes" in this town, but nobody ever gets real specific about the reasons. I had to think. The script had lost some humor—was that it? Was it Dawn, and studio politics? Was it my performance or nonperformance?

The big thing I got from this experience is how important it is to have control. This was a lesson in what happens when you are at someone else's beck and call. You have to just draw your own boundaries in those situations.

It would be easier if people were just more straightforward. Then, if down the road you become the greatest thing since sliced bread, fine. They knew you when. But people say things to you like, "Look, we think you're really talented, and I know we'll work together soon." Yeah, right. What does *that* mean?

Looking back, I could have been more determined about the script. But one day I realized that I was expendable, and it affected my participation. Dawn said at one point, "We can get another writer," and when she said that, I realized that that meant she could also get another *director.*

But now I think, fuck it. In the future, if I'm going to get fired I may as well be assertive. I mean, if I was assertive at least I would feel like I went out there on a limb. You know, my attitude all along was get the fucking job, and then you can be the biggest pig in the world—you can be Alan Parker. I got nervous. I cooperated. Dawn said not to be arrogant, and to be a team player, so I behaved and acquiesced.

I don't know if Disney will put the project in turnaround [a declared status which makes the project available to other studios or buyers willing to pay all previously accrued development costs]. I have heard that they tend not to do that. But I'm left with this wondering. Am I done? I mean, they passed on the project, but does that mean they are passing on the creative team as well? And then there was Dawn's impending thing. [According to the January 6 edition of *Daily Variety*, Steel's Turner deal was dead.]

I dropped off a Christmas gift to Dawn's office before I left. It was a book of photos of Marlene Dietrich. It was going to be a gift celebrating the start of the *Power of No* shoot.

I told Tina Andrews, the writer. We have a fine relationship.

I'm attached [as director] to something called *God Bless the Child.* Rene Russo and Sam Jackson are attached as well. Next I'm touring the South with nine other filmmakers with *In Search of Our Fathers*—Chapel Hill and Vero Beach.

I'm ready for a resurrection. I have no money from the development of *The Power of No*, no pot to piss in. I'm going to be a juror at Sundance for documentaries. That will be good. I like to ski, and they pay expenses and a small per diem. And next week I'm one of twenty producers meeting with foreign TV people at a symposium. I'll pitch my *On the Waterfront* story.

My agent said, "These things happen. We got close, now we just have to move on. That's all you can do."

Look, the problem for me is that I'm very competitive. Not to take anything away from Matty Rich, but I think, based on his film [*Straight Out of Brooklyn*], what is he doing directing *The Inkwell*? You look at it, and mine. So his is dramatic. Big deal.

I don't run a race to come in second.

ROB MINKOFF, Director

Some people say to people above them, "I want to be a director." That's one way. And depending on who you tell and who you know, they'll either help you or not, obviously.

But that's a big barrier for most people—the willingness to admit, "That's what I want to do"—because there are so many people who can't do it that say it, and it frightens all the people who can do it. They don't want to come across as another person who just says, "I want to direct."

It's too often stated, but it shouldn't prevent people who really believe in that and believe in themselves from expressing it.

ADAM DUBOV, Director

It's a weird business. Although in many ways it's so antithetical to the concept of making art, only an artist not knowing the ways of the business can deal with it. In many ways it kills the souls of artists, it really does. It's pretty vile.

BERNARD JOFFA
January 13

You're my barometer of how I feel. Sometimes I like seeing you, and other times I hate it.

[Joffa's hair was now in a short buzz cut.] It's a rebirth. My hair was thinning and I decided to confront it instead of combing it over. I went to AFI and saw some old friends and I think they all thought I was dying of AIDS.

My father took a huge turn for the worse, and my sisters and I decided to fly him here. So I met them in Miami and took him to

Phoenix, where a clinic wanted to double the chemo. We thought about it for three days and decided no.

Then we took him to the Livingston Clinic in San Diego, which is like one of the Mexican "quack" clinics where they do not use chemo or radiation, which you legally must do in this country. They have a sign outside that says, "We do not cure you of cancer, but we can give you the tools so that you and God can." It's a wonderful place. We have all been there for weeks and it feels great to be with the family. My father was sleeping six hours a day from depression and now not at all.

I feel that we have done the very best we could, and that is a peaceful feeling.

I've been on a hell of a journey since I saw you last. I was offered a project which I was associated with a few years ago. It's called *Barry*, and it's the story of the first woman to become a doctor in South Africa. It's sort of a *Yentl* story. She went dressed as a man and had a scandalous affair with a South African governor.

I got along very badly with the producer, so I begged off of the project. This past month, after two years, the writer came back to me, and said that Miramax in London had seen my film and would like to finance half of it, and the other money would need to be raised. But the producer would be involved as Executive Producer, and I said no. The good news for them is that they are now interested in Chris Menges [a former D.P., and director of *A World Apart*]. It was hard for me, though, because the writer has become my best friend.

In November, Chris Silverman called. He said that there was a low-budget feature the director had dropped out of, and would I like to read the script? They had lost a high-profile director, and had seen *Senzeni Na?* and were making an offer [of $40,000]. Karen Black and Emilio Estevez were attached. I received the script on a Thursday night and they wanted to sign the deal Saturday morning.

They said it was a "cult movie"—whatever that means. I guess *The Rocky Horror Picture Show* was one. It was called *Blood & Water*, and it was supposed to be a spoof of people who make "snuff" films.

Well, I read the script and in the first scene a woman is fucking this guy. Right after they finish, she stabs him in the back, and then whacks off his hand. It was disgusting, and horrible, and not something I wanted to be involved with in any way. So I turned down my first Hollywood film!

ADAM DUBOV, Director

If you are fortunate enough to get the big rush treatment when you get out of film school, you should really find—if you possibly can—some way to pull something down out of that initial rush of excitement while you have it.

But if your stuff is of a more personal bent, I don't think you can make a good film out of any piece of shit they throw at you, any stupid high school drama or whatever. You'll do a shitty job if your heart's not in it and you don't like it.

ALAN SHAPIRO, Writer-Director

I've been sent a bunch of scripts people wanted me to direct, and I didn't think I could do a good job, and I didn't think they were very good. There was a period when I was represented by CAA, and I got offered a whole bunch of great movies, and I didn't do any of them and used to really regret that, like, "Fuck—I would have had a bunch of features made already by now." They got made.

I knew Scott Rudin for a long time. He really liked me. He was the president of production at Fox and used to hand me scripts all the time. I remember he gave me *Less Than Zero* and I felt that it had nothing redeeming about it. I didn't get it. Another one, *How I Got Into College.* Just a whole mess of them. I didn't do them, and I'm glad I didn't.

But there's still a little doubt.

On *Home Free*, they want us to do a rewrite with less violence, for the Davis Company, who has seen it. But the ship may have sailed. I mean, *Sarafina!* and *Bopha!* were both huge financial disasters, and

South Africa is now considered "passé." Michael Cimino followed *Deer Hunter*—a great film that has never left me—with *Heaven's Gate*. And then Westerns were passé, until Kevin Costner revived them with *Dances With Wolves*.

Then there is *The Year of the Zinc Penny*. The woman who gave me the story which became *Senzeni Na?* gave me this book a while ago, and I took it with me to Phoenix. It is by a man named Rich de Marinas, who teaches in El Paso. I called and they said he was on sabbatical in Missoula, Montana. I left word and he called me the next day. After talking to me he said, "Your take is absolutely right." It was published in 1989, optioned by MGM. A screenplay was written and then the option expired in 1992.

I found my movie!

It's about an outsider, like me and you—the making of an artist. It's about a kid with a Norwegian mother and an Italian father. He is dumped with his grandparents in Montana for six years. He is abused, and then comes to L.A., where he is reunited with his mother. He lives, though, in a restricted apartment, which they had then—no kids allowed. Every time they come to check, all the kids run down into this hideaway. The kid fantasizes about being a flying ace and dying in the arms of all these different beautiful women.

I want to buy the rights and produce it myself. It's now my obsession. Richard Green of the Pleshette Agency [Rick de Marinas's agent] is playing agent games. He tells my agent that there is now renewed interest in the project. The only way I will ever get the chance to make a film is if I own the material. I have talked to the author about cowriting it with me, which does have some value. I also told him that if money is an issue, he should take the offer from anyone who is offering more, because it will never be me.

It's so personal, and so quirky, this story, it could easily be screwed up. But it's my vehicle, an American piece I relate to 1,000 percent.

ROBERT BENTON, Writer-Director

I've been very fortunate in the books I've chosen because both *Kramer vs. Kramer* and *Nobody's Fool* allowed you to make movies of them, whereas certain material looks on paper like it's film material but it's not—it sounds visual but the action is really too interior or small. I know that people tend to think that there's not a lot of action in *Nobody's Fool*, but there is, compared to a lot of extraordinary novels where the real action is interior and the beauty is in the voice of the author.

I made very big changes in the book—showed the author, Richard Russo, the script with great trepidation and explained to him why I made the changes, and he understood. When we were shooting, I called him constantly to help me out and he was very generous. In areas where I changed things he understood the changes and helped me with further changes.

P. J. PESCE
January 13

Pesce edited The Desperate Trail *on the eleventh floor of the CNN building on Sunset Boulevard, close to the Cinerama Dome theatre. This is Hollywood's business district—a bad neighborhood in denial, perhaps, because of the large number of banks and entertainment companies, mostly record labels.*

On the wall was a memo from MPCA headed "Desperate Trail Post-Production Schedule." It began:

1/7/94 First Cut
2/4/94 Director's Cut
3/1/94 Final Cut
A technical schedule through April followed.

"They're leaving me alone," said Pesce. "But I'll need another week or two, at which point I'll have my agent or lawyer intervene."

Pesce had shaved his Sam Elliott-like mustache and wore a cardigan sweater and '70s-style low-cut suede Nike sneakers. Around the editing console were Snapple, honey, aspirin, and Skoal snuff—the last being a habit Pesce had quickly picked up from Bill Johnson, his editor.

Johnson, a friend though not a client of Pesce's agent, David Kanter, had been the editor of two Fox TV movies. He worked his way up in New York, eventually assisting the editing of Something Wild, After Hours, *and* Year of the Dragon, *then serving as second editor on* Married to the Mob *and* Miami Blues.

Twenty-six-year-old Michael Benson was working as Johnson's assistant. Benson's sister is married to Kanter, and he has known Pesce for years. He had P.A.'d on Patriot Games, Dracula, *and* The Player, *and apprenticed on* Untamed Heart *and* Flesh and Bone.

Johnson used the Avid 4000, a Macintosh-driven system which cuts at twenty-four frames per second and digitizes all the footage.

All were in agreement that Craig Sheffer's performance was weak. "It will add at least a week to what we're doing," Johnson said. During the cutting of the scene where Jack and Sarah partner up, Pesce looked at Sheffer's image as he stalled, clearly forgetting his dialogue. " 'Lines? I have to remember lines?' " Pesce huffed. "You'd think for five thousand dollars a day he'd remember his fucking lines."

For the film's score Pesce wanted Carter Burwell, who composed the music for Miller's Crossing.

"It all depends on what Turner says," Pesce said about the prospects for a non-video premiere. "We're hoping for a theatrical release."

GARY ROSS, Screenwriter

Tom Hanks eating the baby corn was not in the script of *Big*—he came up with that on his own. When Kevin Kline said in *Dave*, "She's half American and half Polynesian—she's Amnesian," he made that up. He is brilliant with words and wordplay.

You need to afford people invention at every stage. Everything has to be a dynamic process and you have to stay open, including in the editing.

JOHN KEITEL
January 23

Keitel worked at Midtown Video's open house at its new Santa Monica facility. The space was a large open area surrounded by edit bays. On the west face, several offices were literally torn apart by the earthquake that had hit exactly a week earlier, on Sunday the sixteenth, at 4:30 A.M. Placed inside the offices were mannequins in hardhats. The doorways were banded with police tapes which were not merely decorative.

It was my third day in the new apartment. To be totally honest, I was hung over, and after the earthquake happened I just went back to bed. Monday morning I just prepared for work like it was no big deal. I had no power and couldn't listen to the TV or radio. Nothing in the apartment was battery operated.

A funny thing happened. Carter was trying to call me, every fifteen minutes, for hours and hours. Finally he calls my mother and says, "He probably picked someone up last night and isn't even home." Can you believe that? And my mother says, "No way."

LIZ CANE
January 25

I saw *Grumpy Old Men*. It was pretty good. What shocked me more than anything was that they really overcame some of the problems of the script. Stuff that really didn't work on the page seemed to come out all right in the film.

This friend of mine, Kayo Hatta, just sold her film *Wedding Gift* to Miramax, which is going to give her finishing money. It was supposed to be ready for Sundance but it wasn't. She has slaved away for about five years on the film. It was originally going to be her thesis.

Caveh took *I Don't Hate Las Vegas Anymore* to Rotterdam, where there is a festival. I really admire how far out he went with his film. There are a lot of people who probably won't like it. I also saw *Sleep with Me*, as a work in progress. Meg Tilly was really good in it and the audience was into it.

Todd Brunell, another friend from UCLA, is doing very well

right now, editing educational films and making a lot of money. Our 401 group, as I call it, got together for the first time in a while, because two of the people who have been working in Ethiopia came back and then left again. Another friend, this woman, is art-directing films for [Roger Corman's company] Concorde. She says the conditions are the lowest—worse than a lot of student films.

In early January, I shot High 8 of this guy Bob, who was one of the kids in my *28 Up*–type project. He's a musician now, really fat, and he wears this red shirt and looks like Elvis. He has this band in San Francisco. He is really an artist. He tells jokes, and is smart and witty and entertaining, and he has a great memory. It made me think about shifting the focus of the project from five or six kids to just him. I sent him the tape and told him, "This is the tape that will make you famous."

That's What Women Want is going to play at the Red Vic Theatre in San Francisco with two other women's films for one night.

I haven't been able to rewrite the mother-daughter script, but I want to and then show it to you because I know it needs work. I realized recently that I tend to be a workaholic, and it's tougher for me to create deadlines for myself. But I have to stay at it, thinking in terms of volume, and exploring different ideas.

It's really a matter of faith.

MARCO WILLIAMS
January 31

I got back yesterday from [serving as a documentary juror at] Sundance. I had a lot of fun, I really did. I saw only one film in competition. All the others were documentaries. I saw a couple of special films.

Not all the documentaries were great. There were a couple I actually hated and a bunch that I liked. I was definitely inspired by seeing films, and I learned a lot. I forgot what documentaries are like. It was a lot of fun.

The only narrative I saw was *Fresh*, which I liked a lot, and I also thought that the kid actor who got the special jury award was certainly deserving.

The jury didn't really vote, we talked. We could have voted, but were all desperate to talk, because we were asked not to say anything about what we thought of the films to anyone, so that there wouldn't be any rumors going around. So for me at least, and everyone else, it was the first chance to discuss the quality of the films, and cinema in general. We talked for three or four hours, expressed our preferences, and never really voted. On just about everything there was a consensus. In some instances maybe for one person or another it wasn't his or her first choice, but they agreed to it. There was never a need to say, "Let's sit down and have a vote." I'm glad for that because that would have meant you could vote but not necessarily be in a position to persuade someone to see things differently.

It seemed very crowded and certainly did get worse in the second five days. I think, for me, having been there before, and having a responsibility, I opted for a different tack. I decided not to hang out and catch up with people. I decided things would come to me. It kind of worked out.

I also had a small agenda. I wanted to speak with the people from American Playhouse, and I did, then really tried to make some contacts. I tried to speak with Matthew Modine a little bit, although that didn't really work out. I got cold feet. I wanted to talk to him about a project and then got nervous, and then when I got my courage back he didn't have time. But he did give me his telephone number in New York, so that's fine.

I knew what I wanted out of it and wasn't flailing desperately in the wind, hoping that some important contact would come along and stick to me. I just went about my business, and it was a little saner that way. When I was there two years ago I never saw any films, I just kept going to Z Place because I thought it was so important to be there to meet somebody or talk to somebody. It's not true.

I was there for the awards. I had a good time.

I saw Stephanie Allain at the very beginning, at the opening night party I said hello to her and chatted with her a little bit, and then I never saw her again. I'm not a fan. I don't begrudge anybody their success, but I sort of have frustrations with people.

I'm working hard on this project God Bless the Child, and trying to get it out there, and get the script to Matthew Modine. I think it's going to pan out at some point. I'm fairly aggressive about it, and I feel good.

I'm going away again next week, to Berlin for four days, and then on a tour with my documentary for ten days on the Southern circuit. I'm going to go to Berlin and try to follow up on some contacts that I made when I was at this conference in San Francisco for European coproducing. Follow the momentum a little bit.

JOHN MCINTYRE
February 10

I met McIntyre at work in FilmRoman's animation workshop in North Hollywood. A boom box with headphones sat on his drafting table.

We start with the audio track.

Essentially any bits of acting—the turn, the spin—we write them or draw the hands moving or little silhouettes of what the body's doing. Or we have a film frame to show when the body enters. Does it start in frame or out of frame or whatever?

This all goes to Korea, where they're animating on paper, then it's scanned into computers. Disney also doesn't have physical cels anymore. They make phony cels, collectibles, and most people buy them thinking that they got a piece of film. The final version of this isn't on film, it's just on video. It's all still done on paper, though.

Out of thirteen shows this is show twelve. I think I'll be working on ten. At one point there were five timers, maybe six, and now we've got four. I worked on the first two shows and will work on the last one. I thought it was just blanket credits, but I'm glad there will be specific credits per show.

I'd like to direct. I think it's doable after a couple of years of timing and layouts as well. To do a season of layouts would be nice. Having the experience. To direct, you should be able to lay these out really well on models, do it well. I'd also like to do storyboards.

The difficulty with this show is they have a lot of different locations and a lot of different characters, whereas *The Simpsons* tends to keep using the house settings and stuff. Here in one show I think we had 115 different characters, which had to be done in models and all. In *The Simpsons* they have had crowds, especially this season they've had everyone in almost every show. Which is a nightmare. A couple of them were really slowed down for that reason.

The backgrounds here have a lot more detail than *The Simpsons*, which are cel backgrounds, very flat, no more detailed than the characters. These backgrounds are based on the *New Yorker* magazine stylings from the '50s, with a lot more detail. Brick walls in *The Simpsons* would have one or two bricks. For this one, we draw every brick.

Here's Washington Square North, East, Waverly Place, everything's familiar [from NYU film school days], and they were catching it at six in the morning, four in the afternoon, it brought you right home. They work off of photos and the *New Yorker* paintings, different angles, whatever they need to pull it off. I've learned on this show that the backgrounds can really do a lot.

McIntyre took me outside, across the street, and into another structure.

This is an old security building. This is the vault here, which is supposedly the safest place during an earthquake. These are all complete shows, all the blue notebooks, and these are files of the characters. Here's Conan O'Brien. I think he was in show one. Here's Schwarzenegger. Here's *Home Alone 24*. Here's Leonard Maltin; they took the beard off. Gene Shalit. This is a critic's screening of *Indecent Proposal 6*, where the Demi Moore character wouldn't take any money.

There are hundreds of models for the show. The hope is that we get to start reusing them next year. Jay [the Jon Lovitz character] is all over the place this year. Hawaii in one show, California, with a thousand locations for each.

Three of us volunteered for cleanup crew after the earthquake, and we came here in hardhats and masks. It was pretty exciting, like *Alien*. We went up into the building, a producer from *The Simpsons* and two guys from *The Critic*. All we heard was walkie-talkie voices, no actual voices. And we had two big aftershocks, the 5.1 followed by two or three more, and the whole thing started swaying, and you could hear it grinding.

The guys jumped off their ladders and we heard frantic talking over the walkie-talkies, and we're still gathering up scenes, until the producer said, "No show's worth this!" and the rest of us went out. There were so many shocks within a few hours it wasn't worth it, but we went back two or three days later and got it back again.

We had a premiere party but I couldn't find James Brooks. It was really crowded. I went to a meeting with some of the producers, but I didn't get a chance to talk to them. There are a lot of layers of people to get through, like on any film. I think there are sixty or seventy people working on this in some capacity.

I've got six weeks left. There's no retainer—we're cast off.

I was offered another job at Games, Nickelodeon's animation, on *Rocko's Modern Life*. It's a smaller group of people. I heard about the job and went over there a month and a half ago and just applied for it, thinking that *The Critic* hadn't premiered yet and I didn't know what would happen.

They're offering $1,300 a week, which is a couple of hundred more than I'm making over here. It's for two seasons in a row. Back to back, no hiatus. Maybe fifty-four weeks—a long deal. Each half hour is made up of three shorts. So it would be forty-eight times three cartoons. The chances of moving up there would be very good.

I'm kind of "wheeling and dealing," and today I'm going to ask the producer of *The Critic* for advice.

Theresa and I have been spending much more time together, and we're more in love than ever. In fact, I just can't picture her not being in my life. So we're going to get married. I was going to propose this Valentine's Day, but I just couldn't get it together. My father told me about this balloon ride where you end up at a restaurant. Maybe we'll do that.

P. J. PESCE
February 15

The first screening of The Desperate Trail *was held at the Lightstorm screening room in Santa Monica. Pesce was showing his film to about twenty-five close colleagues, who packed the small theatre.*

"Thanks for coming," Pesce greeted the crowd. "It's nice to surround myself with friends at this stage—"

"Yeah, both of them," cracked one audience member.

"Anyway, you can see the film, and give me your comments, and then hate me when it comes out and I haven't used any of them."

In attendance were producer Albert Berger (King of the Hill) *and actor Elisabeth Shue, as well as* Desperate Trail *D.P. Mike Bonvillain, editor Bill Johnson, and assistant editor Michael Benson.*

The cut ran ninety-nine minutes. Pesce had used, for his temporary underscore, Ennio Morricone's music from The Untouchables *and Carter Burwell's from* Miller's Crossing. *There were four or five "Shot Missing" cards, the first of which elicited a laugh from the audience because the missing "shot" came in the middle of a shoot-out.*

Afterward, there was an informal exchange of reactions. The ice was broken by Neil Mooney, a musician, who cracked, "Well, it's no Body Waves." *Paul Schiff, producer of* My Cousin Vinny, *the American remake of* The Vanishing, *and the* Young Guns *films, said, "We really want to see what's happening inside the stagecoach when it's held up—but the only reaction shot is the wife's." The audience murmured their agreement, before Pesce groaned, "I know—goddammit! I want to shoot myself."*

Generally Pesce took the criticism well, and it was delivered honestly and directly, with none of the pomp and circumstance—or media coverage—of a studio premiere. In fact, the atmosphere more closely resembled a film school class. The only difference was that Pesce couldn't go back to his dormitory and direct his roommate through a short-end worth of retakes.

The consensus seemed to be that shot coverage was lacking, particularly in the opening stagecoach robbery sequence. The crucial scene, which established the personas of the Sheffer, Fiorentino, and Elliott characters, did seem confusing and short on reaction shots of the three leads.

"I couldn't really tell who was sitting next to who [on the stagecoach]," one viewer noted.

After another observation regarding the lack of coverage on a different scene, Pesce shook his head in agreement, then laterally. "Goddamn you. . . ."

ADAM DUBOV, Director

There's a real humbling thing about being a director—it's not strictly the domain of the megalomaniac. You put your butt on the line, and then once it's done, everyone takes a poke. You have to swallow it all, the good and the bad.

February 17

After the screening I sort of licked my wounds. I drank and felt bad. I guess I wanted a better reaction from the start, but that's just me being lazy.

The big news is that Carter Burwell has agreed to score the film if we can pay him his money. What really gave me a hard-on was that he compared it to the [work of the] Coen brothers. He said it has the same violence and humor.

MPCA offered me two films. One was a Western that was too similar to mine. The other was a thriller, which was not well written. It would start when I'm done editing. They'd probably pay me like $40,000.

Kanter is crazy about the film. He wants me to hold out.

FRANK DARABONT, Writer-Director

My favorite moment in *The Shawshank Redemption*, that I didn't know would be so special, is just a shot of a bus driving away, as Morgan Freeman's character says, "I hope the Pacific is as blue as it has been in my dreams." This gave me a lump in my throat when I first read Stephen King's story ten years ago. And now an audience is watching it and I'm watching it, and I get that same lump. It's all come full circle. There is absolutely nothing like that feeling of an audience reacting to your work—nothing.

LISA KLEIN
March 10

I just wrote a *Murphy Brown* and gave it to the Turtle Agency on Monday. So now I have two samples.

They submitted the *Seinfeld* to the Disney Channel for a sketch show on Monday, and on Tuesday morning they called. They loved it. I had the meeting, and it went well. They asked me to write a sketch.

The show is done in Orlando. One of the other writers in contention wrote for *Saturday Night Live*, so I don't know what will happen. The money is good, $2,100 a week. I would go to Orlando for six months. It's Writers Guild, too.

I finished another draft of *Waltzing Matilda* two weeks ago. I'm going to do a quick rewrite in the next few days.

After we got the positive feedback on *Seinfeld*, I had this pumped-up conversation with my agent. I don't know what happened. It was like someone else had crawled into my skin. She said, "Yeah, that's great," and I said, "I'm totally stoked," and then when I got off the phone I was like, "What just happened?" But I think it was having been validated by the first submission. Being accepted just made a difference.

P. J. PESCE
March 10

Pesce next screened The Desperate Trail *at the Ocean Avenue screening room at MPCA, in Santa Monica.*

Present were many of the faces from the first screening, as well as producer Ron Yerxa, David Kanter, MPCA's Brad Krevoy and Chad Oman, Anthony Drazan (director of Zebrahead*), and screenwriter Michael Angeli, with whom Pesce was considering collaborating on a story about Paul Hill.*

Pesce wore a leather vest and held an unlit cigar. "First of all, please be aware that there is still production sound, so don't be alarmed by that. Also, the last shoot-out uses Led Zeppelin music, because it's the right mood—don't be alarmed. Bill?" He gestured to editor Bill Johnson.

"We're still on digitalized images, so there are two tapes," said Johnson.

"*There will be, like, a forty-five-second intermission while the reels are changed. So, don't be alarmed.*"

"*The message here, clearly, is 'Don't be alarmed,*'" added Pesce.

After the screening Pesce again addressed the audience. "*There are many people here who have seen the film three, four, five times. They've sort of became* Desperate Trail *experts. So I just want to ask the first few questions only to those who have just seen it for the first time.*

"*How is the opening—the first twenty minutes or so—working for everyone?*"

A collective nod indicated that it was working well. A woman in the front row exclaimed, "*I really loved their relationship. I love this film!*" *Pesce leaned down and kissed her. The crowd laughed.*

Michael Kastenbaum said, "*P. J., the stagecoach sequence . . . I don't know, it seems like the guys on the hill are watching, and waiting, and the stagecoach is traveling way too far—*" *Seth Kastenbaum, Michael's brother and his coproducer on the thwarted* Whore II, *agreed.*

Pesce cringed, having heard this many times before. "*Well, both Kastenbaum brothers agree on this one point. Maybe it's just a genetic defect.*"

The question of Fiorentino's performance in the partnering-up scene was raised. Someone thought she and Sheffer should have had "hotter sex."

The ending, in which we see that Sheffer has survived a brutal gunfight when he visits Elliott's grave with Fiorentino, was discussed at length. Many wanted it cut, while others felt Sheffer's movements after severe bullet wounds to the chest should have been more limited. Others thought a stronger final image would have been an earlier crane shot which left Elliott, Sheffer, and Fiorentino on the ground, their futures in question.

Brad Krevoy, Desperate Trail *producer and cochairman of MPCA, raised a hand in objection.* "*You have to be careful, P. J. With these low-budget movies, sometimes when you end them too abruptly, people think you ran out of money.*" *Behind him, Pesce's agent David Kanter roared with laughter, slapping Krevoy on the back.*

LIZ CANE
March 11

My friend Patrick Drummond is directing a low-budget feature he wrote. It's a thriller about homeless people and artists. He's raising money, using his own, and making deals with friends who will help him in post—deferments, etc. Plus he's worked with Jim Brooks and the Marxes, so there will be lots of creative support.

There is a job opening up at the audio-visual lab at UCLA. A woman who was there is going to North Carolina. So I'd really like Patrick's film to start in July rather than June. The new person needs to be trained, because one of us always has to be around.

Someone in the 401 support group had an idea to do an anthology. We would each do a ten-minute film, on ourselves.

In the meantime, I'm writing. I'm trying to make the deadline for this Disney fellowship, which is supposedly open to minorities and women, but I've been told that minorities tend to be chosen over women. I had committed to editing this student's film, but then I flipped out, because I realized the deadline for Disney is April 15. So I had to cancel on her. I felt bad, but it's important to prioritize writing and give myself deadlines, and stick to them.

FRANK DARABONT, Writer-Director

It's very tough to get a foot in the door, and a difficult business in which to maintain a career. A lot of people seem to be in it for the money—they're the ones who seem not to last or whose work doesn't seem to be terribly significant. Caring about what you're doing doesn't necessarily mean you're going to make a good movie every single time, but at least the effort will be honest.

Teddy Roosevelt spoke of those who try and don't try. The person who really deserves the credit is in the arena, with blood and sweat on his face, because he is the one who's trying. And even if he fails, he'll never have to be one of those people who never tried in the first place—"those sorry people who know neither victory nor defeat."

It's really all about persistence, I think—giving 100 percent and not giving in. It's not easy or fun, and this town tends to lead people around in circles. But nevertheless, persistence will out. I've gotten letters from people from time to time, and I always try to be inspirational. Realistic about the chances and the amount of work it takes, but inspirational nevertheless.

P. J. PESCE
March 22

Last night I came home a little stoned and was watching television, and there was this show about the Independent Feature Project, this documentary someone had made about people at the IFP. It was just terrifying. There were all these bad films and bad filmmakers just struggling and going onward, insanely believing in themselves. Looking at them objectively, they had no reason to believe in themselves.

I was thinking, "Is this going to be the net result of this whole movie? Am I going to finish this and not do anything and be right back where I started?" The next thing I do I want to be the opposite, like a Mike Leigh movie. I want it to have no plot. [Laughs]

I went to see *The Hudsucker Proxy* the other night, and there were like five ads in a row for movies before it, and each one looked stupider and more contrived than the last. And the audience was howling, hissing, spitting at the movies. This really lame-brained-looking thing with Joe Pesci as a bum. *The River Wild* ("This river could kill you." "Well, I did this once when I was a child, and now I'm back.") Forget it!

Columbia is interested in *The Desperate Trail*, so we're screening it for them in the middle of next week. The chances of a studio picking up a movie like this are not big. Krevoy was talking to them and they were looking for a Western, so who knows? We'll see. Sam Elliott is well liked, they know that. They get that.

Chad and I have a couple of things we're trying to get together. Did a lot of work on the music and everything, lots of tightening and trims.

I feel like I'm such a hard guy sometimes. Like, I just talked to the editor and he said, "We printed out the video version and there's a shot missing, but it's not a big deal," and blah, blah, blah. And I said, "What do you mean, 'it's not a big deal'?" And he said, "It doesn't affect the story, there's no dialogue in it, na, na, na."

I just sat there for a minute, thinking, "What am I—the only person who gives a shit?"

And he says, "It's like a bad meal—we can just put it behind us." And I went, "No, we don't have to put it behind us. You're going to redo it." And he was like, "Okay, okay, okay." I said, "Yeah, *okay*. Redo it, let's do it properly."

I mean, am I being a hard guy? I don't want copies of my movie going out improperly. He fucked up. When he was putting the thing together, he fucked up. And it takes time to redo it and to output it and everything else, but that's not my fucking problem. It's my movie and I want it to be done properly, and I want anyone who sees it to see it in its entirety properly, not with one single shot missing. Am I being crazy?

It was his mistake. He should have offered to do it and let *me* decide. We get along fine, really well, it's just that when I'm the boss I guess I don't take any shit.

I just feel, like, already one version of the damn movie leaked out and was over at New Line and people were looking at it. And it wasn't the finished version, or anywhere near what it should have been. Probably some jerkoff from Turner leaked it.

ROB MINKOFF, Director

Being a director isn't about being "above the line." It's about being *on* the line. That's what makes it exciting. It's their work, they're going to be responsible for it, they're going to be criticized for it. So they're on the line. They put themselves there.

JOHN KEITEL
March 23

My birthday party was fun. It was basically watching the Oscars. I had gone to San Francisco for the weekend to celebrate with friends from college. One of my best friends from college was in town and we had dinner Saturday night. That was very festive, so by the time Monday actually rolled around, I sort of eased down into it.

It was fine. I feel better about not being nominated this year. I feel like no matter what, thirtieth birthday or not, there was no way I could have beaten Steven Spielberg [*for Schindler's List*]! So I'm just going to save it for the next time.

I talked to a friend of mine, David Desmond, an attorney who just graduated from law school at UCLA, and he's very excited about helping me with *Ground Zero*. So we are kind of a team now. I didn't invite Carter. We hadn't been talking for a while. Last week I called him, and we had dinner Wednesday night.

April 18

I finished the latest draft and have been circulating it. I gave it to my thesis advisor. I've been getting a lot of feedback and making changes.

I'm doing the AIDS Ride from San Francisco to L.A. I raised $3,000. You fly up there, and it's a week long. They really take care of you, with campgrounds, food, etc. And Tanqueray is underwriting it. I may shoot High 8 and have it sent down daily so they can assemble a video photo album. About seven hundred people are signed up to do the ride.

I've had a little breakthrough since breaking up with Carter. That really played havoc with my self-esteem. He was just such a big part of my identity, and now I've reconnected with friends who I wasn't hanging out with. It was a mistake. You need that group of intermediaries.

MARCO WILLIAMS
April 18

The southern circuit was not that inspiring. The year and a half of touring with *In Search of Our Fathers* has taken the surprise out of it. I found myself getting asked the same questions and giving the same answers. Duke and North Carolina State were slightly better. But I've basically decided not to tour the film anymore. I'm not getting anything from it.

On *God Bless the Child*, we got a nibble from Matthew Modine, whom I met at Sundance, but he passed. It's out to actors for the lead, which is white, because Rene Russo and Sam Jackson are playing supporting roles.

The material is controversial. It's about a black father and a white surrogate father who ends up adopting a black child. I wouldn't play it that way but the writer, Dan Gilroy, doesn't want to rewrite it because he knows he will have to anyway, once we get an actor.

The producer is Damian Jones, who was at Working Title and now is on his own. So it's tough, because it's three first-timers.

The elevator ride of an actor reading it, liking the script, then turning it down, is tough. Charlie Sheen read it, but a deciding factor was that he had just worked with a new director [Adam Rifkin] on *The Chase*. Bill Pullman read it and called Damian from his trailer on *Casper*. Hopefully we will meet with him this week. His film *The Favor* may break out and we can put a package together. He showed some range in *Malice*. D. B. Sweeney has been discussed, but I'm not that wild about his work.

I met Modine again in Atlanta when I was touring, but he wanted the script revamped. We chased James Spader for three months. I don't even know if he actually read the script. The script is really good, but it's a matter of dealing directly with these people. We talked to Addis/Wechsler, and to [personal manager] Dolores Robinson about Jason Patric. But he's eccentric, they tell me.

Dealing with the agents is the toughest thing, getting through that. I'm not overly optimistic. I've just learned—after all the shit I've been through—that if something is meant to happen, it will.

I was offered a teaching job at a new film school in Winston-Salem, at the North Carolina School of the Arts. The dean is Sam Grogg, who was the cochair of the Producer's Program at UCLA [and former head of independent FilmDallas]. I went for five days and snooped around and want to go back and check out the living situation, etc. They have a $15 million endowment, and will work closely with Wilmington, North Carolina, where the film business is.

I need to give them an answer by the end of May.

P. J. PESCE
April 18

I'm really nervous. There's a screening tonight at the DGA for exhibitors and studio people. Columbia passed on it. My father's in town. I'm freaking out.

The Samuel Goldwyn Company has a script, *Hero at Last*, that I'm really interested in doing. It's about these waiters.

Dan Algrant's film Naked in New York, *presented by Martin Scorsese, had opened the previous Friday in limited release. Algrant was called "a talent to watch" in the* Los Angeles Times.

At the Directors Guild in Hollywood on April 18, when The Desperate Trail *screened again, approximately 250 people attended, including MPCA principals Brad Krevoy and Steve Stabler, coproducer Chad Oman, Josh Charles, an actor from MPCA's film* Threesome, *and Wally Wolodarsky, a* Simpsons *producer and writer-director of MPCA's just-wrapped* Cold-Blooded.

This event had more of a "premiere" atmosphere than the earlier screenings. Before the film, Pesce said, "If people want to say hello after the screening, that's fine. But not now. I feel like they've all just placed a bet at the two-dollar window."

Krevoy was the first to speak. "Welcome to this screening of a work in progress, The Desperate Trail," *he began. "You are here because you are friends and colleagues, and we value your opinion. We had similar screenings last year of* Threesome *and are very appreciative of the results. And tonight we present another great new talent, P. J. Pesce, who will speak in a moment. We hope you like the film, and if you do, please tell your friends, and the people at the studios. Also, please keep in mind that this is a rough cut, with no music, and it is not color-corrected."*

Pesce was then introduced and kept his comments brief.

"You've heard this speech before. It's temp music, temp sound. I showed

it to my father the other day, and he asked me, 'Whose idea was it to put those black lines in?' and I said, 'No, Dad, those are dissolves.' So, those black lines are dissolves, everyone."

As usual, Pesce's appearance in the film's poker scene drew giggles—especially his violent death. An often-discussed sequence in a hotel room between Sheffer and Fiorentino was received particularly well. Also, the long crane shot before the tag ending had been extended.

I thought it went really well. Miramax is interested, they want a screening. And MPCA has offered me a project called *Deep End*, but I don't think the script is very good. There seems to be a little buzz, though. People are talking about doing something with me.

The film runs ninety-four minutes. They still want the ending cleaned up. They want it to work better. The idiot who directed *Amos & Andrew* [E. Max Frye] told Krevoy that fifteen minutes could be cut. That is so irresponsible!

LIZ CANE
April 21

I've been crazy trying to meet the deadline for this Chesterfield Fellowship. Ten fellowships are awarded, each for $20,000 a year. It's cosponsored by Disney and you have to commit to writing two scripts during that time. You meet with people, I guess, three to five times a week.

At Disney they have basically the same deal. I submitted this new script, a romantic comedy. It was pretty crazy, focusing all my energy on it.

April 27

I'd like to work on the ending of the script. I wonder if I could resubmit it to Chesterfield.

I've been kind of manic and scared to submit the script to Disney for their fellowship. They make you sign a release in case they do anything similar.

I want the script to be in the best shape possible. It's funny in places. Aside from a couple of friends, only the Marxes have it. I'm a little nervous about their reaction.

Patrick is shooting his film late this summer. They may have Jon Savage to star.

BOBBI THOMPSON, Agent

New directors should be concentrating their efforts on getting together a script that they can attach themselves to, whether it's one they write, or collaborate with a writer on, or one they can acquire—some sort of material, be it an idea or preferably a screenplay, that can be their calling card in meetings, and hopefully get made. That has value. If they're writers, they should write. If they're not, they should find writers to work with them. If they have agents, they should ask their agents for material, as much as they can get.

They need to have a property to push the envelope—that's the easiest way to get into features. There are other things one can do. It's not the only thing to do, but it's the key thing.

JOHN MCINTYRE
April 30

I'm glad *The Critic* is back [renewed, but moved from ABC to Fox]. But the writing was uneven. The character was too bitter for you to care about him, and they should have stuck with the critic show set. They got too involved with the other characters too quickly.

Fox will start by showing the last seven episodes we did, which won't help. Parts of the shows were funny, but it was often heavy-handed, with long, isolated shots of Jay to elicit audience sympathy and stuff like that. But I am glad that another animated series is on prime time again.

The Simpsons has been doing esoteric and strange stories, like "Springfield Snake-Beating Day." But they were picked up for three more years, so I guess it's hard to not have to stretch a little.

So, I'm officially engaged! It happened on my birthday, April first. I wanted to pick a night when Theresa wouldn't think it was weird that I put a tie on.

I hired this company to have a helicopter fly us from the top of a building downtown to the Tower restaurant. So I met the pilot in the lounge of the building, and he said, "Hey, man, it's too foggy. I can't fly in this." So we took a limousine ride for a couple of hours instead, and picked up a couple of friends, and drank champagne.

The following week we did the helicopter flight. I'm scared of heights and proposals, so I took the opportunity to take care of both.

We're looking at mid-September or early October, a small cere-mony at the beach, or an inn. Her parents don't have much money, so I think I'll just pay for it.

On the show I'm on, *Rocko's Modern Life*, there are all these kids. Twenty-five-year-olds. One of them was telling me about an ani-mation seminar he went to. He said, "There were a lot of people your age there." *My* age. I'm thirty-one!

I'm doing timing. But I'm also mingling with directors. People are telling the producer, Joe Murray, that I should do a lot more. He really like *Melbridge*, which seems to show people that I can sus-tain a story for a half hour, and that I can write. So people are starting to see me as more of a creative type, writing and directing. I'm getting anxious to do that soon, get to the meat of this and do more. There are new projects and pilots at Nickelodeon maybe I can get plugged into.

I pitched *Kitchen Casanova*, a short animated film, to Hanna-Barbera. They liked it, although it's not the kind of thing they're doing right now. Believe it or not, they want to do things that are more sophomoric and gag-oriented.

But they want to pitch it with me to the Cartoon Network. I'm going to do it anyway, so I'm willing to do boards. They want to pitch in the beginning of July. It was satisfying. I'm also taking a class in animation drawing on Wednesday nights, just to get back into it.

ROB MINKOFF, Director

When you "in-between," somebody gives you a stack of drawings and says, "There needs to be two drawings between each of these," and you do them. The timer decides whether he wants the action slower or not, and then does a chart which says, "Do a drawing halfway in between." In Disney animation, the animator *is* the timer. It's a pretty exacting job.

P. J. PESCE
May 11

This weekend there was some major drama. Bill, the editor, is on another project, so we have this great editor, Lois Freeman-Fox. She won an Eddie Award for *And the Band Played On*.

Krevoy called her on the sly and asked her to make all these changes without telling me. Basically, anything with any heart or guts in it. And of course Chad is in Hawaii [on vacation]. So we had to make the changes and then, slowly, pull them out.

I'm really nervous. I've been sitting here for three or four hours just going nuts. Miramax is about to make an offer on the film. [Cochairman] Bob Weinstein saw it this morning, I met him at the screening room. So hopefully the deal between them and TNT won't get blown.

ADAM DUBOV, Director

The distribution of films is kind of at a sorry state, because most people concede that at the moment there are a couple too few players, because both Miramax and New Line have gone "uptown," as it were, and are bigger companies now and not in the business of picking up small, weirdo movies anymore.

JOHN KEITEL
May 13

Keitel had recently completed the AIDS Ride, a charity bicycle trip from San Francisco to Los Angeles.

It was mind-altering, a week out there with all these people. By the end of the first day, everyone's layers of jadedness were peeled away. It was a common goal, a common purpose, a focus with no distractions, a real bonding experience. And it was physically beautiful, too.

There was a sixty-seven-year-old guy on the ride. He had lost fifty-two friends to AIDS. I made some really good friends—these two guys—and we were like the three musketeers. And the closing ceremonies were really emotional, and really well done. They're approaching $1.5 million raised. It was really successful. I ended up raising $3,500 but a lot of people raised in the upper five figures.

We took lots of pictures. At the closing ceremonies they brought out a riderless bike, and Melissa Etheridge read this moving piece about why the bike had no rider on it.

It was great, absolutely fantastic, and the best thing is to just get away like that, come back a week later and read my screenplay. Because I was so totally removed as the writer from it on this trip, I had so much more objectivity. All those hours on those back country roads. I didn't think you could have experiences like this anymore.

MARCO WILLIAMS
May 18

I had breakfast with Dan Gilroy [screenwriter, *God Bless the Child*, and husband of actress Rene Russo] a couple of days after the *L.A. Times* review of the film he wrote [*Tracers*], and I said, "Congratulations!" He said it was the only good review, and he was so surprised that he even went to see the film, and he said it was for shit. His version of the script was quick. They ended up drawing everything out. I think it was a film for video. But because of this one review he decided to go out and see it.

I had a good time in North Carolina. It's not just a film school. North Carolina School of the Arts is a conservatory/college with programs in theatre, dance, music, set design. So I got a tour of that. It was all very exciting.

The last time I went, they had me on a real rigorous itinerary. It was worthwhile, although I told them, "Look, you really haven't given me a chance to breathe here." But if they hadn't put me on such an itinerary, I probably would have known a lot less about the institution. This trip I rented a car and was ostensibly going to just drive around. I got a little nervous when I got there. Nobody had given me suggestions as to where to drive. Maybe they took me a little too seriously!

What ended up happening was that I had a small itinerary. The first day I was there I had a meeting, and a tour of the town with a man named Chandler Lee, who's a mover and shaker in the black and business community. He owns a Cadillac dealership. I was told that he was the only person who could give me a sense of the black community in the town. The people at the film school are not black, they don't know that community. Chandler drove me through it, gave me some sort of historical context, which is what I was really seeking. A little about the South and how it would be living there as an artist.

It was a good trip, and I'm almost certain I will be going. The offer was there a long time ago, and last night the dean of the school called me at 11:30 his time, saying he had just spoken with the chancellor. I had mentioned that I wanted some type of assurance concerning contract. Not that I really wanted more than a year contract, but I wanted to know that after uprooting, nine months later they weren't going to say, "Oh, we found someone we like better." And that short of gross misconduct I could continue on if I wanted.

So the dean called me last night and said they could give me a two-year contract. I wasn't longing for a two-year contract, but I figured you can always get out. So the offer is sound in that regard. They very much want me, and I think the bottom line is they flew me there twice and put me up, so they're really recruiting.

It's really a question of me acknowledging to myself that I'm moving on, at least temporarily.

I told the dean that I wanted to be clear about what they wanted me to teach. It's not absolutely clear, but I understand they're going to have me teach one of the sections of the first-year students, a class of about fifteen, and one of the sections of the second-year students, a class of eleven. And then there's one set of courses that are on the craft of filmmaking, which I will teach with someone. So I'll have about two and a half classes, which maybe is anywhere from ten to twenty hours a week.

My goal for going there is not simply to teach but at the end of the year to have something I have developed or written, so I could go on to make something later on. To nurture my creativity.

The other big concern of mine aside from the contract was that if I got a job—a directing job or producing job of some sort—that it was feasible for me to leave. That's to their benefit, and is probably the capper for me as to why this is a good thing to do. If I were to get a directing job, they would use the salary they were giving me to bring somebody in temporarily, but as soon as I was done with that job, I could come back and teach. It's sort of like having tenure without it being tenure.

So that gives me the facility to make films, although that may be harder once I'm there than from here. Once I commit, I'll tell them the projects I'm up for. One can almost do this with the shortest of notice because what they are trying to design in the curriculum is to have four filmmakers as production faculty, all teaching the same curriculum, so that if somebody has to leave temporarily, one of the other faculty can step in and teach that class until they bring in a permanent replacement. So I would have a kind of security without completely abandoning my dream to make films.

Sam Grogg's wish is for the faculty and film school to be a de facto production company, and that there will be all sorts of equipment to make films, and the students would get to crew or intern, etc. And of course, North Carolina is a right-to-work state, so you can do things for a little less.

There seems to be, as a vision, a sense of creating a film industry in this town with the North Carolina School of the Arts, the school of filmmaking being one of the pillars of that. So the excitement is being in on the ground floor of this evolving situation, instead of coming in after a couple of years. Chandler Lee spoke like a businessman. He said in his experience, those who get there at the beginning are the ones who ultimately reap the most profit, etc.

So, I'm going to say yes, because I have an escape clause. I'll say yes now, and if in a month or two I got a directing job, I can then say I can't come. As opposed to waiting and waiting and waiting to see if one of these directing things comes along.

I would go around August fifteenth. Because I need to move a little bit of myself from L.A., and I have a whole apartment of furniture in storage in New York, I need to get down there. School starts the first or second week of September.

I'm so broke that up until yesterday I owed three months of back rent. I was able to pay one yesterday. They will give me a flat amount to pay for the move, $1,500 or $2,000 or something. I suppose that will cover my costs. If I have to load the stuff up in New York and drive it down, I can do that, and ship the stuff from L.A. I haven't leveraged for a lot of perks or anything. I'm not experienced in that.

I can get an interest-free loan of $5,000 or $10,000. Winston-Salem is a cute, idyllic city/town. Compared to L.A. it's a town, but obviously it's a city. It's very inexpensive to live there. People had two-bedroom houses for $500, with a backyard and a porch and stuff. I'm a little bit concerned with how it's going to be after a while, but there's a lot there. Wake Forest University is in this town, Raleigh and Durham and Chapel Hill are an hour away. I'm not going to get any work done for the first couple of months. I'll spend most of my free time trying to assimilate, as opposed to becoming a hermit in the beginning.

I'm a little concerned about the movie end of things—out of sight, out of mind. And even the notion of whether I'm "in the loop" or "out of the loop," even though I'm in Winston-Salem. It seems as though my agent is not going to be as active because I'm so far away. I have to be a little bit more aggressive and creative to get him to stay on top of things.

Chris Gerolmo's first response was, "Oh, you get to see a lot of good basketball games there, Duke, and N.C. State." Charlotte is not that far, so there will be people I know visiting me. And there is a cosmopolitan feel, not a lot of bumpkins. I never wanted to lay down roots in L.A. If I settle there, it might be great.

God Bless the Child had a little bit of action. We had a meeting with Bill Pullman, the result of which was that he likes the script and wants to be attached. So that gave us what we didn't have up until that point, which was a white lead for this script. And although Pullman is not a star yet, he's in a couple of things now that will be out next year that may catapult him. He's in *Casper* and *Wyatt Earp*. He's very good in *Malice*.

Plus, we had a meeting at his agency, UTA, going over strategies of who to sell it to. It's the same dilemma of, "Can we get this made whether it's at 2.5, 3.5, four, five million?" It seems a little bit hard to get it off the ground because neither Sam Jackson nor Rene Russo nor Bill Pullman are movie stars. Everybody says, "Great package," but no one says, "Here's the money."

We got kind of caught in the Cannes bind, where everybody's at Cannes right now, so we're waiting for people to come back to push it aggressively. There has been some conversation. I had one with a Hollywood Pictures executive yesterday. He said the script was too much like a project they just did called *Losing Isaiah*, with Halle Berry. I was enthusiastic about getting Bill Pullman involved, but my experience is that it doesn't mean anything until it means something.

There are some script points that are an obstacle. It's a little "white knightish." Somebody white comes to the rescue. I think that's an obstacle everybody who reads it is uncomfortable with. My thought all along was that my involvement would counter-balance that concern, but evidently not. So Dan and I are going to outline the changes and he will make them, which could have an effect on how the script is read by people.

The right place for this film would seem to be maybe Miramax, maybe Goldwyn, a smaller company that does good films, good stories. Universal more or less said, "We can't do this without Spike Lee endorsing it," but it's not angry enough to be a Spike Lee project.

I can't really understand why we can't get Castle Rock to make this movie because everybody involved in the project, with the exception of myself and Damian, has a great relationship with them. Dan is writing something for them, Rene is probably going to be in another movie for them, Bill Pullman has been in several of their films. But they're wondering whether they're going to continue to make small films.

I saw *The Inkwell* at Sundance. I thought it was terrible. I was stunned [that it received any good reviews]. I would have walked out, except that I was sitting with the Matty Rich entourage at Sundance. I thought it was really, really bad. I had read the script, and had pitched a take to direct it, but I don't think it's sour grapes.

I just found it insulting, a series of caricatures from the '70s. It's really kind of humiliating as far as I'm concerned, and poorly directed.

There's one moment during a love scene between two adult characters, and the woman is wearing a scarf or something and all the camera shots are from this angle where the scarf waves in her face, so when they kiss you don't see anything. And I'm thinking to myself, "Wait a second, who is directing this? If this is a warm and tender moment in this movie . . ." You don't get it, because there's a scarf in there. Things like that. I was really offended by it. It's not making a lot of money at all. I've been sort of tracking it to see how it would do.

The other thing that's happened to me that's sort of one of those "things that could have been" is that there was a script at Columbia that I was made aware of. These producers had a script called *Chains*, about the Black Panthers. I met with them and they really liked me, but Columbia wants Forest Whitaker to direct it, so I don't think I really have a shot at it.

The irony is that I heard about it because I knew one of the producers. My agency never sent me the script, and the reason, I've come to realize, is that Forest is represented by them. So they're not necessarily going to send it to me. The producers are Janet Yang from Ixtlan [Oliver Stone's production company], someone from Suzanne dePasse's company, and the writer, Anna Hamilton Phelan, who wrote *Mask*.

I met Janet at Sundance and kind of heard about it, and when I realized she was attached to it I called her and said, "I'd love to talk to you about it." And I had a great meeting, but the reality is that it's hard to compete with a front-runner unless he elects to not be involved.

I'm not optimistic about these things. When it happens, I'll believe it. But until that time, better to pursue, thinking that nothing's going to happen. I think the movie business is designed to disappoint more than surprise. But I'll keep my fingers in as many pots as possible.

LIZ GLOTZER, Producer-Executive

It's not often we would take a leap with a director who has a dubious track record. We must believe they will be great for the project. When we hired Ron Underwood on *City Slickers*, he had made one feature—*Tremors*—that we all genuinely liked. It wasn't that he came in and gave a better meeting than the next person. We were faced with a few guys who had done a few movies that we weren't really impressed with, and a relatively inexperienced guy who had done a movie that we really liked, and we thought, "Well, maybe he'll be really good." We'd rather take that chance than work with someone who's done five mediocre movies. Of course it's a risk.

Often when we work with first-time directors it's because they have written a script and then attached themselves to direct. We wouldn't go out of our way to attach a first-time director to a script, particularly if they hadn't written it, but there are cases where it's happened. Billy Weber is a top editor who came to us with a script [*Josh and S.A.M.*] that we loved. We felt confident that if he developed the script to that stage, he could probably direct it, but—given the fact that he'd never directed before—we wouldn't have offered him a movie.

LISA KLEIN
June 7

My sister died. It was really sudden. She was never sickly, like a sickly kid. Several years ago she had had an aneurysm, and had Epstein-Barr, and went through periods of not being real healthy. The bottom line is, her heart stopped. She died in her sleep. It's not real easy to explain, she just became really weak. She went through bouts of depression and stuff like that, and her heart stopped. She was forty-five years old.

I've been through this before, with my brother, but it doesn't make it any easier. It makes it harder—one more unexplained death that doesn't make any sense. And I know there's a lot of frustration and anger with that on top of everything else. It's just there, and it's constant, and it puts everything else into perspective. Like when I was home I didn't care about my career anymore. I went home for quite a while and for the past month have just been sorting things out.

I quit waitressing. I started working this other job, just to have something, because it was impossible to focus on my writing. It just seemed so stupid and unimportant and required this drive that I just couldn't get. So I'm working at an event management company that a friend of mine works for. I do a little writing for them, nothing like scripts, just copy.

The Orlando job didn't come through. They went with a writer who had far more experience, including *Saturday Night Live*. The money was great and it would have been an opportunity, but in retrospect I would have had to leave anyway. It was nice that they loved the *Seinfeld* I wrote and that in the interview they seemed to like me.

Peter and I are meeting with the agents on Thursday. Right before I left I gave them *Waltzing Matilda*, and they were all stoked about starting to send it around. Well, nothing happened. They didn't send it anywhere. Now they're saying, "Well, it was pilot season, and we just weren't focused on features." All of my friends with agents say the same thing, though. You have to really stay on them and call them every day.

FRANK DARABONT, Writer-Director

Write a script, but make it the best goddam script you can write or you won't sell it. Chances are, years later you'll look back and say, "God, this was really shitty." But having done it, you sit down and write another one. And if you keep doing it, sooner or later you're going to be good enough to sell them and get them made.

That's been my window of opportunity—I look at myself as a writer first and everything else second. I've spent years trying to be one thing and one thing only, and that's a good writer. And I think I've come to the point were I can finally say with a straight face, "Yes, I'm a writer."

LIZ CANE
June 21

Patrick is hoping to start shooting his film, *Night Canvas*, in early August. The movie was pushed back. We have been meeting with actors. There are about four leads. And Patrick is rewriting.

It looked like he had the money about a week and a half ago, but the people financing it wanted control. I hope it doesn't get pushed back again because the crew is working for a fraction of what they usually do, and they will have to take other work. The cost will be about $1 million, including donated services, like film processing at DeLuxe.

Jim Brooks and Polly Platt wrote letters on Patrick's behalf. But I guess because he doesn't have a [directing] credit, the Hollywood system won't back him. He did write a nice proposal, though.

I used all of these deadlines for fellowships—the Disney, the Nicholls, the Chesterfield—to keep real busy on my script. I just kept using the extensions I would find out about to get the script to friends and get feedback. It's called *Don't Shoot Me, I'm Available*. I got good feedback from Richard Marx.

I should probably submit it to the Sundance Writers Lab. Half of the projects from there go on to the Production Lab. Eventually I'll send it there but I want to get it into the best shape possible. I'm also thinking of four or five ideas to sink my teeth into for the next script.

Kayo Hatta had her film *Picture Bride* at Cannes and is doing real well from it. She's trying to figure out what to do next. They're not releasing the film until January. It's too small to compete with the holiday stuff.

And Rory Kelly is getting so much attention from *Sleep with*

Me. He wants to shoot his next film as a quickie, which I think is smart.

P. J. PESCE
June 21

The looping session with Craig Sheffer went great. Sheffer said, somewhat surprised, that he really likes the movie, and he obviously didn't think he would. He said he comes off in a way he never has before, and he will be happy to do anything he can in terms of publicity, etc.

Also, he admitted he was wrong about a couple of things we fought about during production. One thing was his accent. I kept urging him to do, like, a Boston accent because the character was a bit of a Milquetoast, and he wouldn't do it. So during looping, because the sound in the beginning was so bad anyway, he went ahead and did it with a little of that air about it. It worked really great.

MARCO WILLIAMS
June 28

I've agreed to the teaching position, and I will go next week to North Carolina. They're having some sort of faculty retreat, and I'll spend some time looking for a place to live. Tentatively, I expect to be out of L.A. around the middle of August.

I feel a fair amount of apprehension and trepidation. It's not what I have been dreaming of doing. Even though the components are attractive, it's not by my own design that I'm leaving. I would have rather made a film and taken the opportunity to teach second. Now it seems that the pattern will be to teach first and make films second, which will probably be fine once I get there.

It's a mind versus heart thing. All the elements are there for me to be excited, which I am. But emotionally, it's about severing ties, even if it's just temporarily.

I was thinking about it this morning, actually. I was living in New York and made a decision about applying to graduate school. Things were good for me in New York, although not great. But it was part of a conscious plan. I had envisioned it. I would look at graduate school, getting into one of the crafts unions, applying for a grant to make a film. I had these objectives.

But this time around, *this* came to me. It doesn't feel the same, I'm not leaving with the same sense of confidence. Where this development will take me, I really don't know.

This will be a door to some other film opportunity, whether it's immediately back here in L.A., or some projects generated in the state, or in the South.

One thing that's tricky about moving is that there is something to be said for writing from a place that you know. And I think probably why I didn't write much initially is that I was still feeling like a New Yorker. Now I'm just starting to think about stories situated here, not in New York, and I'll be moving to the South. But I have a feeling there are a great number of stories rooted in the southern part of this country that I will discover, and there won't be many black directors in that area. So maybe it will be a capital for me.

All of that is clear to me and I'm sure it will work out. It's just the trepidation of moving toward the unknown. The decision has been made. I have not made it public. I'm still trying to figure out how to negotiate or navigate the film community here at large, whether it's positive to say I'm going out of town to teach, or whether nobody professionally should know. I'm having voice mail set up here, to give the impression that I'm in L.A.

Thus far I've kept it at a very low profile. The only people who know that I'm leaving are my friends. A few of them are in the movie business, but I haven't told my agent, or the agency. Or any of the people I'm dealing with on projects.

I think the way I'm approaching this is to initially not tell anyone, and try to at least create the semblance of being here. My biggest concern is that the simple way to assess me not being in town is that I'm not available, which is contrary to the agreement I have with the school.

The initial three months, through the fall, I will not tip my hand. And then just see. If there seems to not be a lot going on, then it's probably okay and the situation can dictate things. If there are meetings and scripts to be read, I'll just make a point to come back here. Of the current faculty there, I would be the only directing faculty member with a clear connection to Hollywood. So I want to ensure that my schedule is Tuesday, Wednesday, and Thursday, allowing me to have Friday off so I can come to Los Angeles. How much leverage I have remains to be seen. The current faculty would probably like those days off because they make for a long weekend.

My agent doesn't call and rarely sends a script my way anyway, so it's kind of ludicrous. When I was in Berlin last year, I had a call to be in L.A. in two days for a meeting on *The Power of No*, and hopped on a plane, showered, and drove to Burbank. If I can do it from Berlin, I can do it from North Carolina.

ROBERT BENTON, Writer–Director

I would love to direct for as long as someone lets me do it. If somebody won't let me direct, I'll try to write screenplays. If someone won't let me write screenplays, I'll try to produce. And if they won't let me do any of that, I'll try to teach.

P. J. PESCE
July 6

Sam Elliott's scenes from The Desperate Trail *were dubbed at Fidelity Sound in North Hollywood.*

Much of the session involved changing some of the expletives in the film to broadcast-standard dialogue. Elliott suggested "Doggone it!" for "God damn it!" Pesce countered with, "He could just say, 'Dammit, Hollister,'" which they eventually agreed upon.

On another line in a saloon scene, Elliott became frustrated after eight unsuccessful takes. "You know what it is?" he muttered. "It's being here instead of in a fucking bar in Santa Fe."

"Well, that's always going to be the case," Pesce answered.

"It's not the reading of the line," Elliott said forcefully. "It's the quality of the sound."

"What I hear is the emotional sound of the first one—"

"Well, you should listen to the production [sound] again—it was pretty fuckin' intense," snapped Elliott.

*They watched the entire scene once more. Elliott seemed to relent.
"Okay, let's try it again."*

"See, you're a lot more in control of yourself," reinforced Pesce.

*Later, Elliott questioned the problem with an existing line of his: "You
got a safe in this shithole?"*

"Your buddy Turner doesn't like the word 'shit,' " explained Pesce.

*"Don't call him my buddy," snorted Elliott. "Trouble is, this isn't
Turner fare at all, this movie—and that fucking Chad [Oman] never
should have taken money from Turner. We wouldn't be in this situation in
the first place." [TNT ultimately put up the entire $2.5 million,
$100,000 of which was used to pay off Trimark for the verbal agreements
they claimed they had on the picture.]*

"Linda's pretty flat in this, isn't she?" Elliott said later.

*"She's a fucking prima donna," Pesce answered. "She got a great part,
and she didn't even deserve it. It hurts me, it really does. Craig apologized
to me, he was pretty good in the looping. He was willing to do anything I
asked him to."*

"It was pretty weird on location—the shit between the two of you."

"Yeah, it was pretty unprofessional. . . ."

*There was a pregnant pause. Then Elliott sighed, "Well, the movie
looks great."*

When the looping was finished, Pesce and Elliott embraced.

I'm attached to this project called *Fran's Thing*, developed at the
Chesterfield Company, which was brought to me by Rob Weiss
[director of *Amongst Friends*]. I met Rob when he first came out
here. He passed on the script and was gracious enough to send it
my way. He's sort of floundering now. He wants to direct *American
Psycho* [a film version of Bret Easton Ellis's critically lambasted
novel].

Fran's Thing is about a girl in the Bronx, an Italian-American
sixteen-year-old going to Catholic school. It's like *The 400 Blows*. I
love it. I went to Catholic school my whole life. It's truthful, not
pushed.

Ken Orkin, who is one of the Chesterfield guys, loves the
Western and the short, which is like the tone of that script. I met
with the writer last week and we hit it off. His name is Carl Capo-
torto, and he played the handsome younger brother in *Mac*.

The other project is *Bad Men*, which is about existential hit men, which Jon Shestack, a producer who I knew from Sandollar and Limelight, sent me. He did *The Last Seduction* with John Dahl.

I'm thinking of writing, maybe alone, maybe with Rob Weiss. I'm glad I didn't end up doing *Sketch Artist II* [an MPCA project Pesce was considered for]. Because it's one thing for a forty-five-year-old hack who doesn't even care that there's no prep time. But it would have sucked, and I would have felt bad about it. It would have been, like, a downward move, or lateral. And I just would have been going for the money.

Maybe I need to keep struggling, pushing up to four-, five-million-dollar projects, just keep everything moving forward. That's what matters.

I'm wondering about Kanter, and if I should be getting another agent. But I think he wants to wait until this is done and screen it for people. I want to set up a screening in New York even if I have to bankroll it myself.

ROBERT BENTON, Writer-Director

I trust Sam Cohn, my agent. I give him things to read and trust his opinion on things. It's not a conventional agent–writer/director relationship.

I've had Sam say don't do something and I've put it aside, because I value his opinion that much. If I like something Sam believes in and he says, "We're gonna take it here," and then it gets turned down, I don't try to second-guess him. He knows far better than me where a picture should go, who I should work with, and what I should be getting paid. He does that and he does that brilliantly.

To have an agent who you trust—not only to make a deal but whose opinion about your material you trust—is a great privilege.

LISA KLEIN
July 14

It's getting really busy right now [at the event management company], which is great for distraction purposes, because it's taking up a lot of my time. What I wanted to make sure to do was write at night, which just last week I actually sat down and did. I kept saying I was going to do it, and I couldn't.

The job is obviously not what I want to do. The whole nine-to-five thing is very odd for me. It's definitely an anachronism. I did this when I got out of college—I got a job before film school. It's a regression in a way, because I lost those years, but I don't want them back. It's not like I lost all this corporate headway.

It's fine. There's some minor creativity involved in the job, and I'm committed through the end of the year.

As far as writing goes, there was a project I was doing before I left with a couple of my friends. They came up with the idea, though I am pretty resistant to doing something that is not my idea, just because obviously I have a hundred things I want to do. So to do something else is tough. We met about it a few times and they sort of convinced me. They're really gung-ho.

I agreed to do it, but when I went home a lot of things changed, and I didn't really think about it. They were being cool, then started putting the squeeze on a little bit. You know, "You going to do it or not?"

Part of what's going on with me is indecisiveness. I just can't really focus or make a decision about anything. So if it was easy and I absolutely didn't want to do it, I could just walk away. But it wasn't easy, because part of me really wanted to do it. So finally I said, "I'm going to sit down and try," but it took me weeks to do that.

Last week I actually sat down and started working on this. Again, it's another sort of distraction. People say, "How can you work during the day and do this?" But for me it's, "How can I *not* do this?" It's easier for me to come home at night and do this than get up in the morning and do that. One objective a couple of years ago was to have nothing to do with the industry, because I don't like it. I just don't. There just is really nothing attractive about the industry to me.

To me, it's just sitting in a room and writing. I've even been contemplating, lately, saying "screw it" and writing a book, or moving to New York and writing a play. It sounds like I'm five years old and I want to be a ballerina, but I know I want to write, so the medium is almost secondary.

That was the one decision I made, and that I wanted to write during the day. I thought it would be more productive. The idea of interacting with people and having to be "on" just scared the hell out of me. When I first got back, I thought there was no way in hell I could do it. I was completely incapacitated. Now I can do it if I have to do it, but I don't know how effective I am. Basically, you're a salesperson and you're out for tips, that's really your only money.

I wasn't waiting tables because I wanted to wait tables. It was all right, but I don't feel like I would be serving myself or the restaurant right now. In this job there are a lot of meetings, a lot of dealing with people. It's a different level. I'm hiding behind a mask, I guess, a little bit.

Have you read *Waltzing Matilda*? That's a script that was finished before I went home. They [the Turtle Agency] were excited about it and couldn't wait to send it out. It's gone nowhere. It went to somebody who they knew who's doing made-for-TV movies, which we don't think it is [right for]. And when Peter and I met with this guy, and he said, "This really isn't an M.O.W. [Movie of the Week]," we said, "We know, we don't know why they sent it to you in the first place." So it's sitting there, and we have to push them to do anything.

Our attorney got frustrated and said, "Okay, I'm going to do it. I'll send it out for you guys," and that's where we are now. This is Larry Weinberg.

I'm starting to think it's me, and I have this weird agent jinx. I have this fantasy that everybody else has an agent who's gung-ho and aggressive, sending stuff out constantly, talking up their clients, blah, blah, blah.

We met with the people at the Turtle Agency two or three weeks ago, maybe. We went through everything. What happens when we meet with them is we kind of walk out and think, "What the hell just happened? What did we say?" Kind of checking ourselves to make sure we heard the same things. But it was very positive, the usual schmoozing. We kind of went in there wondering, thinking maybe we just need to sort of end this, and maybe they'll feel the same way.

They were the opposite. "Let's do this." I said, "I really want to write something about my sister, it's really important to me. I don't know that I can do it now." And they were pointing me in that direction, saying they thought for me it would be a good catharsis, and they thought it would sell. That was their advice.

With *Waltzing Matilda*, their style is that when people call in and want material, they send it out. They're not about to send it to twenty people and try to get heat on it. And I don't understand that. [Their explanation] is that you're building interest, people are calling and they specifically want a romantic comedy, and that's what you send them. It didn't make any sense.

It wasn't that easy to confront them. I was still in a little bit of a stupor. Peter conveyed it better than I did. I think it did come across, and we may have put them on the defensive a little bit. I mean, they came up with their own reasoning. And then, we talked to Larry, and that pissed him off. And he had a conversation with them.

It's one of those things where you just walk away from the conversation and don't know what hit you. I don't know, man. I've gone from apathy to frustration on this. Lately, I've just thought, ah, screw it. I just want to end this, move somewhere else, sit in a corner and write, teach at night, and just not be part of this whole thing. Because it takes an incredible amount of energy, and your mind is elsewhere.

Before, I could expend a lot of energy and worry and pursue and do all of that stuff. Now I can't. Maybe that will change, but there are too many other priorities right now, too many other things on my mind.

When I started this, it was never about the money. It was always about whatever I wanted to do. Screenwriting vs. playwrighting vs. novel writing vs. advertising. Believe me, I want to see what I do on the screen. I do. Or performed, or read. I don't want to live and die in obscurity with my writing. I truly believe that some of the stuff that I've done is pretty entertaining, and that people would like it.

But I wanted to get to the point where I was somewhat autonomous, and had a comfort level with whomever was representing me, so I could live wherever I wanted. The one thing you can't help but do is compare. Like, if I go see a *Sleepless in Seattle*. I happen to think my script is funnier. When I saw *When Harry Met Sally . . .*, I just though, man, this is great, I don't think I could ever write something like that. I think my ego is healthy enough that I think I could write whatever I want to write.

If I got to the point where I was really exposed and people kept rejecting stuff, I could say I'm really not talented, or my talents don't coincide with what's going on here. But my frustration right now is that it has just not seen the light of day. Nothing has seen the light of day, really.

What I'm learning, too, is you don't talk to someone who's read something of yours and they tell you it sucks. They always say, "Yeah, I thought it was really good! But it's not for me." At first you think, like, "Wow, that's great, they really like it." But then you realize that if they really liked it, they would have bought it. So screw that whole thing. But hardly anyone saw it. So I don't really want to do this stuff for my friends and family to enjoy and act out in the living room.

I'm far from writing any masterpiece. I think I have, however, written some stuff that should be in development, should be considered, should at least be being rewritten. Whether it's the ideas that I think are really good, or the writing, I think I should be farther along than I am.

I really want to write this thing about my sister. I don't have a story, I just really want to do something. I don't know when I'll be ready. It's a weird sort of paralysis. It's so much bigger than any of this, it really does put things in perspective. It's enhanced the feeling about wanting to get out of this whole thing.

I'm not worried about the job, that's fine. I'm just worried about my sanity a little bit. And this whole career thing. There's no way to measure how long it's going to take, or what's good. Is it about talent? I'm hearing all these stories that lead me to believe talent has little to do with it. That's pretty frustrating, too.

GARY ROSS, Screenwriter

The job of the artist is not to bitch about the system. The job of the artist is to find a way to get it done. This is an impossible thing to do when you think about it—to find a way to do it.

BERNARD JOFFA
July 28

My dad died. Cancer is a gift. It makes you get your life in order. He went very peacefully. He just said, "This is it," and he went to bed and died. We were all there, all of the cousins and nephews and grandchildren.

I wrote a screenplay while I was there, with Greg. It was a project brought to us by an actress named Bonnie Rodini. She had written the first draft and met with Donald Sutherland about it. He liked the material quite a bit. It's called *The Story of an African Farm*, a novel written by Olive Schreiner in 1880, I think. It's a classic in South Africa.

The script was too literary as Bonnie wrote it, and needed to be turned into something with cinematic language. Somehow she raised money for Greg to do a rewrite. We spent a month doing it. It's the story of a girl who is abandoned as a child, literally left to die. The story deals with her when she is older. If you haven't been shown love as a child, you die lonely. It's a love story about a woman who cannot love. It's an epic tragedy.

Why am I drawn to this? Because it is my story. We are forever drawn to our own stories. When I was a boy, because of my heart thing, I could not feel love, either, because I didn't feel worthy. I felt despair. The other character realizes you need to find fullness within yourself. It's a character-driven love story.

It was an unbelievable time to be in South Africa, with the elections going on. It was wonderful to see the country liberated, and was liberating for me. So many people told me to come back to South Africa. I could make films there. I could make a living there. So the question is, do I give up everything and go back? Or make South African films from here?

I'm broke. Totally out of money. I came with enough money to live for seven years and now it is gone. My house is totally paid for and worth $300,000, but I have no money.

I haven't dealt with Ronda on anything in over a year. If she doesn't like this *African Farm* script, I think I will not work with her anymore and seriously look for another agent. No—I take that back. What can Ronda do for me now anyway? When I make my first film, she will be my best supporter.

I still am glad that I turned down the other picture. People ask me how I could have, but it was not a picture I could have gotten excited about directing. I do have a few things going on, though. *Home Free* was read by a producer in England who offered to put up 50% of the money, but it had to be matched by U.S. funds. I think they are trying to attract Will Smith. I don't know, I guess he is a big name now.

Also, I was just about to option *The Year of the Zinc Penny* when my dad passed away. They want $5,000, which Chris thought was fair, but that is a lot of money for me right now. So there are three things I am attached to now. They always told me in film school to have at least ten.

FRANK DARABONT, Writer–Director

When Stephen King's *Different Seasons* came out, I thought it was an absolutely brilliant collection. One of the stories, *Rita Hayworth and Shawshank Redemption*, stayed with me. It elicited a tear, and made me cry, and said something so lovely about human dignity and the human spirit. By the end of the story your spirits just soar, and I thought, "Wow, that would make a great movie."

King was pleased with a short film I had made of another of his stories, so I approached him about optioning *Shawshank* in 1986 or '87. Apparently no one could see that there was a movie in it.

The thing that amazed me was that when I heard *Stand by Me* was coming out, I had the same reaction at the time— "How the hell are they gonna make a movie out of [the novella] *The Body*?" It didn't seem immediately obvious to me as a movie. Then when I saw the film, I was so taken with the job that everybody did, that Rob Reiner did, and that [screenwriters] Gideon and Evans did. Maybe I have grown a little bit as a writer, maybe now I could see the potential of *The Body* to become *Stand by Me*. But for some reason it was *Shawshank* that really seized my attention.

MARCO WILLIAMS
August 11

It was stiflingly hot—well over one hundred degrees—the week Marco Williams packed his belongings to leave for North Carolina. I visited him the day before his departure.

He wore dreadlocks, sandals, a Women's Arts Coalition T-shirt, and surfer shorts. In the one-bedroom apartment all that remained on the wall was a mounted film reel. Boxes were everywhere, including sound transfer tapes from Williams's various projects—"MOTHER'S DAY," "James Berry phone calls (Springfield)," "United Way of America 'I'll Be There.' " In a box on the floor was a videocassette labeled "POWER OF NO Director's Test," the sole souvenir of Williams's roller-coaster year on the brink of breaking into the Hollywood studio system.

I've been competing for sound space with my neighbors. It's so hot that we have our doors and windows open and we each blast our music to drown the other out. But I invariably lose because my stereo is smaller. The neighborhood is mostly Hispanic. Oddly enough, we have grown closer since the earthquake, which created some sense of community.

We screened the South African film, *Uncommon Ground* [formerly called *Nana*, which Williams produced], at AFI. One woman got up, she was really moved. She said she had spent some time in South Africa, and the film was so moving she started to cry. So it was perfect, everyone started feeling their emotions. This woman had let it all out.

We went to the Electronic Cafe, which is a place in Santa Monica with a series of video phone hookups so you can transmit via video through the telephone throughout the world. We had sent the film to South Africa for the kids there to see, and then we had a linkup to South Africa, a big event. Lots of people from the screening came to that, and wanted to talk to South Africans about what was going on in South Africa. Amy [the director] and I had talked about what we wanted, but I don't think either of us expected that it would be that successful. It was quite surprising.

We're working on trying to get a distributor. There's some interest at KQED. We're seeing if someone from KCET might be interested, trying to get on *P.O.V.* I'm going to be in New York in two weeks. We've sent it to HBO. I chatted with Sheila Nevins. It's not really their sort of thing—they do sensational stuff. It's surprising they produced *I Am a Promise* [about a school], which won the Oscar last year, because they usually deal with murder and drugs and all that. She said, "The funny thing is, *Promise* won all these awards, but nobody watched it on television. Our biggest-rated thing was on gangs."

I'm going to this Independent Television Service conference August 19–20. Maybe they'll throw me a bone. If I don't make a film soon, I'll die.

There was a party for Chris Gerolmo, who was leaving town for the shoot of *Citizen X* [a movie he was writing and directing for HBO]. I didn't want it to be a party for me too, although they wanted that. I didn't really feel like celebrating what I was doing. Liz Cane was there.

I never envisioned L.A. as being my home forever, so this is fulfilling that, if anything. I always thought that if I had enough money I would eventually buy property in, say, New England, and live there and work here. Or wherever the work was.

The reservations about going is that it isn't on *my* schedule. I wanted to teach, and think I will be a good teacher. I believe I am passionate about the movies and have a keen sense about all phases of it. I thought that sooner or later I would teach, but I thought I would teach probably after making another movie or so.

I didn't spend the last year and a half trying to get a teaching job. I spent it trying to make a movie. So that's where the ambivalence about the move comes in, in terms of personal goals. This was secondary to my immediate goals. In spite of that, this may be part of the path to realizing those goals. I suspect that many good things will come from this.

The fact is that I've been here. And there's much of it that I really don't like at all. It's the idea of going away from it without it being because I have achieved something, or because I have to raise a family.

I can't help but hear that awful saying, "Those who can't do, teach—and those who can't teach, of course, teach phys ed." But I wouldn't mind teaching phys ed. I like sports a great deal. [Laughs]

Secretly there's also that thought—does it signal failure? It's a great honor and a great situation, but will I be back to make a movie? That remains to be seen. Will I *get* to make another movie?

If I had said to myself six months ago, "Okay, I'm going to go teach for two years because that's going to lead me here," it would be very clear. This is one where I don't have a clue. It found me, I'm just sort of along for the ride, the adventure of it. This is the first time in my life I don't have a picture at all.

I know what my agenda is. What I hope to get from this is a steady gig, with this relationship that allows me to leave when I want to leave. To make this two-year gig work so that they want to hire me back for another two years, but then I could leave if necessary.

My goal is to write, basically, four days of the week. I've been sitting on one particular idea for a long time. It's time to write it. And I think this will give me the cushion to write it, because I won't really have to worry about getting paid.

Part of the reason they hired me is because I am someone who has made a couple films from start to finish, is in the Hollywood framework, and have that to speak about. I've spoken to people like Chris Gerolmo and suggested he do a premiere of *Citizen X* down there, just do a little workshop. Show the film, talk to these kids about making movies, writing. Especially since, simultaneously for these kids in the first year, they are writing a feature film script. So why not have someone like Chris who's written a script, and directed? I don't know if it's possible, but I've spoken to some actors I know about doing a workshop. Maybe it can be organized in such a way that they can get paid a little bit. So that element I will certainly integrate.

I don't know how not to be candid about my life and experience, so I'm sure I will talk to them about the movies, and what things are like here. I have a big map of L.A. that I used when I was doing research for the documentary on the riots. I'm going to put that up in my office, so they can see, "This is where Paramount Studios is," etc. So hopefully there's a benefit that I have been in L.A. and trying to work in the industry, which is what they aspire to.

Chris Moore [Williams's former agent] said that sometimes what happens is that you have to go away and reinvent yourself. Even though you're basically the same person, you reinvent yourself by doing something. And I think, in this case, one of the things that probably held me back a little bit was not having something written. What I want to get accomplished is two drafts of two different screenplays, or two different screenplay ideas. One is a passion. The other is probably as commercial an idea as I've had—inspired, actually, by *In Search of Our Fathers*, but taking off into a more commercial thriller. I have some notes on that.

I came out here with a plan, but it was very vague: to finish my documentary, go to UCLA, get at least one master's degree, and try to direct a drama, because I had never done that, and then go from there.

All that worked out. I came out here, got two master's degrees, finished *In Search of Our Fathers*, did direct a fictional film, and thought I was, you know, on my way.

I don't yet have a game plan like I had when I left New York to come to L.A. I don't have a picture, I don't know whether it's going to be enough to have a script, but I believe having a script will be something. At least I may be able to entertain possibilities for writing.

So many meetings I've gone to, I go to with real notes, real thoughts about things. Often there are writers there, but many times not. And if I would be able to demonstrate in their minds that I was able to write, there probably would be a kind of confidence. Since I haven't been able to persuade anybody to let me direct anything—short of Dawn—based on just what I have directed, this might help. Maybe not.

I see myself sitting down and writing. The school will have three or four screenwriting teachers. If I need someone's feedback, Steven Fisher, who's just been hired, is a writer who seems to be completely tied in to Hollywood. So that's my view. I know all the basics for writing. I may not be a good writer, or maybe I am, but through classes at UCLA and speaking with people I know, it's just time to sit down and write a script. I have a beat outline. It's all ready to go.

There's not a lot going on, on the one hand, there. I feel a little isolated to a certain extent. My big apprehension is loneliness. I don't know what to expect there at all.

GILLIAN ARMSTRONG, Director

It's about doing. I went to two film schools, and in the year that I was out in between I had quite a shock. I realized that the time in film school is really precious, you rarely in the real world have the chance to express yourself as an individual. And very few people ever do. It's a hard thing to tell people, because you can't give experience or life perspective. But you have equipment and resources available, and you should use every minute.

It's also a stimulating environment—you can learn from each other.

P. J. PESCE
August 22

I just supervised the video transfer of the film. It looks pretty good. They haven't told me anything about the distribution, or airdate, or anything.

Brad Jenkel from MPCA introduced me to this manager, Kimberly Hines. She set me up with a producer, Gloria Zimmerman, who is doing a film, *Destiny Turns On the Radio*, that Quentin Tarantino is acting in. Two directors have dropped out. It sounds like "creative differences." It felt very much like the producer is actually the one making the movie.

She saw my film and the meeting went well, but she ended up going with someone else.

LIZ CANE
August 25

I've just been working, and helping Patrick think about shots for his film, which he's planning on shooting now at the end of September with the money they have. They haven't raised any more money, so they're just going to do it real down-and-dirty. I mean, they're still trying to get more money, but they've set a date for when they want to start shooting, so we're starting to put shot [plans] together.

He had a casting director, but she can't really work on it because she deals mostly with SAG [Screen Actors Guild] people. And I guess Jon Savage probably won't do it because it's not being done through SAG. I can help Patrick through preproduction, but I don't know what I'm going to do when he starts shooting. I might not be able to be there, because I don't want to lose my job at UCLA.

I did some editing on a student film—I threw a rough cut together for someone who's paying me. We have to figure out some structural problems. A section of the film is not working. It was fun—I've never really taken someone else's material and edited it before. But we didn't have a lot to choose from, either. It was student film conditions. [Laughs]

This woman was happy with my work, but basically we decided to put it together the way she had written it. There was one section where she intercut between three different times with one woman, and one section she never got on film, so she went and shot it in black-and-white stills, and then had that shot on film. That's the section that really doesn't work—it just seems awkward and confusing and stops the film whenever you get to it—so I'm trying to convince her she doesn't need it. She's going to transfer it to video and think about whether she can find any solutions as to how to better integrate it.

I heard from the Nicholls fellowship—no. I haven't heard from anybody else. I think Disney has a hotline you can call but I don't have the number. It's so ridiculous. I gave my script to a couple of people and realized pretty quickly that it needs a lot more work structurally, particularly the first half. I'm realizing more and more that writing, good writing, is rewriting. So I'm trying to get back to doing that. It's easier just to work for other people and learn how to play the guitar, which I am doing.

I saw Marco Williams. He seems to be a really strong person.

> **FRANK DARABONT, Writer-Director**
> There's a certain amount of channeling in the creative process. It's a such a struggle to get the words on the page when I'm writing, but sometimes you kind of go into this trance, and it feels like this sort of Zen state, where you're just trying to keep up.
>
> Those moments are the most thrilling, when the writing really becomes joyful. You look up at the clock and it feels like twenty minutes, but five hours have gone by. That mystical mojo kicks in in the writing and something else takes over.
>
> It doesn't happen often. Writing is mostly trying to chip through a wall with your hand, pebble by pebble. But you leap over that wall, soaring over it, from time to time. And that's great.

P. J. PESCE
September 19

I attended yet another screening of The Desperate Trail *at the Directors Guild of America. Brad Krevoy addressed the crowd, which included executives and producers, Pia Zadora, and* Amongst Friends *director Rob Weiss with his girlfriend, actress Shannen Doherty.*

Krevoy addressed the crowd: "We want to welcome everyone to the first-ever screening of The Desperate Trail. *We think you will agree that P. J. Pesce has a bright future ahead of him, and encourage any of you with projects which might be right for him to keep him in mind.*

"Most of the cast members, Craig, Sam, and Linda are not here as they are working on other pictures, which is a testament to our casting director."

From the back, Pesce yelled, "She's working on another picture, too!"

"Our editor and cinematographer, who did such great work, are here," Krevoy continued but, oddly, did not name them.

Afterward, southwestern food and drink were served, and Pesce and Krevoy posed for a photo op with Weiss and Doherty.

September 20

I sat there thinking, "They're not reacting. This really sucks." But enough people came up to me and told me that the movie was good that I don't feel so bad.

I swear, the whole thing is a blur. I remember at the beginning most of the people coming up to me and saying how much they enjoyed it, mentioning Peckinpah, John Woo, and all that. But the last thing I remember after that is it was all over.

If Kanter was aware of other agents being there he didn't show it. I was very disappointed that only two or three agents from UTA were there and he hadn't gotten any of them. I had asked him to.

If he doesn't know I'm not happy, he's more out of it than I thought. The screenings are the minimum that he can do. All I ever hear from him is, "You've got to keep writing." I'm like, "Oh, thanks." I could tell myself that. I could do that without an agent. I got this movie going myself. He didn't do it for me. He hasn't done anything to help me in keeping myself alive.

Maybe I need to not hire an agent until I'm getting barraged. I just think of, like, Ben Stiller changing agencies. I mean, what the fuck, the guy doesn't even write, you know? First he does *Reality Bites*—why wasn't I being offered that movie?—and now he's doing huge movies.

I feel like Kanter should get behind the movie and bust the balls of the Turner people for distribution. I haven't signed papers with him this year. I could walk. But I don't think at this particular juncture it would be the right thing to do.

Some people were there from Sundance. They were very into it [for the festival in late January]. So that could be a major thing. Airing on TV first would be a deal-breaker. Right now I think Turner's plan is December, anyway.

GILLIAN ARMSTRONG, Director
When I became the first woman in fifty years to direct a feature in Australia, the journalists all had their cliches—well,

she must be strong, aggressive, a manipulator, she must be somehow vicious and malicious and she struggled her way to the top. Then they would meet me and say, "Oh, she's so small! Her voice isn't strong!"

To me it was very insulting. But it's also an uninformed way of understanding what a director does. I was always hardworking and conscientious, and a perfectionist, and I had a gift in the area of visual storytelling since childhood. So maybe I was just good. Half of it is hard work, but half was that I did have talent.

IV

AUTUMN 1994–WINTER 1995

In Hong Kong, I feel I work like a painter. In Hollywood, I also work like a painter, but somehow my hand is tied up by rope.... But I still think I can do something here.

—John Woo, *The New Yorker*,
August 7, 1995

I remember an agent of mine was once frustrated with me. I had made a movie and the studio wanted some changes and I didn't know how to make them—I really didn't understand what they wanted—and the agent said to me, "I just don't understand why you always take the tougher road." And I said, "You think I have a choice? You think there's an easy road and a tough road, and I say, 'See, I'm going to take the tough road'? Tell me where the easy road is—I'll back up."

—Albert Brooks, *Buzz* magazine,
November 1993

P. J. PESCE
October 6

How am I? Lousy. I feel like my vision is getting lost. I mean, if I ever had one. I'm having trouble coming up with what it was in the first place.

I'm writing this script with Rob Weiss. It is an idea we came up with together, and it seems like it should be my voice as much as his, but it's sort of becoming what *he* is into, and what *he* wants to see and do, and I don't know if I'm into that. It's for him to produce and me to direct. We don't have paperwork, though.

I've also been working on a screenplay with Tom Abrams, adapting this book *You Can't Win*. And now he's getting pissed, I think, because I've been getting together with Rob too much. It's a stressful time.

FRANK DARABONT, Writer-Director

Writing has been my door of opportunity to directing as well. That's the flip side of the coin. The writer is a storyteller, and so is the director, but they're really two sides of the same coin—pretty much the same job, but wildly different in the particulars. It's storytelling. Believe me, directing is such a pain in the ass that if I believed someone would really take care of my words, I'd probably be just as happy not doing it. It's just awful. But the words mean enough to me that I will direct if that's what it takes. To make sure the words get protected.

BERNARD JOFFA
October 18

A 21st Century realty sign had been put up in front of Joffa's house.

The "For Sale" sign is about getting money to live in this crazy town. Hanging in a bit longer. This has been a crazy year, workwise, and it's been very tough. But in terms of personal growth it's been the best year of my life.

I'd like to live in an apartment in this area. It's just a matter of getting some money together, which is really hard, but thank God I've got the house to sell.

I'm very lucky. Clearly it's reached an end now, moneywise, but I'm not worried. Two people are staying here who have no place to stay. One is an Englishwoman, the other a South African actor. In South Africa he was a big star. Wherever we would go people would ask for autographs and mob him. Today he is delivering tickets to the Rolling Stones concert for Virgin Records. His first Hollywood job was driving the honeywagon—you know, the toilets—for a film. And he was paid to do this experiment at UCLA where he would take acid.

I'm starting to teach at AFI, two days a week. I'm very happy about that. I just got a call out of the blue from the film school.

Each student has to make three projects in the first year, and I will be at the screening of each project and discuss it with the group.

It's fun. The pay is $5,000 for the year, not very much, but significant for me right now. It's back in the creative loop. The most frustrating thing has been the waiting. This will be a positive way of using my time.

I've always seen myself being involved in a film school in South Africa down the road. And this will be a great experience, having been to the AFI and knowing how they work and now being able to give it back to them. And if I have to shoot a film, please God, make it my problem. They would be happy to replace me.

Hollywood in the past year is the nicest Hollywood that I've ever seen. And that has to do with feeling okay about myself. I spent the first three years in this town hating it—this whole victim mentality. Then you realize that everyone is in the same bloody boat.

I've been out here six years. School for three years, and out of the country for eighteen months. But having been out of the country for eighteen months, I've found this town doesn't have a long memory. You got to be there all the time, be out there. Because ultimately somebody is going to just like your work, or like you enough to give you an opportunity. I don't think it's a matter of being more talented than a hundred other people who are out there. It's just a matter of finding the right material, the right script.

The Year of the Zinc Penny is my biggest love and passion right now. It's just a matter of me getting the money and getting the option. It's available. But this is part of my plan to sell the house, to free up money to buy the option. It only runs eighteen months, and you have to get the screenplay written.

It's going to be another uphill battle for me because it's not a very commercial Hollywood film. But I see it, and I want to do it. I've kind of gotten used to the idea of not being all that commercial. It hasn't hurt John Boorman [*Hope and Glory*]. And Lasse Hallström [*My Life as a Dog*] went on to make *What's Eating Gilbert Grape*. He's a quirky filmmaker.

What's a quirky filmmaker? *I'm* a quirky filmmaker, a quirky guy who likes to make quirky films. But I'm still pretty secure about maintaining my pure aspirations in this business, whatever that means for me. Staying away from *Natural Born Killers* sort of stuff.

It got so frustrating for me with my agent, because she just can't do anything for me until I come up with the right material. I hardly ever speak to her, and she takes months to get back to me. And I understand what it means, finally—don't take things personally. But with Ronda, from the word "go," it was going to be a relationship in which I would have to find the material.

At first I got angry, and I thought, this is the wrong agent for me. I finally resigned myself to believe that she is a great agent, and that I'm not delivering the goods to her. It's hard enough to sell big directors. I'm really unproven. My film was a short film. I'm not viewed as a long-form filmmaker yet.

Chris [Silverman, the junior agent] and I speak a lot. He's now gotten very busy doing television. I'm very happy for him, but it's hard to get hold of him now because he's busy. On the other hand, I think: Great. These are great people to have behind me once I get going. I'm just grateful to have an agent—and a damned good agent—who's really tried. But right now it's all up to me to come up with material.

I had an interesting meeting with someone at Showtime, Jeff Silverman. He loved my short film and seems to be pretty serious about wanting to work with me. He took me out to lunch last week, and we're having lunch again tomorrow, and he wants to find me a writer to work with. I need someone like that.

He wants to try and find a story in my life. He was touched by my growing up with a scar and all of that.

The script that we just wrote, *The Story of an African Farm*, was given to Showtime by a company in South Africa. And Jeff's the guy who got hold of it and he likes it a lot. The coverage was glowing. It said it wouldn't be right for them, though, because it deals with white people in South Africa in 1860, and they would prefer it to deal with black people. The coverage said it's more entertaining and the characters are richer than *Out of Africa*.

I'm going to pitch him *Home Free* now. It will solve that. I guess South Africa has become an issue in that the revolution is over. For me, the appeal of South Africa is not political at all. The appeal is that it's another way of life. It doesn't have to be political. Political messages can be for the newspaper. But it's not my right to tell him that. It's the current consciousness of the world.

BOBBI THOMPSON, Agent

Part of the reason I have focused on foreign directors who can come over here and say something is because it enriches us culturally. When Kenneth Branagh can come over and make *Dead Again* in America, that's good. When Jocelyn Moorhouse, who has a unique viewpoint, being Australian, can do [Raymond Chandler and Robert B. Parker's] *Poodle Springs* for Sydney Pollack at Universal, it adds to it.

I guess for a long time people didn't want to make films in Germany because they couldn't imagine making a film about a good German. It took a long time for *Schindler's List* to be made—for people to palate that, and remove themselves enough from the tragedy and say, okay, there were *some* Germans who had some consciousness about them and changed things.

For you, me, and my mother, it's a good angle—but Hollywood's got their own. I've got to look at it from a different point of view. They're the ones making the movie, putting up the bucks. I've learned that I want to run with people who want to run with me.

To try to convince somebody that what's written on the printed page is actually better than it is, is a useless exercise. You may be able to change their thinking a little bit, but you have to have that passion. I have that passion for *Zinc Penny*, and I've given it to a lot of people to read and they say, "What's in here? I don't understand what you're getting so excited about."

For me, I know there is something really special in there. So that's why I will always work to get *Zinc Penny* made. And it's going to have to be maybe when I'm more powerful in feature filmmaking. I'd like to have a go at the script with the writer of the book.

I need to call him and tell him what's going on, but in a way I feel bad telling him I've got no money. It seems like I'm such a flake. And I am still interested, but I don't have the money and I don't know how best to tell him. I love when filmmakers talk about something they have for ten or twenty years. I think it's one of those.

I've become a monster video maker. In the last year I've shot maybe fifty hours of video. Like a maniac. The whole procedure with my dad, from the moment he got cancer, right through the consecration the other day. I wanted to shoot it to end off this work I had been doing for sixteen months, for closure. And I did it, and I'm glad I did.

It was hard for some of my family to accept the fact that I would be running around with a video camera. I've gotten used to that. My family doesn't know who the fuck I am. Must be pretty weird having a brother who's a filmmaker in Hollywood, I would imagine. I always get phone calls, that I'm expected to video the bar mitzvah, or the birthday party or the football game.

Nobody's born an artist. I think you become an artist because you're unable to identify with what most normal people identify with and you can't express yourself in the real world, so you find something that's abstract. Painting, or a visual thing.

For me, the camera is a great camouflage. You can do whatever you want to at a party, and the moment somebody suggests that they're about to start talking to you, just turn the camera on them. I think all artists hide behind their art.

And if you're able to express yourself in a visual sense, then you're an artist. So, yeah, I'm an artist—I've finally come to terms with that. Janusz Kaminsky [D.P., *Schindler's List*] was at the American Film Institute the year before me. And he wasn't invited to the second year, which is usually quite a heavy thing to live with. There are only thirty-three in the program and they only select five for the next year, so how do you make the choices?

Anyway, Janusz wasn't selected for the second year, so he used to hang around on *our* first-year projects, and help as a gaffer, things like that. Now he shot *Schindler's List* and he's one of the greatest cinematographers in America.

What I'm saying is that maybe two years ago he was also one of the greatest cinematographers in America, but nobody saw it yet. The light wasn't on him.

Embeth Davidtz, a friend of mine from South Africa, came to live in Hollywood, having done a bit of stage acting. And she was struggling. On a Thursday night a TV movie she did had just aired, and she gets a phone call. "Hi, Embeth—this is Steven Spielberg."

And she was in *Schindler's List*, and now she's in major pictures. It's so wonderful to see. Lebo M did music for me for nothing two years ago on my student film, and today he's being paid a shitload for this wonderful Disney picture *The Lion King*.

The videotaping has become my salvation, because even though I'm getting no money, I'm working virtually ever day, and sending them all over the world. It's such a nice way to communicate. My brother, who is living in South Africa, gets to see his nephews and my sisters. Those things I love to do.

I've started seeing L.A. as pretty much home. Tomorrow I get my U.S. citizenship. And then I will have every right, as much as you. It's kind of a big deal for me right now. It represents a lot for me, because growing up, my whole life, my South African passport was the most embarrassing thing in the world. I couldn't get into any countries without special visas.

But I've kind of worked through that stuff. Hollywood has never treated me as an outsider. When I was younger I used to revolve from Shabbat to Shabbat, growing up in a traditional Jewish family. And then that disappeared and Sunday became an important day for me. And then when I finally came to Hollywood I have fallen into Hollywood time, which is measured in trash bags. I know every Friday that's the most consistent thing in my life. If I don't get the trash out on Friday morning, it's not going to be picked up. I think everybody has their Hollywood trash day cycle. It's the only day that involves me with the outside world. It's a kind of cleansing thing as well.

This guy staying with me—this out-of-work actor—came for two weeks and stayed for seven months, and has been the most wonderful friend to have. Even though I'm not working, my life's full.

A girlfriend came into my life, which was pretty wonderful, and then it got to the big commitment question, and I guess I can't deal with that—and I don't know many film people who can—so, sadly, that had to end. I wasn't ready to get married and have children with her. Going in knowing I wasn't ready for that kind of commitment put a different energy onto the relationship. When I was younger and I wanted to get married desperately, it was all I wanted to do. I fell in love and got married—happily ever after—and got divorced in eighteen months.

Where do I see myself in five years? I think that's a very unfair question. [Laughs] And I'm not prepared to give you an answer. I don't predict in terms of five years. I know where I'll be next trash day. Here.

Please God, here. If I'm living here in five years I would have gotten work which would allow me to stay here. But it may be ten years.

I never projected years in advance. I cannot ever recall saying to myself, "This is where I want to be when I'm twenty, thirty, fifty." I think you're just setting yourself up for failure. Must be the most terrible pressure.

I went to the AFI and wasn't going to go the second year because it wasn't really so important. Then I get there and everyone is fighting to get into the second year. So I made a film that was really so un-Hollywood, and I got into the second year. Of those who tried so hard to get in, many didn't.

But that's been my whole life. Growing up with a scar made me have to deal with life on a day-to-day basis, just to get through the day. If I could get through every single day, I was doing well. And I honestly feel no stress right now.

LISA KLEIN
October 26

They would like me to stay at this event management job. The money's fine. But it's not what I want to do. I'd rather starve and write.

I really want to do what I came out here to do. The important thing is that I haven't been writing any scripts. I'd get home at nine or ten. This month I will finish out the job, and go back to writing at night.

I'm not doing the script with the two guys. I started the rewrite and was on about page forty, and they did not want me to rewrite their stuff. They wanted me to take their treatment and flesh it out. I wish that they had told me sooner, because they said, "We'll be flexible."

They read my first twenty pages and loved it. I wrote twenty more and we had a meeting, and I told them where I was going with it, and that I really wanted to, and they said, "You know, you're changing our stuff." And I said, "Well, what if this is better?" And they said, "No, no—we want it to be *our* stuff." So I never even showed them the other twenty pages, and we parted as friends.

I realized I'm not Joe Eszterhas, but I'm still not going to be a servant to someone's treatment, and just flesh it out and put dialogue to it. There's no way. They should get someone else to do that, or do it themselves. I hope I'm a little better than that, even though I'm unproven.

Monika Skerbelis at Universal still really likes my script *Guardian Angels*. And it still needs a lot of work. It really does. This draft maybe I'll be proud of. I'm halfway through the rewrite and I want to finish it within the next couple of weeks.

I'll do this job until the end of the year, go home for a little while, hopefully go to Australia for a month, and then come back and figure my life out. I'm not even going to think about it until I get back. If I have to go back to waiting tables, that's what I'll do.

I feel like I have to put all my energy back into this. I don't know how it got lost, but hopefully it's there.

I want to work on a book. I want to write something about my sister, although I don't know if I'm ready, but that's the cathartic thing that I want to do. Not to mention the ten other projects that are sitting in limbo.

I love writing. I could have said this before but I don't think I meant it. I need it more now. If I can put my life back together, this other stuff is sort of gravy. It's not sour grapes, me going "I don't really care." I care and I *do* want it. But I kind of want it for her, rather than to satisfy my own ego.

My brother died also, that's it. So there's this only-child–orphan thing, and it's a weird kind of pressure. My mother's been great, but there's been a weird pressure there, too. If I have a cold, she freaks out. She doesn't want to see me stress out over this. It's nerve-wracking, and it's scary, and I'm a little lost. She wants me to keep my life together, and more than anything else to be happy.

When I left home this last time was one of the most difficult things. I find myself saying that a lot—"That's the most difficult thing I've ever done." Because ever since my brother Peter died, there have been a lot of most difficult things I've ever done. And this career stuff is just forgotten. Leaving home was tough. My mother has been here a couple of times, and she'll probably be back for Thanksgiving. I'll be home at the end of the year. There is sort of a need to know she's around, and talk on the phone. But I don't think I can move back home.

My sister would have wanted me to speak at her funeral, and I did it. I wrote something for it, and that was a huge thing. And my mother is doing the same thing. She wrote a column within a month of her death. It was beautiful, not-a-dry-eye-in-the-house kind of stuff.

That was a concern with my mother and a concern with me—like, okay, it's in my family, is it going to happen to me? So it does run in my family. My sister was actually manic-depressive, bipolar. I don't know if there's anyone in Hollywood who does not suffer from that. So that scares me, that it's going to happen to me—at a clinical level—we all feel highs and lows. That's a fear. Plus I feel like I should have chosen podiatry or something, something that I know would have at least offered some stability.

When I was home, there were these producers who approached me to write the screenplay for this book called *Replacing Dad*. They're raising the money, and it's all pretty iffy. If they pick the director first, I'll have a chance, but the director will probably choose his or her own writer. If they pick the writer first, it will be me. And that would be great. But I didn't care because of what was happening. This came through Monika Skerbelis, who is like my guardian angel.

NEAL JIMENEZ, Writer-Director

I've written two scripts based on books that were commissioned by studios as favors to producers—in one case Martin Scorsese and in the other Rosalie Swedlin. Because these two people have a lot of clout, the studios want to treat them with kid gloves. [When] Scorsese comes in and says, "Develop this project," they say, "Go ahead and find a writer."

I've basically been used as a favor to two producers with clout, and the studios at the outset knew what the stories were going to be and had to know that they really had no intention of ever making these films. But I'm not sorry I did them, because you're always writing your next calling card on one level.

I've gotten calls sporadically, like to enter the Sundance competition. I sent something mainstream and a woman called me and said, "You know, I really like your work a lot. But you and I know this is not for Sundance. But as soon as you have something right for Sundance please call me." It was just nice that she called, because usually they just send cover letters. But I would love to rewrite the script, have it be great and have Monika get the credit, if it were made and she shepherded it through Universal.

She's sent stuff out to agents and gotten me meetings before. She would do it again if I asked her to. I want to help her, now. I want this to come through and make that happen.

I want to switch agents very soon. Turtle is completely ineffective.

A friend of mine has a friend and he gave *Seinfeld* my script, and they called my agent, because the scripts all have their name and number on them. My agent called me and said, "Oh, yeah, I got a call from such-and-such at *Seinfeld*. She really liked your script. She liked the *Murphy Brown* better because *Seinfeld* would never buy a spec. . . ." And I said, "You realize that script was sent by my friend Sherry."

The way she called—like she had sent the script—was, like, *out there!* It made no sense. I wasn't expecting anything out of it, but I had totally forgotten that their name was on the script.

It was just hubris. They do nothing.

I mentioned to Klein that Radioland Murders, *a recent Universal release, bore a striking resemblance in concept and title to her USC film* Radio Wars.

We had sent the *Radio Wars* script to George Lucas. We got a letter back—"George does not read anything . . . blah, blah, blah," whatever that means. We heard from a friend of mine who works at Skywalker Sound that he is extremely paranoid about stuff.

I heard *Radioland Murders* was written a long time ago and went through a total rewrite. I wish there was a way for me to find out if he saw *Radio Wars*. There's probably nothing we can do about it. I heard it's terrible and it's been universally panned. I guess I need to hurry and see it.

I wanted to write a screenplay about a writer who writes a script, and then goes to a theater and sees it on the screen. Then I saw *Only You*, which I only went to see because of the similarities to *Lovestruck*. So then this writer would say, "Wait a minute!" and hire a lawyer and go through the whole thing, and at the end win this lawsuit. Yeah, the little guy wins! I was going to write a script to that effect because I thought that would be my revenge.

A lot of people said I was on the right track [with *Radio Wars*]. I'm going to reserve judgment until I've seen the movie. Ten-year-old kids called me! Relatives called me, when I was at home and stuff. "Lisa! Your movie's in the movie theater now?" This kid who went to see *The Flintstones* saw the trailer to *Radioland Murders*.

In five years I would like to have autonomy. I would just like to be at a point where I've written some stuff, my stuff is being made, and I'm not living in L.A. New York—maybe Boston, maybe Chicago. I'm not going to fall into the New-Mexico–Jackson-Hole—Wyoming trap, because that's really just L.A., but prettier.

It's been a weird few months. For a while I just wanted to be sad and cry. I guess now I'm at the point where I know that I have to make a choice. I have to either move forward with my life or stop. And I don't want to stop. There are a lot of things out there for me, and for my mother and my nephew. I can't just let everything go.

I guess this is my rebuilding phase. And this job is a little bit of an escape from reality, my distraction. And now that the high-pressure part of it is winding down, for the first time in a while I'm thinking about trying to rebuild my life a little.

I'll go home for a while, do the Australia thing, come back at the end of January, and say, "What the hell am I going to do now?" If my mother had her druthers I would be a doctor or a lawyer or something—or an accountant, a seamstress, something that would be nine to five—she really likes that. She likes that comfort level a lot. She likes that I'm doing this job.

You want to feel that what goes around comes around, that there is some equity. That all this will happen and then . . . something. Just a little bit of hope.

LIZ GLOTZER, Producer-Executive

Jeff Maguire wrote *In the Line of Fire*—he's in his early forties, and it's his first big produced script. He was about to give it up. He sold the script for close to $1 million. Now he says the people that wouldn't return his calls last year are wining and dining him but he says, "I'm not sure I was that bad of a writer then, and I'm not sure that I'm such a good writer now."

P. J. PESCE
November 4

The Desperate Trail *officially premiered on October 20, 1994, at the Hamptons International Film Festival on Long Island, New York.*

The film was reviewed in both Hollywood daily trade papers. "The shadows of spaghetti Westerns maestro Sergio Leone and Sam Peckinpah loom large over the imagery of The Desperate Trail,*" Daily Variety's Emanuel Levy began. ". . . tale's quality and its characters never match helmer P. J. Pesce's technical savvy, speedy pacing and thrilling shootouts. Despite splashy directorial debut, lack of narrative originality and uneven writing will keep enthusiasm at a modest level. There are also serious questions whether Turner Pictures will air the Western on TNT, or just send it straight to video." Levy concluded by calling the climax "well-orchestrated, strikingly shot and framed . . . a corker that provides both dramatic and visual satisfaction, keeping the picture at least two cuts above the usual Hollywood Western."*

In the Hollywood Reporter, *Frank Schock called the film "an old-fashioned, traditional Western, [whose] filmmaker has been eager to point out that it is an homage to the classics of Hawks and Leone. Although the comparisons don't do the film well, this low-budget effort, shot very quickly, does reveal an emergent talent. It won't reverse the recent trend of Westerns being shot down at the boxoffice, however, and the producers, Turner Entertainment, might think twice about putting this one in theaters. . . . The film looks better than it had a right to, although the director does have a tendency to overdo the Peckinpah slow-motion action scenes, with the blood flowing fast and furious."*

I met a few good guys at the Hamptons festival. This guy Mark Malone, who made a film called *Killer* [released theatrically as *Bulletproof Heart*]. All these guys are making these gangster movies now, and they all really suck.

The venue for the festival was a little cheesy—a four-plex, that was it. The biggest names there were Treat Williams and Quincy Jones. But Williams paid me a real compliment. He said he knew Sergio Leone, and that Leone would have loved the movie.

At the awards ceremony, the most popular film was The Last Good Time, *directed by Bob Balaban.*

Twenty thousand dollars' worth of soundstage services and the Silver Cup was awarded to best director of an American independent feature— P. J. Pesce.

Darryl Macdonald, the festival director, read my name. I was lighting a cigarette. My girlfriend, Lisa, poked me and said, "P. J.! They said your name."

I went up and said, "I'm overwhelmed. I didn't expect this." And I thanked Mike Bonvillain, who was there, and MPCA, and the festival. I thanked Turner for putting a million dollars into a film that's going straight to video. [Laughs] I forgot to thank Lisa, which was really stupid.

JOHN MCINTYRE
November 10

I got married September 17 in Santa Monica, at the Unitarian Church. We had about sixty people. My family came from back East. We had a reception at a German restaurant.

The wedding plans and pressure was unbearable. We fought

every other day, and then were really happy. The money poured out of us and there are still plenty of bills. But we turned out happy we did it, because in August we were considering eloping. Finally it all made sense. I know it's normal, but we couldn't rationalize it at the time. It was crazy.

Two days later we went to France, and took a tour for a month with an organization from Seattle. Theresa used their book a few years ago when she went to Europe and it was great, a little more attuned to us because it was inexpensive. I would not recommend taking the bus tour. It wasn't the crowd we expected. The average age was about sixty-five.

Right now it's very romantic. I moved in with Theresa in North Hollywood. It feels a lot more secure already. In one sense it's not a lot more involvement than we had before, because we would see each other a few days a week. But now I'm never going home to my apartment. The first week we got back we both realized we were expecting that. And I still call this "her house." So it's kind of like a permanent holiday or something. She has two bedrooms, and it's packed. I have a three-foot workspace. I stay at the office to work if I have to. I had to give the big duck to Duck Soup.

It's fun right now between us. The pressure is off.

She's at Rich Entertainment, still. Her film *Swan Princess* comes out on the twentieth. She was an assistant animator. She's been hired as a key assistant on the next project. She's got an incredibly steady hand, and she drew the prince character. He's rock steady. The drawing doesn't wiggle.

The film was completely traditional, cel-animated. Disney is doing computerized animation, but for Rich it may be an economic thing—they don't have the money to invest in that system. This is their first feature, and if this one is a hit, they'll start investing in more technology.

It looks really good—a solid, epic Disney-type film with some really great, memorable moments. In fact, it's so good that Disney pulled *The Lion King* three weeks ago in mid-release to rerelease it the day *The Swan Princess* comes out. It's clear that it's just to stop the competition and discourage anyone from doing a feature of Disney caliber and getting credit for it.

My big news now is that two days ago I got promoted to storyboard and assistant directing, which also means writing. The fun thing about *Rocko's Modern Life* is that you do everything. So I'll get a three-page treatment and be able to write the dialogue and board the show. We work in teams. Jeff, another guy from Film-Roman, is becoming a director, so I'll be his assistant.

I can't wait to do something, because I feel as if I've been idle the last four months. Not that I haven't had enough work to do, I've just been unbelievably frustrated, and I made it very clear to them.

It's a little more in terms of hours and a couple of hundred more a week. I was a little disappointed in that. But I'm thrilled. It's exciting. You get a story from the two writers who are in-house, and the creator is writing as well.

That's the great thing about this show. Everything is in-house, and the creator is trying to be somewhat comparable to old Warners. The result isn't quite that, but it's far better than at Film-Roman, where we were the work-for-hire factory, and there was no contact with the writer-creators. Here, they have encouraged me to write treatments, and I've given them summaries for ten stories. A year ago I was just dying for this, you know? I'll be real happy to have it.

I've learned so much in the last two years. I wouldn't have even have been ready for directing or boarding a couple of years ago anyway. Getting more experience. I feel like if I continue in the next few years, I'll be in a good step-by-step plateau system. I'll be able to learn as I go without being in over my head.

At *Rocko's*, one of the directors who left and got his own show inspired, along with the creator, about six of the characters, and the look and sense of the show—that handle on how it gets on the air. I want to create my own, too.

I'd rather be in television. I like the punch of shorts, and what you can do in shorts. That's definitely one thing I've discovered this year. I didn't know what was better, but having seen Theresa go through that feature and all the work she did, that's not the kind of thing I want to do. Even if I did it well, I wouldn't be happy. I'm more into the Warner Brothers style, Tex Avery, stuff like that.

A lot of the mentors are gone. I'd love to work at Chuck Jones's new studio. But I really don't know how much he is there and has that kind of mentor situation going. I think he comes in twice a week to supervise. I don't think he's conducting armchair discussions or anything.

I'm still dying to make my own shorts, like *Kitchen Casanova*. I showed the boards to the woman in charge and she wanted me to pitch it to the Turner Cartoon Network, but I was getting ready for my wedding. It was May or June, and it was frustrating. I was staying up late trying to do the boards, and they were just not going to get done. And they had these pitches every two weeks or so. I was missing one after the other. Finally I packed the whole thing to move. Hopefully now, by December or January, I can get back to that and bring them a finished board. I don't think I would do it unless I had someone else's money and backing.

For me, *Kitchen Casanova* would be something that I could show in festivals. I really miss having a short film to show. I never really achieved what I wanted with that. I made shorts and got ready to make a great film when life got in the way, and I had to get a job. But I don't think I'll ever stop wanting to make shorts. I'll finish the boards and then come up with thirty seconds or a minute.

ROB MINKOFF, Director

An animation director works with all the different artists on the picture, from the actors through every phase of the process, from storyboarding to the layout process to the animation process. In a way, you're working with the artists as individuals, sometimes in the context of the whole piece.

This is unlike a live-action film, where you have all the actors in the same room, and you set the lights, and everything is right there for you to photograph. In animation you're making the film in bits and pieces, and you have hundreds of people who will provide you with those bits and pieces. And you have to work with each artist to make them understand how what they're doing will influence the rest of the film. Because everyone is thinking that they're a soloist, and they're not. What they're doing has to blend into the rest of the orchestra. So it's being the arranger and conductor or orchestrator of the film.

Theresa and I want to go to this festival in France. We thought, We have to make a film and come back here. It would be great to show a film in that area, and then go around to Ottawa, and do the festival circuit. It's funny, the film was like a secondary thing. I miss that community, people who are doing this in different styles. It's comparable to the art world, wanting to show your paintings and go to galleries and whatnot.

Going to NYU got this in my blood, and I can't *not* want to make a film. Most of the people I work with have no desire or inclination to make their own short films. They didn't get into it to make short films. Theresa has a drive to be creative. For her, it's doing a children's book.

In five years I'd like to say I might be doing features, but not Disney rehashes. Not *Roger Rabbit*, either. A feature as original as *Nightmare Before Christmas*.

I could be supervising sequences, directing shorts or fifteen-minute segments, and having a team of creative animators who I'm directing, or who are working for me. Or be working on a Nickelodeon show or Hanna-Barbera, and just being the creative director or producer on it. Also, doing a lot of the writing as well. That would be the one major thing I'll be doing, writing and controlling a film from the starting gate.

The other thing I want to do is build a family. We're probably getting a house in the spring or summer. We'll have a child in two years or so.

LIZ CANE
November 11

Patrick Drummond's shoot happened. It sounds like it went well.

I was there through preproduction, and the first weekend. It was pretty intense. Everything kind of came together when it had to. It's low budget, but they had a good-sized crew which worked really fast, shooting seven or eight pages a day sometimes, six days a week. Long days.

He was great. Really in control, calm and decisive. He seemed perfect for directing. He almost didn't need an assistant once they started shooting. He was going so fast, he didn't need a lot of what we thought he might. I haven't seen any of it, but I will see a rough cut soon.

It was pretty impossible to get a name cast. He got this guy Michael Zelniker, who worked in some Hal Hartley films.

Patrick's wife Joan is the lead. I went to the wrap party and he seemed very relaxed. It was really a big relief. And people seemed to have been brought together working tightly on the film. It may look like a $1 million picture, and goods and services might have cost that, but he spent about $270,000.

RANDA HAINES, Director

I became very good at being a script supervisor. Five years into that I started thinking about directing. I had a reputation for being good with first-time directors, because I would be very tactful when I made very helpful suggestions. I'd whisper in the director's ear, "Maybe you could try . . ." and then the director would say to everyone, "Okay, we're going to try a shot where we do this." I began to want to be the one saying things out loud and see if I really knew how to do it.

My dad came down this weekend and we worked on one of my scripts. Writing has just taught me the importance of rewriting. For me, at this stage and at this level, it is, it's getting better—I can see that. I'm studying structure, and I can see what I need to do, and sometimes it's really hard to figure out how to do that. It's such a struggle to stay focused on it and keep working. It's amazing how much you can work on a feature script.

I have friends who have been working on one script. I'm sure they have other things. I do, too, other treatments and files and script ideas, but I try not to get into developing them so I can keep my focus on this one. And I know a number of people who have done that for years, and a couple of them are getting somewhere with it now. It just seems like you need a lot of patience.

My 401 group from school is not really together. I have this friend who moved to New Orleans about a year ago and is teaching now. It seems like everybody is working, some of them in the industry, some just making a living. Writing, but not having time to be social. But sometimes that is very connected to working.

The first year out of film school is very tough transitionally. [At school] you're running and working so hard and have all these ideas about what you can do, and you're in such a position of power and control, and then when you get out, there is no structure for you at all. All the loans and money problems. I feel good about the fact that I wrote a couple of scripts and managed somehow to keep one foot in filmmaking one way or another, whether it was helping on a student film or being assistant camera on an educational or whatever. And then also, having the little A-V lab job is a gift, and I feel terribly lucky to have that. I feel good about my progress.

I do have ideas for documentaries and other really low-budget projects, and sometimes I just think I should go off and do them, like Penelope Spheeris did *The Decline of Western Civilization*. It's another approach to getting accepted and being able to make films. I can't do what Patrick did, because he had a house to mortgage, and he had his mother and wife's brother, and people on the sound side of the industry. I don't have that kind of capital and support. He had a group of people who were just determined to make this thing happen.

Five years from now, I would like to be in a position where I can make films. I don't know if that's overly optimistic or not. I just want to be in a position before I get too old, or become less excited about my ideas, to get people to give me money to make films. It doesn't have to be a lot of money, and I don't know if it's the studio, or what it is exactly. It's just going to depend on the scripts, and who's interested.

I used to think, Oh no, I have to direct, I have to be in control of my work. But if I could get a good chunk of money for a screenplay I would probably be pretty happy to sell it. Although I'm sure it would be a lot harder to do it than to just think about it—to give it up, and let someone else destroy it. [Laughs]

Unless it's something really low budget and you get a star attached, like Rory Kelly [*Sleep with Me*] did, or what Alexander Payne is doing. [Payne eventually directed *Meet Ruth Stoops*, a 1996 Sundance hit starring Laura Dern.] That's possible. Right now I'm writing something that's not big-budgeted. It could be done for under $4 million.

I have days when I wonder if I am doing the right thing at all, and wonder if I should be teaching. It gets very grim. I didn't touch my script for two or three months this summer. I was always ready to be there for Patrick, and then it didn't happen. And then I did the editing, and Patrick was going to shoot, and there were like five weeks of intensive preproduction in which I wasn't able to do anything but help him with casting. And then there was the shoot, feeling a little bit like, am I doing the right thing going back to this job and not being there, even though he doesn't need me?

After all the intensity of being with him in that preproduction phase I went into a little bit of a depression, and knew that I had to get back into my script. And it was a struggle. It's a struggle to see what you're doing. When the script is alive in your consciousness, it's a lot easier to be hopeful. The longer you are away from it sometimes can make it harder to get back in, but it also helps you throw away what is shitty. I've thrown away a good third of it in the last couple of months.

I don't think there is any one rhythm. I think it depends on the project. Sometimes you write something really fast and it's great. I'm still not exactly sure what I'm doing with this script. It's kind of more open. My first feature script was not that good, and I'm not very proud of it. But I was really happy to finish it. I'm just figuring out the whole feature-length structure.

Some of it is good, edgy and funny, and I may come back to it someday. But I had never written a feature script as a film student. It's just a whole different thing, trying to get the skills of that structure so you're not thinking about it so much and are able to be creative.

I think if you're resonating with what's out there, things can happen. You just have to keep doing your work. Also, sometimes it's not a matter of staying with whatever rhythm you think you should be on, but relaxing and fucking around. That can give you insight. When my dad was here we were playing Nine Inch Nails, Led Zeppelin, and Nirvana, just goofing around.

It seems like people who do finally break in tend to have a lot going on, like Tarantino. And John Dahl wrote so many scripts. Sometimes it's harder than for others. I'm lucky that I don't have to contend with a lot of personal stuff. I haven't had any major tragedy. It's a luxury to have a job that allows you to do some writing.

It would be nice to have more happen than what's happened. But in a lot of ways, the more I write, the more I realize that it takes a while. It doesn't seem that people these days are just going to have faith that you're a good director without you being a good writer. So the writing has been good for me. If I never get any-where with it, I'll be kind of frustrated, though.

I feel like I just really need to stay positive, have faith, be patient, and struggle. It's hard when you're trying to do something on your own. And easy to get really depressed, or isolated, and lonely. It's good that I have these ways of collaborating with people. It keeps my hope alive.

RANDA HAINES, Director

I wish there was some great practical advice, like if you do A, B, and C, you will get D, but there really isn't any. Everybody has to make their own path. If this is something you really want to do and you believe in yourself, you have to keep forging ahead no matter what happens. Surround yourself with a network of friends who can give you a lot of emotional support during the hard times.

It's perseverance, following every lead. I used to wake up some mornings and, without being aware of it, I had been crying in my sleep. I would think, "Why am I pursuing this? This is so hard to get at, it's never going to happen. I gave up a successful life as a script supervisor. I've made a terrible mistake."

But somehow I would get out of bed and make the phone calls and do what I had to do, and I guess I never stopped believing in myself. I was so focused and sure of what I wanted. It's important to acknowledge that what you're trying to do is next to impossible—and then go do it anyway.

P. J. PESCE
November 15

Brad Krevoy told me that Amir Malin, who used to be Ira Deutchman's partner in CineCom, wants to distribute *The Desperate Trail* theatrically.

I asked Pesce about a laudatory feature on Linda Fiorentino in the then-current Premiere *magazine, which said, "Ironically, as she turned down A-list projects [*Top Gun, We're No Angels*], she was agreeing to do films like* Shout, Queens Logic, Chain of Desire, *and* Desperate Trail.*"*

This is the second time this has happened. The same fucking thing happened in *New York* magazine. The fact is, she's a huge fucking pain in the ass and doesn't do what she is told. But fucking journalists just eat up whatever you tell them and spit it out any way they are told to. [*Author's note:* I thanked Pesce for his kind words.]

November 22

These guys are planning to release *The Desperate Trail* on video on December 28, and they've been planning that, and doing nothing otherwise, for months. I don't think they ever had any other plans. I think anything they've ever said to the contrary was to shut me the fuck up. They could care less.

If they would have given me just six months with my movie. I wrote it, conceived it, directed it, I was in the room for every single cut—I mean, my blood is on every frame of that fucking movie. And they could give a shit. They say: Okay, great, thanks. You did a nice thing. We're going to make $2.5 million for your labors, for which you were paid $50,000. But in spite of that we're going to fuck you royally *that* way. We could care less that you could take the movie to film festivals, that it could help your career and reputation immensely.

So a lot of people, over Christmas vacation, can watch the movie.

I'm tremendously disappointed. I got another call from yet another distributor the other day, saying, "Yeah, we'd like to talk to you about whatever you're going to do next. It's really too bad about *The Desperate Trail.* We saw it and liked it a lot, but we were all under the impression that New Line was going to distribute it, and we also heard that Miramax had gotten shot down by Turner because they didn't want anybody to distribute it."

It would only cost TNT money. The longer they have to withhold the video release, the more interest they have to pay and the longer it's "on the books." It's strictly shortsighted bottom-line thinking. Kanter has tried. The people at Turner are just not interested.

Dennis Miller from Showtime, who I spoke to myself, said, "It comes down to that we want to get our money back for our investment. We're not willing to wait around." For them, a theatrical distribution is very much a risk. If they put money into distribution, and prints and advertising, they're not going to make it back. At best, it's only going to increase their video revenue, and they don't even know if it's going to increase it enough to justify it.

They're not even willing to go through the trouble to get someone who is interested to do it. They just don't want to deal with it. They don't believe in the movie at all.

Why should another party put up all the money for distribution? Whatever they do, it's going to benefit Turner as well, so why should they take all the risk and put up all the money? It's not right. It's not fair.

It's a crowded market. The Western has once again been put deep into the ground by foolish Hollywood thinking. They made a slew of Westerns on the heels of *Unforgiven*, and a slew of crap Westerns sunk to the bottom. *Geronimo, Bad Girls*. And then they say, "See, we told you the Western is dead, nobody wants to see the Western." They make these gimmicky movies, like *Maverick*.

Talk was circulating in Hollywood that Linda Fiorentino's performance in October Films' The Last Seduction *was Oscar material. (The Academy subsequently ruled both the actress and the film, which had premiered on HBO prior to its theatrical release, ineligible.) Fiorentino was being offered big roles and big money, eventually accepting the lead in Paramount's* Jade, *from a Joe Eszterhas screenplay, for a reported $1 million.*

I asked Pesce if he thought Fiorentino's career boost had any impact on the decision to release The Desperate Trail *on video.*

These guys don't have any idea. None. They don't know, they don't read, they don't even watch television. They've never had a film at a festival. And they don't even know that if you're out on video you can't go to film festivals! What do these guys know from Linda Fiorentino? They don't know anything! You would think that just as a result of what's happened they would consider theatrical distribution, just so that the video would be fucking huge! It's fucking stupid!

The scripts are going pretty good. I just came from Rob Weiss's house. It's slow going. We've got certain actors we're talking about. It's a slice-of-life, weird comedy. A bunch of filthy-mouthed vulgarians take over a club.

We sit around a lot and watch daytime television and crack up. He comes up with more and more outrageous scenes, and I try to string them together into some sort of structure. We go back and forth on the computer. We have fun. We definitely have a blast. Occasionally we both get upset with the other for not getting work done. We need to move ahead a little bit more.

Rob gets offered stuff he doesn't want to do. He lives like a prince at Shannen Doherty's house. He's got a deal at Universal. He gets a weekly salary. I don't know what the deal is. He owes them a movie.

The Abrams script is taking a long time. For better or worse, neither of these are real studio movies, I think. It's the stuff that I'm interested in, you know? What can you do? Got to go with what you know and like.

I feel like I got screwed. This movie was entirely my doing. I should have been cut in for part ownership, you know? Why was I not? Why did I put all my imagination and thought in, for a flat rate? These guys will make money off of this movie for years and years to come. I won't see a dime of it. How can that be?

Look, if Satan would have come with a contract and said, "Your soul, and that's it," I would have said yes. And they know that. Does that make it any less wrong to exploit someone and their intellectual property in that way? No. It's still wrong. It's still bad. They will say that they're taking all the risk. But I'll say that's not true. I risked two years of my life. I spent all that time, so we should have at least been partners. I should have been in for some of whatever it could have been. I don't think that's outrageous.

One nice thing was, when we got more money, one of the first things Steve Stabler and Chad Oman did was up my fee [from $30,000 to $50,000]. More than they were contractually obligated to do. Just because. You would think that Turner would have the same sort of thought, then. That they might say, "Okay, take three months and go to film festivals."

Chad is looking for an action movie for me, which is nice and all, but I don't know if I want to be an action movie director.

I'm thirty-three. In five years I'll be thirty-eight years old. I would like to have directed another three movies. I would like that at least one of those be a small, character-driven comedy that I really care about, that means something to me. I would also like to have done a studio movie of the sort that I now know I could really do. Like *Midnight Run*. Something like that, which is a great, smaller studio movie. I could take something like that apart and really do a good job on it.

And I would like five years from now to have enough money in the bank that it's not an issue. Preston Sturges said something like, "Money should not be a player. You should never have so much or so little of it that it's an issue." You should never have so much of it that it becomes a millstone around your neck, or lack it so severely that it's the driving force in your life. And right now, it is.

So, I'd like that. I'd like to be married, and maybe even have a kid. It's not a bad scenario. I think, if I'm on the West Coast, I'd like to be living up in Ojai. Come down here twice a week. What's here? I like the golf courses. I've got good friends here. Especially with the kid, I won't be socializing as much, I'll be staying home. But I need a hit movie to do that, or at least be in pre- or postproduction on a movie.

I just need to be about three steps higher than I am. Either that, or have a girlfriend with a lot of money. [Laughs]

In spite of all the bitterness and cynicism that comes flowing out of my mouth, yeah, I'm really grateful. From the three years before and after me in film school, I could count the number of people on one hand who have directed one feature, let alone two.

A couple of them have done really well. But many, many more of them haven't even had the opportunities I've had. So I can't complain, I really can't, without being pretty indulgent, arrogant and whiny. I'm actually really lucky. Okay, I'm not in the situation that Quentin Tarantino is in, but I'm a working Hollywood director.

Tarantino has managed to be involved with three or four movies which, if nothing else, have screen stories which work well. In the next few years there ought to be too many film students who have seen *Reservoir Dogs* too many times writing dialogue about *The Brady Bunch* between two hitmen. Please don't do exactly what he does! Take a page from his book. Learn that every scene needs to have a beginning, middle, and end, and have dialogue that isn't about what the scene is about. And don't ever write about '70s pop culture again. Thank you very much.

The Desperate Trail *was released on video by Turner Home Entertainment in December 1994. It aired on Turner Network Television several times during the week beginning July 9, 1995.*

Reviews were positive. Most encouraging was Entertainment Weekly, *which in December had graded the video release a D+; for the broadcast review a different* EW *critic called* The Desperate Trail *"the best Western on any size screen since* Unforgiven. . . . *First-time director (and Scorsese protégé) P. J. Pesce reinvents the genre's clichés with panache and includes enough slo-mo mayhem to make Sam Peckinpah proud."* Daily Variety *(which had also previously reviewed* The Desperate Trail, *eight months earlier at the Hamptons festival) wrote, "First-time helmer P. J. Pesce gives a tip of the hat to masters John Ford and Sam Peckinpah in this striking, action-packed and at times brutal oater." (Neither publication seemed aware of Pesce's true feature debut, the Roger Corman-produced* Body Waves.*)*

"We finally got a bad review," Pesce called to tell me the day after The Desperate Trail *aired. But it was less a review than a verbal body slam from none other than Ted Turner, who was addressing the Television Critics Association on the subject of TV violence. "I thought it sucked," Turner said, as quoted in the* Hollywood Reporter. *"Jane [Fonda, his wife] and I couldn't even watch it. . . . That was a film we picked up for nickels and released to video first. . . . I'm not proud of everything we make."*

While it may have been nickels to Turner, his company did not "pick up" but actually financed the entire $2.5 million production of The Desperate Trail. *After his blunt, adolescent critique of the film, Pesce began referring to the entertainment mogul as "Beavis Turner."*

The Desperate Trail *earned a 4.5 Nielsen rating and was the second highest rated basic cable program the week it aired.*

KEVA ROSENFELD, Director
Directors I knew told me, "You won't believe what it looks like on the set." I said, "I've done it—I already know what it's like." But I have a very vivid memory of being driven to

the set and seeing so many trucks and so many people that I started to giggle. I'll never get that feeling again. All those people are working for you. You don't even know their names. Seventy or eighty people, each with a job to do. "How did this ever happen?" I thought.

By lunch time, we were behind schedule.

MARCO WILLIAMS
December 12

Williams telephoned me from the North Carolina School of the Arts, where he had been teaching for three months.

My feet are freezing. My sense is that there's kind of a cold spell everywhere, but it's real cold here.

I enjoy the teaching. That part's been good. The town, I'm still getting adjusted to. It's really a small town in feeling. But I like the teaching, I really enjoy that.

I'm glad the term is over. I was starting to run out of steam. There were some areas I needed to work on, and it was good to have a chance to do that.

I think about how long this will go, from time to time, and I really can't say. I keep saying I'd like to do it for at least two years after this, because a new facility is being built that's going to be a kind of back lot, and I think it would be great to be here and be able to utilize that facility.

Then there are times I think I really don't know if I can last in this small-town atmosphere. But what's started to happen and should improve in this year is that you come here from Hollywood and everyone perceives you to be a big fish. People are beginning to contact me about various things. And while there hasn't been anything sterling, there have been a couple of projects that initially sounded interesting. So I wouldn't be surprised if while I'm here I either discover an idea of my own or someone else's project that is really worth developing.

Next summer is the Black Theatre Arts Festival, something that happens every two summers in Winston-Salem. It's a huge thing where black movie stars as well as stage stars come down here for a two-week period to participate. I think that will tell me if there's a real creative vein in town for me.

Beyond that, I'm still trying to generate different projects.

Actually, I've got a documentary TV series in development. We got some development money. It's like the *Declarations* series but should be much better, with me directing one of the hours of a four-part series. The theme is addressing violence in America. Mine is about individuals who have had experiences of violence in their lives, yet have responded or dealt with that violence by developing grass-roots organizations. There are a couple of candidates in Phoenix and Chicago. It's a great proposal this guy up in Berkeley wrote. So I'm just starting to research that.

Things are as chaotic as you might imagine with something being built from the ground up. But it's been fun. I didn't expect to make friends right away, but the only wish would be to feel that I'm being part of the community. But I also recognize that that will come with time.

It's been good.

JOHN KEITEL
December 14

Right now I think that the most important thing about getting a movie made is having a good script. If it's a given that the person who is the director can direct, that director still needs a good script that he or she believes in. To talk about "directors" in the general sense of the word, though, is to group Paul Verhoeven with Ingmar Bergman. You know what I mean? There are so many different animals. I think there are so few good scripts.

Somebody I was talking to recently said he was reading many screenplays recently, and he can tell the literacy in America has declined. I asked, "Were you reading screenplays ten years ago?" And he really hadn't been. But even if he had . . .

Everybody thinks they can write a screenplay. Everyone is getting together 100–120 pages in screenplay form and putting it out there. There's a huge glut of screenplays. I don't necessarily think literacy among our writers has gone down. I just think a lot more people are considering themselves writers. Or they want to be involved in this very seductive-seeming, glamorous business.

If I believe in something, the tenacity comes through. I'm not a result-driven person. If I get up in the morning, it's not imperative but I would love to have twenty pages written by the end of the day. But if it's not happening, and the process isn't right, I'll be happy just thinking and figuring out what's wrong. And being much more concerned about the quality.

I don't know if it was arrogance or just sheer naïveté, but making my documentary, when USC wanted to know "What is this all about?" my attitude was "Because it fucking hadn't been done before," at least not where I was coming from. USC had not done something like this. And it needed to be done. I needed to see two people on the screen that I could identify with. And who better to put up there than yourself?

I told my professor I literally wanted it to be shown in the Castro and for gay men to watch it and say, "Finally! Some normal people with everyday neuroses who happen to be gay."

What I have learned the most from film school is this: Everyone's got a story to tell, but so few people have the time or are willing to put in the time and the hard work to figure out the film. A novel is different, because you can wax poetic in a novel. You can do anything in a novel. In a film you have to have a structure. You have an allotted period of time for the most part. Let's face it, you can make a five-hour film, but who's going to see it unless it's made into a miniseries? And then that has its own unique structure to it. It's that hook.

That's where I am with my script. It's so different from what you read. The idea of minorities figures in, but it's a lot less pansocietal than it was.

I want this done by Christmas. I want the week between Christmas and New Year's to let it be. New Year's is my favorite holiday. It's worked for me in the past when I prepare for it. It really does mark time for me. I will use that to slingshot into 1995.

More and more the responsibilities at work have been put on my shoulders. I'm the last of the legacy of USC film student grads at Midtown Video, and the guys before me are all moving on. One's doing a lot of commercial work, one is editing. I know this job has fulfilled its purpose.

I realized with a couple of phone calls I could take Tuesday through Sunday off, and I did. I went home after work, packed up my computer, got in the car, and drove to my mom's in Laguna Hills. I knew there would be no distractions there. I knew it would be like going back home during high school, before finals and all. I knew even the furniture would get me focused, and my mom would see to it that I ate.

I spent one week there, and came out with pretty much not *the* draft, but I had made these critical decisions that aligned it all. And that would enable me to take it where I wanted it to go. So that is what I've planned to do again starting this evening. I'll drive down there again and go through Christmas.

L.A. is such a hard place in which to focus. I think James Baldwin said he could never write in New York. He had to leave New York. Then he usually wrote about New York. Jack London said the same thing about San Francisco. He could never write in the city. I feel like that's good company. [Laughs] I'll do the same thing and hope for the best. I'm going down there and I know why.

I think I've learned something about writing. You have to check out. Three hours, in a day when you have to do other things, doesn't work. You need to put yourself in a situation where your environment always brings you back to the purpose at hand. You really need that. Being where I live, with people I know, and the gym, and I can always do this, that, or the other thing—that can screw you up.

Everything in the past two years had been related to my relationship and subsequent breakup with Carter. Two years ago to this day I was preparing to go to Chicago with Carter, spend Christmas with my family, then go off to Europe for three weeks over the New Year. Two years ago I was also looking forward to Sundance.

I know there's two sides to a story, but Sundance was when I realized that these two were just not going to mix, Carter and my work. Carter, over the course of four years, could never figure out a way into this world of mine. That was an ongoing problem in our relationship from day one. I recognized Carter's potential and our visions were really in synch, which is why the relationship took off. But we did acknowledge the problems early on, and I realized the risk I was running. Do I help him through all this—and is there a relationship on the other end? Or do we both move on, in which case am I just a caretaker?

I probably wouldn't have been able to tell you this two months ago. But when I first came out in my senior year of college and had my first boyfriend, these floodgates opened. Even with taking this step there was this real feeling of loneliness. I had good friends and objectively a bright future, but I was seriously lonely. I wanted companionship. That led to a boyfriend, and another and another. These lasted three months or so, culminating in a four-year relationship with Carter.

That whole period of time was about learning that nobody else is going to let you off the hook. That's almost what I was looking for, somebody to make me complete.

So whether it was Carter or someone else—because I've dated people since then who would have been happy to have not necessarily serious relationships but serious dating situations—I have turned them away each and every time. My excuse was that they weren't meeting my expectations. But really what it is, is that *I'm* not meeting my expectations. I'm not doing what I need to do. And not until I garner that security, until I achieve this achievable thing, will I be able to seriously look at another person and think about "forever."

One thing the making of my film made me respect is my family. Particularly my mother, and what she instilled in me and my brother and sister. There's a legacy there, and that is where my strength and my ability to be arrogant or tenacious comes from, or to be all these things a director may need to be. But I don't want to employ all that stuff until I've got the product. And believe it or not, I feel like it's so close.

The past two years have been largely about healing. Do you realize how process-oriented I am? Friends of mine joke about that, that in some ways that's the most important thing to me. I mean, I want the results eventually.

My favorite poem is "Ithaka," which was also Jackie Onassis's favorite. It was read at her funeral. It's basically about the journey. Ithaka is the goal, the island you're trying to get to, but it's going to take you a lifetime to get there, so you better enjoy the journey. If you do, Ithaka will not disappoint you when you get to her, if she's poor and lonely, because what she gave you was a journey.

I like to take responsibility for where I am and who I am. But it doesn't mean it's not an ongoing process.

The other thing besides coming to terms with this process, and personal stuff, was coming to terms with L.A. As much as I would live nowhere else, L.A. can make you feel like there's always some big party going on that you weren't invited to. And even if you are invited—even if it appears to be an event—you still feel that way. It's kind of coming to terms with having made a film in film school that you feel good about, and other people feel good about, that garners a certain amount of attention. Thinking you're going to capitalize on that somehow, but not knowing how you're going to capitalize.

It's not like the NBA draft—like they said in *Premiere* magazine the year before I attended film school—really, unless you're all set and ready to go and have that script. It's not like they have to fill so many slots on so many given teams, and that they're going to the film schools and saying, "Okay, who's the best? We'll take the best." There's so much more at work.

Not being a person who has regrets, I've looked back on some interactions, like with [producers] Craig Zadan and Neil Meron, and felt like I really hadn't capitalized on them at all. I just guess there are many ways to go about it, and the way I usually do is that I don't look for mentors or people who will help me along the way, and maybe that's my arrogance. In some way I don't want to have to be beholden to anyone. I don't want to trade a part of what I might think of as integrity. That's why I think you almost have to look *back* and say, oh my God, he or she was my mentor.

I also think there are fewer things more daunting than trying to get a feature film off the ground. Anyone can make a documentary. I don't mean to put down documentaries, but they're easy to make—all you do is get a camera, find an interesting subject, edit creatively. But feature filmmaking is getting the story and getting the money, and the only way to do it is focus on doing it.

I have a cushion saved up. I'm becoming the obsessive person I need to be, to get this draft done. Taking these writing retreats is new and different. Oddly, for the past two years I've felt like I couldn't leave L.A.—maybe because of Carter—even for a week at a time. It seems strange.

I think I need to give myself time, and still work fifteen to twenty hours a week at Midtown to slow the drain on my money. I feel like the spring of '95 is it. It's time. And however it's done, at Columbia, Miramax, or this quasi-limited partnership I have with David Desmond, an attorney, to set out to make this film, it's time.

I want to be a director. That's what I see myself as. People say, "Are you going to sell the script?" I don't think that way. I think of directing my script, and I don't care how that's done, it just has to be done.

If somebody offered me a lot of money for the script and it never saw the light of day, I guess I could live with that. If somebody gave me a million dollars—although I don't know why somebody would buy this particular kind of script for that much . . . It would have to be at least enough to pay off my student loans and leave a cushion to get another project up and running.

In five years I would have made this film and proceeded, but I don't know what level I would be at—if I were to have a three-picture deal at Warner Brothers or be truly an independently spirited filmmaker. I would have made this one and at least one other one, and really engaged in professional relationships to get other people's films made, in a producing capacity. I'd like to be teaching a course at UCLA or USC, as a returning professional. That doesn't have to take five years.

There is another alternative, something I've had the opportunity to do in the past two years. That's to dabble in journalism, in writing, and I've enjoyed that. I don't see myself as giving up film altogether. But if I fail in terms of not getting to make another film easily—which, if I don't, will haunt me for the rest of my life—once I've made it, I'll probably feel a lot freer to write in other areas.

I don't consider myself a screenwriter. I want to direct the films and in fact don't need to write every film I direct—or the next one, even. I do consider myself a writer, though, and could definitely commit myself to writing a lot more in other areas. I'm getting the process down, and good writers are hard to come by.

What had really gotten me through these two years in a way is this: Invest in the one or two people you connect with. Return people's phone calls. Make it habitual with the people that matter. Don't garner a reputation with a good friend of not being able to come through. Try to have dinners, once a week, every two weeks, keeping in touch like that. Out of that everything else grows.

Beyond that, it's been a coming-home process for me. There's this annual holiday party that acquaintances from Stanford have—one gay, the rest not. This year I felt so much more like I had done a whole circle. I wasn't the person I was ten years ago, but I came back to being the person I was, in a sense. It was stabilizing. I saw people like my best friend from film school. He and his wife just had a baby and I went to the hospital, Cedars-Sinai, and even that felt not at all like an "other" experience, and I thought: How can I make this part of my life?

In five years I will have kids. Maybe not, but maybe. After I do the film it is a major priority. But first I have this other baby I need to deliver . . . *Ground Zero*.

Keep Ithaka always in your mind.
Arriving there is what you are destined for.
But do not hurry the journey at all.
Better if it lasts for years,
so you are old by the time you reach the island,
wealthy with all you have gained on the way,
not expecting Ithaka to make you rich.

Ithaka gave you the marvelous journey.
Without her, you would not have set out.
She has nothing to give you now.

And if you find her poor,
Ithaka won't have fooled you.
Wise as you will have become,
so full of experience,
you will have understood by then
what these Ithakas mean.

—C. P. Cavafy, *Ithaka*

AFTERWORD

In a 1994 *New Yorker* interview, Pauline Kael was asked what kind of person it takes to become a movie director.

"Let's be brutal," Kael answered. "It takes a person who can raise the money to make a movie."

Kael's response *was* brutal—brutally accurate. However, funding features no longer means raising millions of dollars. In the past four years *Clerks, Crumb, El Mariachi, The Brothers McMullen,* and many other acclaimed movies costing well under $100,000 have heralded a golden age of guerrilla narrative and documentary filmmaking. This generation's credo may well be, "Forget the car for graduation, Mom and Dad—finance my directorial debut."

Sadly, though, as instant auteurs emerge regularly from the independent scene, opportunities at the studio level continue to shrink. Many films that inspired the subjects of this book as they came of age in the 1970s—*Taxi Driver, Badlands, Scarecrow*—would have slim chances of being produced today.

If the film school graduates I've followed have learned anything in their first years as professionals, it's probably this: No one really cares if they can direct. What studios and independents *are* concerned about is material. Few executives won't look at a new speculative screenplay, but the odds against an original script getting made are pretty high. More often than not, a sold spec will result in future writing opportunities.

The spec market—where the term "high concept" was born—is hardly a forum for creative expression, however.

"The biggest box-office draws are pictures catering to the intelligence of the twelve-year-old," said producer Arthur Fellows to John Huston—incredibly, over forty years ago, during the making of *The Red Badge of Courage*.

'Twas ever thus.

Most young filmmakers have none of the resources to participate in Hollywood's ongoing romance with bestselling novels and comic books, extravagant star salaries, sequels and remakes. And this blockbuster mentality is virtually blind to the possibilities of original, creative work from new talent.

As long as there is a movie industry, the debate will rage as to whether film school is worthwhile. But if it has no other value, affording filmmakers the opportunity to take artistic chances is enough.

If it's become so hard to make it on creative talent alone in the professional marketplace, what's left? Well, there's always luck, which few success stories don't include. Perseverance counts for something, too. And over the four years this project has spanned, the seven graduates—while enduring riots, floods, fires, earthquakes, a mad bomber, and one rather high-profile celebrity murder trial—have certainly continued to persevere.

In the months before the publication of this book, their professional activities continued:

LIZ CANE worked briefly as a copywriter in home video marketing but turned down a permanent position to focus on her scripts. In the Spring of 1995 she wrote a segment for a TV pilot, *Apartment X*, which was produced by colleagues from UCLA film school. Cane is currently at work on two new screenplays.

BERNARD JOFFA served as the AFI's only directing instructor in 1995. After he did consulting work for the South African cable company M-NET that summer, they hired him to write and direct a low-budget feature, *A Woman of Color*. He has sublet his house.

JOHN KEITEL left Midtown Video in August 1995 to begin as an editor on A&E's *Biography* series. He then rewrote his screenplay—now called *Defying Gravity*—and filmed it in the spring of 1996 on a $60,000 budget.

LISA KLEIN spent much of 1995 traveling, including a trip to Australia. She also began teaching Jewish History to second and third graders, and working with a group of teenagers on a documentary about the Holocaust.

JOHN MCINTYRE sold his concept and storyboards for *Kitchen Casanova* to Hanna-Barbera and was hired to direct the $300,000 animated short in September 1995. McIntyre is still happily married to Theresa, with whom he has purchased a house in Studio City.

P. J. PESCE and Rob Weiss sold their screenplay, *Milk Bar*, to Savoy Pictures for $400,000. Pesce then directed two unsold network pilots and an episode of ABC's *The Marshal*. In late 1995 he and Tom Abrams were hired by Universal to write a screenplay for actor Chow Yun-Fat. Pesce is renting a house in the Hollywood Hills.

MARCO WILLIAMS finished his first year of teaching at the North Carolina School of the Arts. In June 1995 he took a leave of absence and moved to San Francisco to direct an installment of a documentary series for public television, *Making Peace*.

AUTHOR'S NOTE

I may as well have been a mushroom; I grew up in the dark.

When I was six years old, in 1965, my parents took me, in our Country Squire station wagon, to my first drive-in. The double feature was quite odd—*The Sons of Katie Elder*, a Henry Hathaway Western with John Wayne and Dean Martin, and *Son of Flubber*, the sequel to *The Absent-Minded Professor*, which again starred Fred MacMurray.

From then on Flubber was Flaubert as far as I was concerned. If I learned anything as a kid, I learned it from the movies. By age sixteen I had become my high school's newspaper movie critic and resident filmmaker. It was pretty clear that playing left field for the Mets—my only other acceptable vocational choice—had taken a back seat to my true calling: I was going to Hollywood to be a film director.

The following year I pushed my way in (after an initial rejection) as an early admittant to New York University's undergraduate film school. My instructor for Sight and Sound—the seminal production class—was Martin Scorsese's mentor, Haig Manoogian. An old-school drill sergeant with a passion for cinema in all its forms, he has been accurately described as the Chuck Yeager of film schools. Robert Siodmak's *The Crimson Pirate* was one of Haig's favorite "pictures"—he never called them anything else—but he was also apt to wax rhapsodic over obscure contemporary stuff like *The Duchess and the Dirtwater Fox*.

At NYU the challenges were considerable: taking your chances shooting on the subways without a permit; pulling a star-making performance out of your predental roommate at 3 A.M. the day before a project was due; making nearby Washington Square Park look interesting despite the fact that *everyone* shot exteriors there. And of course there was keeping a cordial relationship with Haig, who was fond of making ominous pronouncements like, "You're either going to make terrible pictures, Frolick, or terrific ones."

Our three-pronged technical attack featured Filmos, man-handled World War II news cameras which were wound with actual doorknobs; outdated battery-powered Nagra reel-to-reel tape recorders; and ancient Steenbeck editing machines notorious for shredding the best scenes they were fed.

Having attended summers, I graduated in three years, less due to distinguished academic achievement than to a deep need to begin working in the motion picture business. I left New York in 1979, a few months before Haig Manoogian died. The following year *Raging Bull*—"A Martin Scorsese *Picture*"—was dedicated to his memory.

Immediately following NYU, I set my sights on Hollywood. I'm not sure why I failed to heed my Jewish mother's alternating refrains. One was that I was "in too big a hurry." The other was that I should have my head examined because "show business is full of whores and thieves." At the time, these seemed like fear-driven, Old World sentiments from a woman who had been raised during the Great Depression.

Sixteen years later, her words seem uncannily prescient and wise. The movie business is indeed filled with—among others—whores and thieves. One wishing to pursue a career in motion pictures must dance with wolves in sheep's clothing, self-described creative types whose passion is not for cinematic greatness but for financial gain. When films as mediocre as *Cocktail* and *Stargate* manage to spin the turnstiles, the message is clear: you can still get rich off the sizzle, not just the steak.

But I was hungry for steak at age twenty. Woody Allen, Robert Altman, Terrence Malick, and Scorsese were my heroes both for their superb work and for their apparent creative autonomy. The notion of material wealth was a minor consideration, as it seemed to be a natural byproduct of artistic success—in the film business, at least.

During my last two semesters at college, I read and evaluated soon-to-be-published novel manuscripts for the fledgling Orion Pictures. That credential—along with my B.A. from NYU Film— landed me my first job in Los Angeles in the fall of 1979.

My senior film project had been a comedy in which I, playing myself, tried to convince a producer of schlock films to hire me. As life does imitate art, the week I hit L.A. I was put on the payroll by the affable, polyester-wearing producer of several grade-B "block-busters."

They were the kinds of movies in which the president of the United States would appear in one scene to explain the plot, and usually be played by Richard Widmark. One was a romantic thriller about a scientist and the test-tube fashion model he creates. My boss had his own opinion as to why the picture bombed: the lead actor was such a "blatant homosexual" that he couldn't kiss his costar with his mouth open.

At the production company I moved from analyzing novels to screenplays. I read more than three hundred scripts and wrote marginal recommendations on exactly four. Around the office I was dubbed the Assassin for my brutally honest opinions. (Often the material I was covering had, unbeknownst to me, already been purchased by the company.) After six months, the Assassin was terminated with extreme prejudice.

Soon afterward I was hired by International Creative Management as a "floater," or temporary secretary, in the motion picture department. During this eighteen-month period I worked for, among others, ICM president Jeff Berg and superagent Sue Mengers. It was Hollywood boot camp for me—a crash course in deal making, client relations, and office politics.

My next position was as assistant to Tamara Asseyev, the Academy Award–nominated producer of *Norma Rae*. This familiarized me with the machinations of producing: solicitation of and negotiation for material, story meetings with writers and studio executives, the pursuit of creative elements. Three years as an independent producer followed, during which time I developed a feature film project with Robert Duvall, which has since been made as *The Stars Fell on Henrietta*.

In 1988 the Writers Guild of America went on strike. I *began* writing—briefly for television, and then for entertainment journals and, finally, this book of seven different stories which I feel, oddly enough, reflect my own singular experiences in Hollywood.

ACKNOWLEDGMENTS

M any thanks to my agent, Suzanne Gluck of International Creative Management, New York's quickest closer since the
Broadway musical version of *The Goodbye Girl*.

To Steve Katz of Katz, Golden & Fishman, for sixteen
years of expert professional counsel and three decades of friendship,
and to Jennifer Justman for her precise, prompt, and comprehensive legal work.

To my brother Stuart, for invaluable editorial assistance, and for
introducing me to the movies. Also, to my high school English
teacher, Barbara Miller, who shared my growing obsession and
encouraged me to write about film.

To Marsinay Smith, Kari Paschall, Susan Jensen, and Sara Bixler
for attention to detail, common sense, and follow-through. And
Ann Marlowe, for masterful copy editing.

Thanks as well to Stephanie Allain, Gillian Armstrong, Robert
Benton, Pieter-Jann Brugge, Frank Darabont, Adam Dubov, Liz
Glotzer, Randa Haines, Neal Jimenez, Karey Kirkpatrick, Mark

Kruger, Rob Minkoff, Keva Rosenfeld, Gary Ross, Alan Shapiro, Steven Starr, and Bobbi Thompson.

Also to Gigi Agrama and Dwora Fried, Denise DiNovi, Arnold Dolin, Arlene Donovan, Saundra Saperstein and the Sundance Film Festival, Randy Levinson, and Bill Stuart.

My parents, Carrey and Sy Frolick, have been unwavering in their support for the choices I have made in my life, a quality I aspire to with my own children. Speaking of which, thanks to my kids Dominic and Cristina for treating my erratic temperament as an occupational hazard rather than a personality flaw. And to Gabriel, for waiting to be delivered until after I delivered my manuscript.

Peter Borland, my editor at Dutton, is an answered prayer. Despite living in an age of specialization and exclusive contractual agreements, he let me burn bridges, dig ditches, eat boxes of chocolates, and philosophize like a Philistine while I worked on this book. Thanks, Peter, for the humor, wisdom, and friendship.

My wife Kym, from the outset, gave me unconditional encouragement despite the financial hardship of a four-year project. Then she gave me the emotional support without which it would not have been done.

Finally, my immeasurable gratitude to the book's seven subjects. Fate smiled upon this project and presented me with a set of truly fascinating individuals. Creative filmmaking usually involves taking risks, and these directors demonstrated their capacity to do so by allowing me to watch them struggle, conceive, budget, write, plan, present, suffer, delight, agonize . . . and occasionally even direct.

More impressively, though, they expressed—with startling honesty and eloquence—their fears, hopes, and dreams. They did this regularly, over the course of three years, usually for the price of a cappuccino or a cheap breakfast, and often despite great emotional resistance. By participating with such commitment, they shattered a belief I mistakenly held dear: that the best stories are written.

They are not. The best stories are told, heard, and—most definitely—lived.

Beverly Hills, California
December 1995

THE PROFESSIONALS

STEPHANIE ALLAIN is president of production at Jim Henson Pictures. As a Columbia Pictures executive, she supervised the first studio-produced feature films of John Singleton *(Boyz N the Hood)*, Robert Rodriguez *(Desperado)*, and Darnell Martin *(I Like It Like That)*.

GILLIAN ARMSTRONG was the first woman to direct a feature in Australia in fifty years when she made 1979's *My Brilliant Career*. Since then, her films have included *Mrs. Soffel, The Last Days of Chez Nous,* and *Little Women*.

ROBERT BENTON co-wrote the screenplay for *Bonnie and Clyde* and directed *Bad Company, The Late Show, Places in the Heart,* and *Nobody's Fool*. He won Academy Awards for Best Adapted Screenplay and Best Director for 1979's Best Picture winner, *Kramer vs. Kramer.*

PIETER-JANN BRUGGE attended film school in his native Holland. The films he has produced or executive-produced include *Glory*, *The Pelican Brief*, and *Heat*.

FRANK DARABONT adapted for the screen and directed *The Shawshank Redemption*, for which he was nominated as Best Director by the Directors Guild of America and the Academy, and for which he won a 1995 Humanitas prize.

ADAM DUBOV directed the independent feature *Dead Beat*. He is an alumnus of UCLA's undergraduate and graduate film schools.

LIZ GLOTZER, president of production at Castle Rock Entertainment, attended USC's Peter Stark Producing Program. She was producer of *Sibling Rivalry*, and executive producer of *The Shawshank Redemption*.

RANDA HAINES was nominated for the 1986 Directors Guild of America Award for *Children of a Lesser God*. Her work also includes *The Doctor*, *Wrestling Ernest Hemingway*, and the television movie *Something About Amelia*.

NEAL JIMENEZ is an alumnus of UCLA's graduate film school. His screenplays include *River's Edge* and the autobiographical *The Waterdance*, his directorial debut and winner of the 1992 Sundance Film Festival's Audience Award.

KAREY KIRKPATRICK attended the USC Filmic Writing program, where he received the Jack Nicholson Screenwriting Award. His produced work includes *Honey, We Shrunk Ourselves* and *James and the Giant Peach*.

MARK KRUGER wrote the movie *Candyman: Farewell to the Flesh*. He was vice-president of production at both Turman-Foster Productions and Scott Rudin Productions.

ROB MINKOFF attended California Institute of the Arts. His directorial credits include *The Lion King*, the fifth highest-grossing film—and the Walt Disney company's highest-grossing film—of all time. He has just directed his live-action debut, *Into the Woods*.

KEVA ROSENFELD, a graduate of USC's film school, is the director of the documentary *All-American High*. His first narrative feature, *Twenty Bucks*, screened in competition at the 1993 Sundance Film Festival.

GARY ROSS is the co-screenwriter of *Big* and the writer of *Dave*, both of which were nominated for the Academy Award as Best Original Screenplay.

ALAN SHAPIRO graduated from NYU's undergraduate film school. His work as a writer-director includes *Flipper*, *The Crush*, and *Tiger Town*, winner of the 1984 CableACE Award for Best Dramatic Film.

STEVEN STARR attended film school at the University of Wisconsin. He escalated from the mailroom at the William Morris Agency to eventually head their motion picture department before leaving to direct films. His credits include the independent feature *Joey Breaker*.

BOBBI THOMPSON was vice president of the motion picture division at the William Morris Agency, whose director clients have included Robert Altman, Whit Stillman, Gus Van Sant, and John Woo.

The typeface used in this book is a version of Bembo, issued by Monotype in 1929 and based on the first "old style" roman type-face, which was designed for the publication, by the great Venetian printer Aldus Manutius (1450-1515), of Pietro Bembo's *De Ætna* (1495). Among the first to use octavo format, making his books cheaper and more portable, aldus might have grown rich printing as he did a thousand volumes per month—and extraordinary number for the time—had his books not been mercilessly pirated. The counterfeits did, however, spread the new typefaces throughout Europe, and they were widely imitated. The so-called Aldine romans were actually designed by the man who cut the type for Aldus, Fracesco Griffo (d. 1519). Griffo fought with Manutius over credit for designs and was later hanged after killing his brother-in-law with an iron bar.